The Last Sermon of Christ

The Last Sermon of Christ

An Expository and Analytical Commentary
on John 14–16

Michael Cannon Jr.

RESOURCE *Publications* • Eugene, Oregon

THE LAST SERMON OF CHRIST
An Expository and Analytical Commentary on John 14–16

Copyright © 2012 Michael Cannon Jr. All rights reserved. Except for brief quotations in critical publications or reviews, no part of this book may be reproduced in any manner without prior written permission from the publisher. Write: Permissions, Wipf and Stock Publishers, 199 W. 8th Ave., Suite 3, Eugene, OR 97401.

Resource Publications
An Imprint of Wipf and Stock Publishers
199 W. 8th Ave., Suite 3
Eugene, OR 97401

www.wipfandstock.com

ISBN 13: 978-1-62032-339-7

Manufactured in the U.S.A.

For my beautiful daughters Tiffany, Lydia, and Amanda who have taught me how to love and cherish God's gifts every day.

Contents

Preface | ix

chapter 1	Troubled Hearts	1
chapter 2	Heaven	9
chapter 3	Do You Know the Way	18
chapter 4	Seeing God	28
chapter 5	Doing a Great Work in the Kingdom	37
chapter 6	That Name	46
chapter 7	Gospel Obedience	56
chapter 8	A Very Real Comforter	64
chapter 9	Four Promises	74
chapter 10	Class is in Session	84
chapter 11	The Peace Dividend	97
chapter 12	The Gospel of Unity	108
chapter 13	Love that Bears Fruit to God's Glory: Part 1	120
chapter 14	Love that Bears Fruit to God's Glory: Part 2	129
chapter 15	Friendship	138
chapter 16	Realizing the Real Purpose of Our Appointment	146
chapter 17	Taking Their Hate Out on You	156
chapter 18	Part 1: Pass It On	167
chapter 19	Part 2: Inspiration and Illumination	176
chapter 20	Perseverance: Running On Fumes	187
chapter 21	The Spirit and the World	197

chapter 22	The Unity of Trinity in Revelation	209
chapter 23	In a Little While	219
chapter 24	A Loving Father Wants You to Ask	229
chapter 25	Understand and Embrace the Incarnation	241
chapter 26	Peace in Despair	151
	Bibliography	261

Preface

This is the first of a series of three books covering the last acts of Jesus Christ. The first volume is his last sermon, the second volume is his last prayer, and the third volume ends with his last breath from the cross. In the days before the crucifixion, Jesus brought all of his teaching into a tight grouping contained in a sermon, a prayer, and in his discourse during his trials and from the cross. His heart is on display as he turns his attention to the disciples in the upper room teaching them to see the New Covenant and calling them to serve one another. Much of the teaching they heard that night wouldn't be understood until sometime after the crucifixion but the words were all there for them to reflect on.

As Jesus lifted his heart before the Lord in prayer, the disciples were privileged to hear God the Son speaking to God the Father and praying for himself, for them, and for all that would follow them. He prayed for God's glory to be manifest and for God to empower the Church to do the same. In this prayer from our great High Priest, we are treated with an intimate conversation within the divine Trinity showing us the purpose of all things.

And finally, in the last hours of the life of Christ, till the last breath of Jesus, he is aware of the eminent arrival of the Kingdom of God and he is focused on finishing the work that he has been called to do. There is much intrigue about the events leading up to the cross in those last hours. The response of religious man in stark contrast to the righteousness of Christ helps us to see the truth of his words and we hang with him as he takes his last breath.

The material gathered in these volumes has been a labor of joy to gather and teach. Those last sleepless hours of our Savior's life are to be treasured by His people in every generation and we ought to hang on each and every word He spoke.

Take time to explore John in these chapters that give us rich detail of the last thoughts, the last words, and the last moments of our Savior's incarnate life here on earth.

1

Troubled Hearts

John 14:1

"Let not your hearts be troubled. Believe in God; believe also in me."

John Chapter 14 is a fascinating part of the farewell address of Jesus because it shows us clearly the heart of our Savior and his love for his disciples in a time of not only their anxiety, but his own anxiety, knowing that the shadow of the cross has now grown dark across him, and there is no place else for him to go. There is no ministry that remains except now to these disciples, and then ultimately to the cross itself. Even in his own humanity as he was troubled by the prospect of his suffering, he now turns to minister to the disciples in their time of trouble and anxiety.

Christians have taken great comfort in the teaching of Romans 8:28 and have quoted that verse as a testimony of their confidence in God's love demonstrated in his grace for those that belong to Christ. It reads very simply, "And we know that for those who love God all things work together for good."

Sometimes that verse is regarded by unbelieving ears as escapism or avoidance, as if when we have no other real answer, all we can do is say, "Well, God will take care of it because God loves me." Now to the Christian, it's a comfort, and it's words of truth that are based on not only our own experience, but on the history of God's working with his people as God time after time has liberated and saved and brought his people to peace and rest, and we know that he does the same for us as well.

We feel anxiety when we face a bleak political, moral landscape, such as the one that appears to be before us now, and we are reminded of the intent of those engaged in terror to kill us, and we wonder what it is that we should do; or perhaps it's even closer to home, we have a sick parent or a sick spouse, or perhaps when one of our young people begins to wander in the way of the world, or maybe our marriage is, as they would say, on the rocks or in trouble. In those times of genuine anxiety and concern, in those times when we feel that our life is on edge, and we wonder if we will fall or collapse or if everything will come down upon our own heads, is there really anything beyond a slogan, anything beyond a saying that our Christian faith offers to us to bring us genuine comfort? Not simply a hope for some future comfort, but a genuine comfort in the present day based upon the realities which we know exist in Christ.

Faced with the immanence of the cross, perhaps we can take some comfort in knowing that our Savior wasn't indifferent to suffering. We've read that as he sat with the disciples he was troubled, and they knew and they could sense this anxiety. In fact, the whole time in the upper room has been a time of tension from the time that he washed their feet till Judas left, and now Peter, the rock of the disciples, the cornerstone of the disciples, the one that was always speaking and always the aggressive one has been told, "Before the morning you will betray me and deny me three times."

They were shaken and troubled. We don't know, it may have been a very somber setting, but it might also be that the disciples at this point were wailing and crying because their Lord had said, "I'm going to leave you, and I will die, and you will wander, all of you will scatter, and Peter, you will betray me." What would their response be? Even if they were quiet, they would be trembling in their hearts for they had committed their whole lives to Christ. They followed Christ. This was their whole purpose in being, and he was now saying, "I will die, Peter will betray me, Judas is gone, and all of you will scatter."

And so now comes a word of comfort in these troubled times. Jesus, though he himself is troubled, now turns to minister to those who are anxious. In John 14:1, we find first a word of consolation. "Let not your heart be troubled. Believe in God." But then Jesus also gives a word of revelation. "Believe in God; believe also in me." Those promises are bound up in the covenant which he has given to them in the Lord's

Supper just celebrated, "This blood is a new covenant." As he has instructed them in the new covenant, he now is giving them the promises of the covenant. "Believe in God because he is the one who has given you covenant promises, and believe also in me," because it is in Christ as mediator that those covenant promises are made accessible to you and to me.

But first these words of comfort. Often in times of trouble, particularly at funerals, we turn to the Psalms. I'm afraid that often it's simply a tradition that you read Psalms at funeral, but to the believer, to the one who has a hope that their loved one has passed on to glory, what they hear in the Psalms is the faithfulness of God in times of trouble.

Such as in Psalm 23, "The Lord is my shepherd; I shall not want. He makes me to lie down in green pastures. He takes me beside the still waters. He restores my soul." Here we have the promises of God given to one who is in trouble.

Or Psalm 46 is also often read at funerals. "God is our refuge and strength, a very present help in trouble." What words of comfort to one who's in trouble, one who feels their world is collapsing in chaos or is coming apart, and here we're reminded God is your refuge and strength. When enemies are persecuting you, when the terrorists want to destroy you, when it seems that your job is about to be lost, when the creditors are pressing down upon you, your refuge is in God, and that is where you will draw your strength from in the day of trouble. He's a very present help in trouble, that is, a help that is present now.

We live in an age of what we would call practical atheism. A practical atheist is one who makes a profession of faith that's credible and real. They believe in God and they believe that Jesus Christ has secured their salvation from sin. They take up religious habits. They attend church. They change the way they speak. They rid themselves of vices in life, but then when trouble comes, anxieties of living, they turn not to God, but to worldly resources. They seek comfort and ease—whether it be comfort by trying to secure an answer to their problem through worldly resources, or whether it be through substance abuse or relational abuse—rather than turning to God, living as it were as practical atheists. We often fail to believe God is our refuge, our strength, and a very present help in times of trouble.

> Deuteronomy 6, verses 10 through 12: "And when the Lord your God brings you into the land that he swore to your fathers,

to Abraham, to Isaac, and to Jacob, to give you, with great and good cities that you did not build, and houses full of all the good things that you did not fill, and cisterns that you did not dig, and vineyards and olive trees that you did not plant, and when you eat and are full, then take care lest you forget the Lord, who brought you out of the land of Egypt, out of the house of slavery."

When God has given his people all of the blessings he has promised, when he has sustained and carried us, having liberated us from sin and delivered us in the redemption of Christ to salvation, when we are enjoying the blessings of the peace of Christ, be careful because in that time of prosperity when our conscience is at ease with the Lord, it is easy to forget about the Lord.

"Let not your heart be troubled," Jesus told them, reminding them to believe in God. Just as we do when we're mourning the death of someone we love, the minister in reading the Psalms is saying, "Let not your hearts be troubled. Believe in God. Believe in God."

If we mention getting through a tough time by thinking of heaven, we often are told that it is simply a psychological device, something that we need to get us through those times. There's no sense of the reality of the present help of God. This Comforter that Jesus said he would send to us, does it really comfort, or do we turn to something else?

Jesus recognized that growing anxiety in his disciples. They had that same anxiety which we experience perhaps even to a greater degree because they had invested their whole lives in Christ who now said, "Gentlemen, we're at the end of the road. I am going to die, Peter will betray me, and you will scatter." Where were they to go? What were they to do? They had left their friends, their vocations, in some cases even their families to follow Christ, and now they would return to what? Jeers and "I told you so" and "Look what you've wasted."

Jesus recognized the anxiety in their lives, and he recognized in that anxiety their vulnerability to temptation, their vulnerability to turn from God, their vulnerability to succumb to the world. Just as when he was in the boat with them and the waves began to swell around the boat, and to break over the bow of the boat, and they began to sink, they grew anxious and they turned to him. They were confident with Christ before the storm. They were excited to be with Christ before the storm, and then as the storms hit and they grew anxious. They said, "Don't you even care? We're going to die! Don't you care if we die? Have you no regard for our lives?" Jesus stood up at that moment and said, "Peace, be still," and he stilled the storms around them.

Second Corinthians, chapter 1, verses 3 and 4 bring comfort to us, reminding us of that scene in the boat. "Blessed be the God and Father of our Lord Jesus Christ, the Father of mercies and God of all comfort, who comforts us in all affliction, so that we may be able to comfort those who are in any affliction, with the comfort which we ourselves are comforted by God."

"Believe God," Jesus says to us. Believe God. He believed God. What were the promises that he himself was drawing on when he said, "Believe God"? Jesus was facing death, and yet he said to his disciples, "Believe God for your comfort," because God had promised him, "I will not abandon your soul in the pit. I will not leave you in Sheol. I will not abandon you to Sheol."

In fact, in the verses that follow, Jesus displayed his confidence in that by telling them that even though he was about to die, he was about to go and prepare a place for them in heaven. He was about to go to the Father to prepare for their arrival to him and the Father. Jesus was ministering to them out of what ministered to him.

He said, "Believe God because I believe God. If I can face death, if I can face the cruelty of their jeers and the slaps and the flogging and the staking of my hands to the cross, if I can face that with confidence in the comforting words of my Father, then you be comforted as well because though I am facing death for sins of this world, and though I know that my Father will turn his face from me because of that sin, I still have a confidence that I will reside with the Father ultimately, and that confidence can see me through the trials which I face today."

When trials and temptations come, they're like the waves troubled by stormy winds, and he says, "Don't let your hearts be troubled." The confusion and the misdirection of all these waves that were battering the boat create a picture of the word "trouble." It's the same with our own hearts. When our hearts are troubled, isn't there confusion and misdirection as our heart is pulled this way and that and moving back and forth?

Jesus was saying to them, "Don't let this happen. Don't become this way. Don't surrender to the confusion. Don't become ruffled and discomposed in your hearts because that is a state that belongs to those who lack knowledge of God."

They're even described in Ephesians 4:14. They are children, we're told, tossed to and fro by the waves and carried about by every wind of doctrine. They lack a knowledge of God, an understanding of the ways of God and the purpose of God, an understanding of the providence of God in life. "What use is doctrine?" we say sometimes. "What purpose of doctrine? It just causes people to fight." Without doctrine there is no real knowledge of God. There's an idea of God, but no knowledge of God, and without the knowledge of God when real persecution and real trouble comes, what will we draw upon for confidence? How will we be able to say, "I know that my God lives, and I know that these events remain within his sovereign hand to guide me because the Scriptures have taught me so"? Without that, we will be carried by every wind of doctrine. The promise of the Scriptures is that we will indeed be tossed and buffeted about by the storms of life. There's comfort in belief.

In the 77th Psalm, in verse 11, the first 10 verses are the state of the psalmist who's in confusion, and he's in despair wondering, "Where is God?" It's the prayer of most of us, most of the time I regret to say, as we are facing life's troubles and we wonder, "Why does God leave us this way?" And then in verse 11, what does he do? He says, "I remember, I remember that my God is able to save."

The comforting words of Hebrews 13:5, "I will never fail or forsake you." It's a triple negative in the original language. We would read it that way as saying, "I will never, never, never fail you or forsake you."

And then notice the second word of our treatment of this scripture. "Do not let your hearts be troubled." Our heart is the fortress of our fortitude. If our heart begins to tremble, then our resolve is ultimately lost. It was Pharaoh's heart that turned hard and deserted him and directed him.

In Exodus 25, we're told it's the heart that moves people in their giving to God. In Deuteronomy 6, we're told it's the heart that is to love God. In Deuteronomy 8, it's the heart that fills with pride and forgets the Lord. In Deuteronomy 30, it's the heart that is drawn away, leading us ultimately to idolatry.

In Joshua 14, Caleb returned from the Promised Land with the other spies, and he said that the land was full and wonderful, and it was a land where God had given them great provision, but the other spies told the people that the land was full of giants and that they could never take it, and we read, "My brothers who went up with me made the hearts of my people melt." And so for their melted heart for 40 years they were made to wander. Why? Because they did not believe, and their hearts trembled, and their hearts melted, and so they were not able to enter into the rest of God.

"Believe in God," Jesus says, and then just like lumber that's cut to be tongue in groove where the pieces fit and lock together, he says, "Believe in God, and then believe in me." Believe in God. Believe in Jesus. Jesus wants them to apply all of the comfort and all the security that comes to their mind because of their study and their meditation upon God and his work with them. He wants all of this to be applied to himself, and he reveals to them a hope.

Some of them would watch his death from the foot of the cross, they would watch his agony and they would watch his bleeding and they would watch his dying, and they would not leave. They would stay there with Christ until he died because even there he was telling them that he was leaving, not in death so much as to prepare a place for them.

The promises that are made by God are fulfilled in Christ. In Hebrews 11, we're told that by faith Abraham went to live in a land, and he was living there in tents, but then in verse 10, we read he was looking forward to the city that has foundations whose designer and builder is God.

In Hebrews Chapter 11:36 to 39, we read simply, "Others suffered mocking and flogging, and even chains and imprisonment. They were stoned, they were sawn in two, they were killed with the sword. They went about in the skins of sheep and goats, destitute, afflicted, and mistreated, of whom the world was not worthy, wandering about in deserts and mountains, and dens and caves of the earth. And all these, though commended through their faith, did not receive what was promised."

These saints of old were looking forward to Christ. "Believe in God," Jesus says, "and believe in me." And then in chapter 12, the second verse, "Looking to Jesus, the founder and perfecter of our faith, who for the joy that was set before him endured the cross, despising the shame, and is seated at the right hand of the throne of God." Believe in God, and believe in Jesus, the founder and perfecter of our faith. The promises of God are made real to us by the mediation of Christ, the mediator of a sure and better covenant.

The late Donald Grey Barnhouse, pastor of the renowned Tenth Presbyterian Church in Philadelphia, included this story in his last book, *The Cross Through the Open Tomb*.

He tells a story of when he was pastoring in France. It was before World War II, and there was a young French girl named Simone. She came over, he says, nearly every day to spend time with his wife. She was trying to learn English, but she also was being ministered to. Following that Titus 2 principle, his wife was ministering to this girl and teaching her practical Christian living. She was a believer.

They had one of those Bible promise boxes with cards that you draw out each day to receive a promise from the Scripture of a blessing from God. He said that she would delight in sitting at the table as they would each draw out the card and read a verse from Scripture which was a promise of God. She liked it so much in fact that she went and took her French Bible and wrote out her own cards and made her own promise box which she kept.

Many years later, as World War II came and went, and as the Germans retreated and the Americans advanced, they had forced upon the French people German money, paper money, which was ultimately worthless. So this young lady with her family and her children was left destitute and impoverished with no means to buy anything at all.

She would go to one of the local shops, and all that the man could afford to give her were the peels off of potatoes, and he would give her these, one peck worth. She would take them home and boil them, and that was all they had to eat. She was emaciated. Her children cried, and they were hungry, and she finally reached the end of her rope, and there was no place else to turn, and nothing else for her to do. She went into her bedroom to pray, and she looked, and on her nightstand was the box of the promises, and she asked God, "Lord, I'll open the box. Just give me some hope in one word."

And as she reached for the box, her hand slipped, and the box fell, and busted open, and all of the hundreds of papers she had written were scattered all over the floor. It was at that point she realized that God actually did answer her prayer. It's not a single promise that you would pull out. In Christ, all the promises of God, all the blessings of God are for us all the time. He withholds nothing. He doesn't parcel it out to us. He gives us all of his blessings at all the time.

2

Heaven

John 14:2-4

"Let not your hearts be troubled. Believe in God; believe also in me. In my Father's house are many rooms. If it were not so, would I have told you that I go to prepare a place for you? And if I go and prepare a place for you, I will come again and will take you to myself, that where I am you may be also. And you know the way to where I am going."

These verses bring us near the end of the activities of the Upper Room Discourse, but deeper into the dialogue of Jesus, which would have taken only as much time as it takes us to read it, not counting of course what we do not have recorded. We find here the capstone truths as it were, those truths that bring clarity to all of the miracles and all of the teaching and all of the parables which Jesus has delivered to this point.

The disciples are in despair and very near panic. They have been told that Jesus is about to be taken away, that one of their own members is a deserter and a traitor, and that all of them will scatter and none of them will be faithful. Even Peter has been told that he will "deny me even before the morning as the cock crows three times."

So we find that now a state of depression is beginning to sink in on the disciples, and Jesus will speak to them words of encouragement. We find here his mention of their ultimate destination.

D. L. Moody noticed that the older we get the more interested we become in heaven. With age comes interest in heaven. He related that to a child recognizing that our whole lives are here on earth and we don't really know much about heaven. We think of it as a big city, perhaps glowing or radiating light. It has streets of gold. There's God in the city, and there will be a day of judgment that gets us there.

But he said as he was growing up, his brother had died, and instead of all the people that he knew and all the things he knows being here on earth, he now knew one person in heaven. And as he continued his journey through life, he lost more siblings and ultimately his grandparents and his parents, and with each passing year or two of his life, those he knew in heaven continued to increase in number, and those relations and connections he had here on earth decreased in number. And he said that along with that, his curiosity and his interest in heaven also changed and grew, and the questions that he had about heaven became more pointed, and his comfort with the idea of heaven became more settled.

What comes to your mind when you hear the word heaven? Do you worry about what your daily routine will be? Are we just going to be issued a harp and find a cloud and settle in and sing "Holy, Holy, Holy" to the same tune for the rest of our lives? And there'll be no sleeping, so we'll sing it 24 hours a day, if there are days. Will there be days? What are we going to do while we're there?

Do you wonder about the location of heaven? Growing up, we look up into the sky and we assume heaven is there, but as we grow older we understand that there is space above us in the sky. In fact, one of the Russian cosmonauts, an atheist, as he was out in space looked out the window and said, "I'm looking outside the window, and I don't see God anywhere." I had a seminary professor that once suggested that if he had opened the door and stepped out, he might actually meet God at that point.

Do we wonder about the appearance of heaven? Will there be streets of gold? Will it be real gold as we know it to be? Will the walls be radiating light? Will there be 12 high gates with angels manning each of the gates. Will it be set on 12 pillars with the names of the apostles around it? Will God be inside the city, and will he actually be the source of all of the light that is radiating out of the city?

Do you worry about recognizing friends and family, that you might be struck with holy amnesia once you get to heaven, and you might pass your spouse in the street and not know who they are, or worse, not really care because they're all the same? Do you want to have those cherished relationships still? Are you worried that you might forget the love that you shared when you were here?

Do you wonder what it will be like to be rid of sin, to be rid of a fear of death when you get there? Some of the first religious questions a child asks are about heaven. "Mommy or Daddy, what will heaven be like?" And we find at the end of our lives while we are more settled and we have a better idea, we still never are able to completely answer that question.

There's so many questions that we have about heaven. Perhaps they reflect our insecurities because we have a fear of what we might lose when we leave the earth rather than what we will gain. Again, will we be able to stay married? Will we be bored? That's the question I get from at least a portion of the population in my household. What if I can't sing well? I'm supposed to sing all the time. What if I can't carry a tune in a bucket? Will the people around me all move away when I begin to sing? Or the more important questions, "Will I get that younger body I had back?" Or more important for some of the young people around us, "Does this mean I'll never get my driver's license?"

The disciples in the upper room have been carried to the very brink of desperation in their journey now with Jesus. They've given up everything. They've walked away from their family, from their vocation. They've invested their whole lives into following Jesus, and now it's being announced to them and made real in their awareness that Jesus is about to depart through death. Not that he's going to the next town, or taking a sabbatical; not that he's going up on the mountain to pray to the Father as was his practice. He had had some temporary separations from them, but now they understand Jesus is leaving. He has carried them as it were, to the edge of a cliff, and they are about to be pushed over the edge. Jesus has just reminded them at the close of chapter 13 and the beginning of 14. "Trust in God. Trust also in me."

They still love Jesus, but their confidence in his messianic mission is beginning to waver because to them death marks the end of the work, and so they're having trouble understanding how it is that Jesus will be Messiah if in fact he's going to die. Jesus is saying, "Just as you believed in the unseen work of God, just as you believed that the God whom your eyes could not perceive was always working for you, just as you believed that, then also believe that I (Jesus Christ, that is), though you will not be able to see me, I also still am at work for you."

The Last Sermon of Christ

And then he begins to elaborate, and he says, "In my Father's house." This is a reference to paradise or to heaven where he is going. Some have tried to think of heaven as a sort of Nirvana. Nirvana is a Buddhist term implying that heaven is simply a state of mind. It's a way of ascending or transcending our present infirmities and becoming more than we are, joining a great orb of energy that will be a utopian paradise. It's a being at peace with yourself and without anxiety in life. That would be heaven in this view.

This is again a Buddhist idea that our end-state will simply transcend the process of reincarnation that people go through, but this is not our Lord's idea, and it's not the Lord's goal for us in life. No, heaven is not just a state of mind that we are able to enjoy here, and it is not a place on earth either.

There have even been songs about heaven being a place on earth, but it's not a place on earth. Jesus is clearly saying that he's going somewhere. He's leaving them, and he's going to the Father, not a place here on earth. Later, his visible ascension would provide to them continued evidence of Jesus' going to be with the Father. It provided the disciples with a concrete idea that Jesus had departed.

A number of places in the Bible give us descriptions of heaven. Heaven, a place so unlike where we are that we often have to depend on metaphors to understand, but there are places, and if we compile them, we can come up with some ideas of what heaven is.

From the story of Lazarus and the rich man, for example, we conclude that we will not be struck with some sort of a holy amnesia, but we will remember our friends and our family. We will recognize those whom we have known in this life. Jesus, even after the resurrection, came to the disciples and seemed to continue to have affection and a bond with the disciples as he recognized them and they recognized him.

In 2 Corinthians, we find Paul talking about getting caught up in a third heaven, and that has given a rise to much speculation. It simply is using the language of Scripture where the first heaven would be where we see birds in flight above our heads. The birds fly in the heavens, and then we know that beyond that is the space that lies beyond the reach of the birds. That could be a second, and then the third is what lies beyond which we do not have eyes to see. We are not able to know. Hence, Paul was carried to that third heaven.

Heaven

The cosmonaut would not have been in that third heaven. Even if he had stepped out, he wouldn't have realized until it was too late that it even existed. There is a heaven that is beyond the realm of the sky and even the place where the moon and the stars are in their orbit. Those would have been clearly visible to the people of Jesus' time and before. They would have seen birds flying, and they would have observed stars that were even above that, knowing that there was a first and then there was a second. Paul was carried to a place that he calls a third heaven. It's not here, but it's not just above our heads, and it's not in the place where the stars are, and so there must be yet a third heaven that he was taken to.

Revelation is the witness of John to things which he lacks words to describe, and so he uses analogy, metaphor and figurative language to give us a spectacular view of all that his eyes were beholding. He sought to use language and described hair as wool and eyes like blazing coals and feet like burnished bronze and tongue like a double-edged sword to explain his experience in poetic or metaphorical language.

In John 14, Jesus is not trying to provide a comprehensive description of all these aspects of heaven. His disciples have a single need at this point. They need reassurance, and they need to know that there is a continued purpose, and that there will be a continued presence of Christ. He limits his explanation to what the disciples need to hear.

The idea of home would be a summary. "I'm going to the Father, to his house, and I'm preparing a place for you there that you will go to." Jesus is saying, "I'm going to my Father's home, and in that home I'm preparing a place that would be your home." The idea of home, just the word home without even placing it in a religious context or religious discussion brings a sense of comfort to us. No matter how far we travel, no matter where our lives take us, we always have this idea of where home is, and we always have as our goal the hope of getting back to home.

Jesus will elaborate on how his atonement, the coming of the Spirit, and his second coming will all mean that they'll be together. He's going to elaborate on that as we go through the 14th, 15th, 16th chapters. That's part of Jesus' teaching, but right here he simply is telling them, "In my Father's house, in heaven, are many mansions." Coming from the Latin, the word is more properly translated as rooms, or actually apartments.

The Last Sermon of Christ

Too often this comforting analogy has been made literal. Just as people take John's struggling to explain what he saw in Revelation, and they try to make literal pictures of what heaven will be like, so here people will take the concept of many mansions or many rooms, and they'll try to come up with something that usually ends up being a health and wealth theology. They'll begin to describe our upgraded housing that we get in heaven, or they'll say it's the apostles that got the mansions, and the rest of us, if we work hard and are faithful and perhaps receive this or that spiritual gift, we'll have to settle with maybe a split level or a nice ranch home. Perhaps our yard size will be based upon how faithful we have been or how much we have worked or how much we've given to the ministry, whatever it might be that earns us a mansion in heaven.

Do you think Jesus was saying to these disciples who had just been arguing about who would be the greatest in the kingdom, "But let me tell you, you guys are getting some nice houses when you get up there"? Jesus had taught them about the laborers in the vineyard and about how it doesn't matter if you come in at the last moment and begin working or if you had been there all day, your pay at the end is the same.

Now as to the translation, mansion comes from the Latin, from the Vulgate, from where it was brought over into the King James particularly. The proper understanding of it is not a house that you will be assigned quarters in as if you were in the military going to a new post.

The word is used for rooms, ordinarily to convey the idea of apartment as I already mentioned. In that day, you had either a palace, or you had a home, or you stayed in an inn. There weren't plantation style homes that we have a history of in the South where some could live in one of those palatial homes while others did not. Inns were larger structures in that day. They had many rooms that could accommodate many guests, but there was always a chance in the disciples' experience of arriving at one of these larger inns and hearing those infamous words recorded in the gospel, "I'm sorry, but there's no room in the inn."

Jesus here is telling them, "There is plenty of room in my Father's house. There is room enough for all in my Father's house. You will never hear, 'There's no room in the inn.'" Jesus is promising the disciples there's a place for them at home, that they have a home, and that he will secure a place for them in that home, and he says if it wasn't so that he certainly would have told them.

Basically, he's acknowledging to them that they are wrestling with the thought, "Why have we come all this way for it all to end now?" And Jesus is helping them at this early stage in his teaching on the afterlife to understand, "This is not the end. This is the beginning. Where I am going, I'm preparing a place for you, and you have admittance to it. There is a place reserved for you. It's not hypothetical. It's not whimsical. It's actual. There is a real place for you. Every laborer from the field will have a room."

And not only is the room prepared for you by Jesus, but it's also made ready for you. He says, "In my Father's house are many rooms, and I go to prepare a place for you." Have you ever arrived at a hotel before check-in time, and you go in, and it's been a long trip, and you try to get a room, but it's not ready yet? You can't go upstairs. The room exists. Your reservation exists, but the room is not ready. You can't go in because maid service has not come and cleaned the room and made it ready for you to go to. It's dirty. You can't go in to a dirty room.

I have been let into a dirty room before accidentally. Trust me, it's good that they have these rules. You don't want to go where some of these people have been staying. It's wonderful what they do to turn these rooms around and to make them right.

Jesus at the cross opened heaven up. He made it ready by his own atonement and by his obedience to the Father. When his blood was sprinkled on the mercy seat, it had a cleansing effect, and atoning effect, to make ready a room for us, and when the veil was torn in two at his death, it was if the doors to these rooms were opened up for us to enter, but unlike an inn or a hotel that is temporary, this is a home. You're not just checking in for a short time. You're checking in to stay.

Jesus doesn't just call it a place, but he says it's a place for you. Someone once said, "A house is made of walls and beams. A home is built with love and dreams." Growing up, we take our home for granted. It seems that most of our young lives are spent trying to get away from home, and then the rest of our lives are spent trying to get back.

We long for the day we can escape from under the authoritarian rule of our father. We assume he must have some anger or some dementia that he's suffering from that he wants to exercise some powerful authority over us. We think we should be able to escape from this oppression. And then we realize that's what has kept our lives in order all of those years, and then once we escape, we find everything exploding in chaos, and we just want to go back home where somebody is in charge.

Not long after—unless shame makes us wander so that we're not able to go home because of our own conduct like the prodigal that wanders off to enjoy the world and cannot return home until he is completely broken—except for those cases, we begin to long for home again, and our hearts seem to be made to desire home. Wherever that home may be, whatever shape it may take, our hearts seem to have a desire for home.

As we get older and our parents begin to pass from this life to their eternal home, many lose their sense of home. They lose their sense of roots. When I go home to see my parents, I pass by my grandmother's home. My dad always called it the home place. It was sold out of necessity, and a developer came and with a bulldozer he removed the home place, leaving the trees. Now as we drive by, we see the driveway and the mailbox still standing, after all those many, many years.

In the front yard we would gather every Easter, all as family, extended family. We'd hide eggs over about an acre's worth of property. Probably some of them are still there to this day. All that is left now are the trees in the circle around a hole where my grandmother's home was, my father's childhood home. And it represents the hole that it leaves in one's heart when the home is taken away, a testimony to the history which we have lived for our home.

My own childhood home still stands, but it now is a daycare center. The place that I grew up, I still pass by when I go to visit my parents. The front yard is now paved. The climbing tree that was in the front by the road is gone, but the yard next door where we played baseball so many days, so many years, is still there.

I stopped one time and I went inside, walked across a porch where my father had bricked, and some of the bricks were uneven. He was younger at that time than I am now. I thought that he could do anything, but now being 44, I would not even touch a project like that. And so there was a place where one of the bricks protruded a bit, and wouldn't you know it, that's exactly where I fell. I still have a scar on my knee from that porch.

And so I walked over the porch where I received the scar. I walked inside, and I could still recognize the walls. I could still recognize all the places where I played. Growing up I would crawl behind the couch when I was supposed to be in bed. All the things that I did in that home I could still picture. I could still hear the sounds; it's still home though I know I could never go back.

All of our desire for security, for home will never be realized in this life because nothing here remains permanent, nothing. We try. We build our homes of brick. We secure our mortgages, pay them off early. We do all that we can to make sure we won't lose our home, but in the end it will go to someone else, and they may even dispose of our home.

We come to realize as we grow older that our roots, even our deepest roots here are temporary. Perhaps to cultivate an appreciation for our real home, we're not able to have a permanent home here. Since the time of Adam and Eve when they were expelled from their home, we have longed to go back home. Abraham when he was promised a very real and a very local home complete with boundaries, but even then his praise was not because he finally settled in his home, but that he was looking forward to the city that has foundations whose designer and builder is God (Hebrews 11:10).

Abraham's heart knew that no matter how deep his roots could be in the Middle East and no matter how secure his borders, no matter how great his estate, his real home was with the Father. Earthly homes are necessary and good, but our real need and the thing that our hearts ought to cling to is not longitude and latitude, not a place of dirt, not a roof, a particular roof over our head, but to be at home with God, and to be content in his service.

In fact, the way we cling to that which is temporary on earth tells where our real hope is and how much we neglect that which is eternal. The home was made ready and a door was opened by Christ, a permanent home that's real where those we love have already been gathering and are waiting, a home with Christ.

3

Do You Know the Way?

John 14:5–7

"Thomas said to him, 'Lord, we do not know where you are going. How can we know the way?' Jesus said to him, 'I am the way, and the truth, and the life. No one comes to the Father except through me. If you had known me, you would have known my Father also. From now on you do know him and have seen him.'"

WE FIND IN THESE and the preceding verses that the disciples are vexed by the information that a traitor is in their midst, that Peter will deny Jesus, that they all will be scattered, and finally that Jesus himself will leave them. We find them troubled, and now they begin to have questions that they're bringing to the Lord. He seeks to comfort them by saying that where he is going he will prepare a place for them and that there will be room for all who desire to come there with him. There is no limit to the rooms, as it were, in the Father's house. The one who enters into the labors in the field early in the day and the one who arrives just before closing time, all will find access to the Father's house.

And in this time of comfort that he is giving them, they want to go with him. Peter, of course, first asks, "Lord, where are you going?" and he wants to go immediately. "Why can't I follow you now?" Jesus replies to him that he would not be able to go, but he is not the only one with such questions.

The disciples hear Jesus say that he is leaving, and he has comforted them by saying that though he is leaving, ultimately they will not be separated. Not only will he bring them to him, but later we will discover that he will send them a Comforter, saying that he will not leave them orphans, but he will continue to abide with them. So within the context of the whole framework of this discourse, they will not only have the promise that they will actually go to be with Jesus, but that he will remain with them in spirit even after physically he has departed.

But here we are in the midst of the discussion, and he has comforted them with the words that the separation will not be permanent. Thomas begins to reflect for just a moment, and he realizes that while Jesus is saying that they will eventually be with him, he still hasn't answered the initial question of, "Where is he going, and how will he get there, and how will they follow him if they actually do not know the way?"

Here we see clearly the need for the work of the Holy Spirit to regenerate and illumine our minds as teacher and guide, for they're not able to grasp yet the spiritual truths which Jesus is giving them, though in giving them he provides a way for them to reflect and understand what he has taught.

There are today teachings that would presume that there are many ways to salvation. We hear it phrased this way: "There are many paths up the mountain," but that's clearly directly contradictory to Scripture. Proverbs 14:12 says, "There is a way that seems right to a man, but its end is death." And Matthew 7:13 and 14: "Enter by the narrow gate. For the gate is wide and the way is easy that leads to destruction, and those who enter by it are many. For the gate is narrow and the way is hard that leads to life, and those that find it are few."

I suppose if I were interested in climbing a mountain, then there would be many paths going to the top of the mountain, but I'm not interested in climbing a mountain. I'm interested in being with the Father. And so Jesus has told them the goal, to be with God. He told them, "I am going to the Father, and I will prepare a place for you. I'm going to the Father, and you will be there with me." So there you have the goal simply stated, to be with God.

But he's also telling them the way. So he has told them the what and the how, the goal and the way. He has told them the goal is to be with God, and the way is via himself. This is, in this exchange of comments between himself and the disciples, one of the most exclusive claims yet by Jesus is that he is going to be the only way of salvation. This is number six in the "I Am" sayings in the gospel of John. In 6:35, we read, "I am the Bread of Life." In 8:12, Jesus said, "I am the Light of the World." In 10:7 and 9, "I am the Gate." In John 10:11, he said, "I am the Good Shepherd." In John 11:25, he said, "I am the Resurrection and the Life."

These words in contemporary culture are offensive, aren't they? There's only one way of salvation, Jesus Christ. And we find when those words fall on the ears of contemporary listeners, they are considered. They are judgmental. They are exclusive, and exclusivity is not permitted in today's culture. It offends two broad groups of people. The first are easy to classify, those that are anti-Christian. What I mean here are those that we would consider to be universalist, which is not Christian teaching, and universalists would hold that all are saved, and they don't necessarily have to go through Christ; so therefore if we say Christ is the only way and there will be those who aren't saved because they are not in Christ, that's offensive to those who hold non-Christian teaching. It's offensive to Muslims. It's offensive to Buddhists. It's offensive to Hindus.

But it's also offensive to a larger group, if you can believe that there is a larger group. I'm talking about those who today choose to live and are comfortable living in a place of ambiguity. We might call them post-moderns. We might call them Gen Xers. You might call them any number of things, but the point is that they are living in an area that they believe to be gray, and they like living in that area.

What is some of the evidence we see of this? We can see where Christian images are tattooed on rock stars' arms. Crosses, big gold ornate crosses are hung from athletes' necks. We see Christian symbolism treated in the most irreverent of ways. We can see that also in the way people approach their worship in the most irreverent of postures and dispositions, blending as it were in this gray area the sacred and the secular, and that is where they're most comfortable, living in this place of ambiguity where it's neither this nor that, and you can't say it's all this or it's all that. Instead they seek to blend secular and sacred together.

This blending of sacred and secular, this tearing down of absolutes is now a mainstay of a generation of people, but why shouldn't it be? We've essentially taught them, and they have experienced that nothing is solid anymore, and there are no boundaries. I was reading someone's blog the other day who said, "I hate worship, but I love to study religion."

We live in a time which is historically unlike any other time in history, and it's a time where history itself seems to validate this ambiguity that people enjoy living in. We know that man can't fly, and yet

Do You Know the Way?

somehow man has walked on the moon. Where are the boundaries? Where are the absolutes?

We're told that there are those people of noble character who are elevated to high position, and then we study in history of Nixon's Watergate, and most of us have fresh in our mind Clinton's Monica-gate, and we wonder, "Where is the character, and where is the nobility of people who are our leaders?" And so once again, boundaries are broken down, and that which is supposed to be special and noble is made common and filthy.

We are told that life is precious and we're created in the image of God, and yet if you were of the Vietnam era, you've learned that we could send people to war and they could come home having accomplished no stated purpose and content to let things go the way they were. Or perhaps you're keeping up with the abortion statistics, and you're considering the millions in that holocaust that have been killed. And so the church says life is special, but culture teaches life is cheap, so once again the boundaries have been broken down.

The church is where we find truth, and yet from Jimmy Swaggert to the Roman Catholic pedophiles we find that there too truth is no longer sacred. You can take that all the way to denominationalism to where people would say with so many translations and so many denominations, "What is truth?" And so rather than calling everybody wrong, they simply are content to say everybody is right, and therefore there must be many paths to truth.

In a world and culture like ours, is there any room left for absolutes? Let me read to make this point further. Do we really need to take time to focus on the fundamental axiom of Christian testimony, that there is a truth, and that that axiom is that Christ alone saves? Do we really need to take time to do that? Can't we assume that in likeminded churches that all would hold that and believe that to be true?

After the church was established, wasn't it clear that Christ alone is the way of salvation? Apparently, large bodies of Christians have forgotten or left that. At a year 2000 Pastor at Peace Conference sponsored by the PCUSA church in Orange, California, the Reverend Dirk Ficca, who's from Chicago, said, "God's ability to work in our lives is not determined by becoming a Christian. So what's the big deal about Jesus?"

And in that same conference, there was a comparison of evangelism to ethnic cleansing because evangelism was seeking to destroy other faith groups and make all people Christian. Ficca said that he wants Christians to abandon their "instrumental" view that salvation comes solely through Jesus, and that Jesus himself is the good news, and that the goal of the Christian faith is the establishment of Christendom.

Have they learned anything since then? In November, 2006, a consultant to the same denomination, a Reverend Robins said, "There are many paths to God, and there is no capital T in truth." She writes Horizon Bible Studies, which are taken up and used as study material by many who are unaware of where the source of material comes from.

A survey taken in that denomination, "Do we wonder if the leaders have an effect?" reports that one-third, or actually 28 percent of that denomination strongly agree that all the different religions are equally good ways of helping a person find ultimate truth. One third of those who sit in the pews and worship and sing hymns like we do each Sunday believe that Christianity is just one of many ways. This is in a mainline denomination.

Martin Luther, the great Reformer, said, "The world is so blind and stupid that it always seeks to explore other ways. It is gullible and willing to follow where anyone directs and leads it. It will try and rely on any method or work suggested to it." Martin Luther certainly understood the preciousness of the gospel. Martin Luther was not a particularly religious man but believed he had been saved by God. He promised to give himself to the monastery and to Christ's work in the monastery as a monk, an action which ironically later he also condemned.

And as he entered into that monastery, he was the type of personality who couldn't be satisfied until every stone was overturned and everything was clear to him concerning salvation, and so he put himself through incredible physical torment. He put himself through confessing sin day after day, moment after moment, in excruciating detail, and no sooner would he leave the confessional, but he would come back afraid that perhaps he had forgotten some other sin. Wearing his confessor out, he finally came to understand the gospel, that we are justified by faith alone.

In spite of Luther's self-flagellation, his flogging himself, his starving himself, his being nearly naked in freezing weather, seeking to suffer enough to earn God's pleasure and merit, he only saw God as angry and as judgmental and unapproachable, and was never sure of his salvation, and he wasn't content with a lack of assurance. And as he began to teach in the University of Wittenberg, and as he began to teach through particularly the Psalms and then on into Romans, he came across the idea that we are justified by faith alone.

With that background then, note his words: "Therefore we dare go no farther or fix our thoughts on anything but Christ, as though there were any other road or way we should or might travel, as the false saints and reason persistently seek to do. For example, those who are known as Carthusians build themselves a special bridge to heaven by vowing and observing poverty and obedience, by abstaining from meat, from wearing linen garments, from resting at one place longer than a night, etc. In this way they suppose that they are on the right road to heaven. But this is a bridge and a stairway made of spider web; the higher they ascend on it, the deeper and more shamefully they fall into the abyss of hell."[1]

You hear here his reflection on his monastic experience. "'I'll forsake the world. It's evil and it's impure. I'll crawl into a corner, fast daily, abstain from meat, and torture my body. God will surely view such an austere spiritual life with favor and save me.' Another monk or priest also aspiring to live spiritually builds himself a different way, saying, 'If I read so many masses, if I pray, clothe myself in wool, and go barefoot, I'm on the right way.'"

Hear him here reflecting on his priestly experience as he says, "No matter how many religious functions I perform, I can't receive assurance of salvation. All of these are ways," he says, "of human design and judgment. They are founded on our own acts and deeds which pertain to this life only. They are all physical matters and works that even non-Christians can perform."[2]

How sobering. When we begin to think about the walk and the pace of our Christian life, do we realize that non-Christians could perform most of the Christian duties that we draw our assurance from? It doesn't take belief to attend a meeting. It doesn't take belief even to sing a hymn. It doesn't take belief to read the Apostles' or Nicene Creed. It's hypocritical not to believe it, but it doesn't take belief to do it.

And could it be that someone would have a false assurance because of their religious activities and traditions and time spent in sacred halls and hallowed assemblies? Even if such people do their utmost in

---

1. Martin Luther, *Luther's Works* vol. 24, p. 35.
2. Ibid.

all sincerity, it is still utterly evil, utterly corrupted, because it is all done without faith in Christ as though Christ were lying when he said that he is the way and the truth. The very fact that people seek such a variety of ways, devising one after another, is ample evidence that they are ignorant of the right way.

Do we not live in the same times that Martin Luther spoke of? Do we not live in a time of such incredible ambiguity where there is such an intense interest in all things spiritual and yet such an utter rejection of the claim of Christ? It's offensive, but it shouldn't be offensive. We shouldn't be offended and upset that Jesus said he is the way. We should marvel that God has provided any way at all. He has provided a way, but rather than rejoice, we're offended by the work of God in providing a way. Rather than protest that Jesus is the only way, I say again we should marvel that God has provided any way at all.

James Montgomery Boice points out three privileges that have been lost that Jesus is addressing that could be retained. Three privileges in the garden of Eden that were lost in the fall: constant and unimpeded communion with God, that is, being able to be in the presence of God, being able to abide with him and speak with him, being able to enjoy the presence of God.

The second one was that they knew God in truth, who he was, with unveiled eyes. They knew the truth of God, maybe not exhaustively. We don't know the limits of their understanding, but what they did know of God, they knew truthfully concerning God. And they were spiritually alive with eternity within their view, the promise of everlasting life attainable to Adam and Eve, but lost in the fall. The fall forfeited all of the privileges. They lost communion, they believed a lie, and they knew death, and this is the condition we are born into—alienated, ignorant, and condemned.

Jesus is speaking now of making things right again. "I am the way, and the truth, and the life. I will take the alienated, and I will reconcile them to God. I will take the ignorant, and I will give them spiritual vision, that they may know the truth concerning God. And I'll take the condemned, and I will bring them back, and I will give them life." Man is on a spiritual quest, and the history of religion and humanity testifies that in one form or another, man has sought spiritual peace and unity and wholeness, and has always done so.

John Owen, another great minister and theologian, said, "By nature, since the entrance of sin, no man has communion with God. He is light, we are darkness, and what communion has light with darkness? He is life and we are dead. He is love and we are enmity, and what agreement can there be between us?"[3] Men in such a condition have neither Christ nor hope nor God in the world, as Ephesians 2:12 teaches, "Being alienated from the life of God through the ignorance that is in them."

And so Thomas is asking Jesus a question, and Jesus is now speaking not only about the immediate context, but he's speaking more broadly about the reconciliation that we have in him. Of the four questions the disciples ask, this one helps us to understand that which is to come.

Notice their questions revolve around these issues. Peter and Thomas ask questions related about communion with God, whereas Jude and Philip, Jude also called Judas, concerning the revelation of the truth about God. And to answer these questions, Jesus in each case points to himself. He says, "I am the way." It's the dominant idea in the three terms, "I am the way, and the truth, and the life."

The two that follow serve actually to explain the first. "I am the way," and truth and life help illumine and explain the first. Truth is God revealed in holiness and love, life is God communicated to the soul, and truth and life are granted in Jesus, so he is the way that the soul gains entrance to the Father's house where truth and life reside.

Just as it is by a path that we make our way to a place, it's by Jesus that we make our way to the Father. The difference is that someone shows the way to travel on a road, whereas Jesus is the way to salvation. That's the fundamental misunderstanding with the idea of a path going up a mountain. Jesus isn't a guide; he actually is the path, and so if there are many paths going up a mountain, only one path is Christ, and so it's not a question of arriving at the top of the mountain. We can't access the top of the mountain. The path is Christ himself.

So what is the way? Let's boil this down in our closing moments and simply answer these three questions. What is the way? The way is reconciliation. We are all guilty not only in Adam, but in our own sin as well. We've affirmed the sin of Adam over and over again. Our lives are a testament to our being born in sin and deserving God's wrath. That sin is removed by Christ who enters into a covenantal union with

---

3. John Owen, Communion with God, p. 6.

his people, and we are so identified with him that his cross is our cross, his death is our death, his resurrection is our resurrection. Our sins are forgiven, and they're cast into the depths of the sea and forgotten, as Scripture teaches.

What then is truth? Truth is the illumination of God's will and God's way and God's person to our mind. Pilate asked Jesus as he was interrogating, "What is truth?" but in an ironic and in a tragic moment, he didn't even wait for Jesus to answer, but acknowledging that in his own mind there was no absolute truth, he simply asked the question and walked away, the same as the culture does today as if to say, "You speak of truth. There is no absolute truth."

Jesus is the Word of God made flesh. He is the manifestation and the embodiment of truth that is eternal. The goal of illumination is to know truth, and the object of truth is God and God is revealed in his Word which was once made Flesh and which spoke to reveal the way of salvation to all men. Jesus is not only the way. He is the right and true way. Once we profess faith in Christ, we have to continue in Christ.

A. W. Pink says, "The whole Bible bears solemn witness to the fact that the natural man is spiritually lifeless. He walks according to the course of this world. He has no love for the things of God. The fear of God is not upon him, nor has he any concern for his glory. Self is the center and circumference of his existence. He is alive to the things of the world, but dead to heavenly things."[4]

Regeneration is life. What is life? It is simply to be born again. It is to be regenerated with a hope to live eternally in Christ, and only those who are in Christ have spiritual life. Luke 15:24: When the prodigal returned, the father said, "This is my son who was dead and is alive again. He was lost and he is found."

Christ grants life to all who come to him, and then he is their life. He grants it, and then he becomes their life. Indwelled by the Holy Spirit, they live more and more to Christ and less and less to self. As we near the end of life on earth, we see death's best stand, seeking to block our way to the eternal, but Jesus says, "Remain in me. I am the life. Death will not take you in the end."

Increasingly, we hear his voice above the roar of the world, and we learn that life's purpose is the same as Christ's, to glorify God and enjoy him forever. Christ came to give life. He didn't come to confuse.

---

4. A.W. Pink, The Gospel of John, vol. 4, by James Montgomery Boice, p 1079.

He didn't come to provide a different way. He came to reveal the only way, the only way there has ever been. He came to make that which was impossible possible. Like the Israelites as they approached the Red Sea with the army and the sword behind them and sea and potential of drowning in front of them, Jesus makes a way through to life.

As when Moses raised his arms and God parted the sea that they would pass through on dry land to the other side, to salvation, so it is with Christ as he raises his arms on the cross and offers to us a way to eternal life and salvation. And so we have the sword behind us as death pursues us, and we have that our physical demise in front of us which would seem to be our end, and yet Christ makes a way, and he is the way.

Have you entered into the way? Have you come to Christ and heard his call? Not the way of the world which leads to death, but the way of Christ which leads to life? He's not a way; he is the way. Luther noted that when Christ is preached, multitudes run forward to hear the sweet and comforting message of grace and forgiveness, but then they don't continue on with Christ, thus proving the parable of the soils in Matthew 13 to be true that some grain will fall on rocky soil and spring up, but lacking roots and lacking proper soil, it withers away. The life of a Christian is one of sacrifice in frightening circumstances. It's one of persecution and service. Facing the sword and the lies of the devil, the child of God will cling to Jesus as the way, and the truth, and will not turn back.

Have you indeed not just come to religion, but come to Christ? Are you in the way, not just hearing of the way? Is your life testimony that you are clinging to Christ as you pass through the parted Red Sea? With towering columns of waters on the side and an army at your back, are you fleeing to Christ each and every day, holding onto truth and not taking any other road along the way so that you may arrive at the other side to receive the promise of life already given in Spirit, but waiting eternally in the place prepared by Christ to which we will go?

4

Seeing God

John 14:7–11

"I am the way, and the truth, and the life, and no one comes to the Father but by me... 'If you had known me, you would have known my Father also. From now on you do know him and have seen him.' Philip said to him, 'Lord, show us the Father, and it is enough for us.' Jesus said to him, 'Have I been with you so long, and you still do not know me, Philip? Whoever has seen me has seen the Father. How can you say, "Show us the Father"? Do you not believe that I am in the Father and the Father is in me? The words that I say to you I do not speak on my own authority, but the Father who dwells in me and does his works. Believe me that I am in the Father and the Father is in me, or else believe on account of the works themselves.'"

WHAT IS OUR GOAL in the Christian life? You hear it expressed if you go to a funeral, don't you? When life is over you hear people say, "He's now with God or in the presence of God." How many times have I heard those who either are unbelievers or are skeptical of the Christian faith say something like, "Well, if God would just show himself to me, or give me a burning bush." In other words, "If God would appear, I just can't believe that which I cannot see," as if we were asking too much of those who are skeptical of the teachings of Scripture, those who would say only an appearance of God will be convincing.

That would be a spiritual mountaintop experience, wouldn't it, to see God? Could there be any experience in the Christian life that would be greater than to see God? And yet that's the promise of Scripture, that in the end we will see God face to face.

Seeing God

As we begin to study these verses, I want you to notice something about the disciples. Notice how comfortable they have been in asking these several questions of Jesus as they have been seeking to interpret his discourse. Peter wanted to follow Jesus immediately. Jesus said, "I'm going to depart from you, and where I'm going you can't go," and Peter who had grown comfortable with the Lord said to him, "But Lord, I will go, and I'm going to go with you right now. You just tell me the way, and I'm there, and I will be there with you."

Then Thomas said, "Christ, if we're going to have to go later, you're going to have to give us directions. Can you tell us how it is that we can get there? I don't know how to get to where you're telling us to go."

While all of this is going on, and while Jesus has been talking about seeing the Lord, we find that Philip's mind apparently has begun to wander. His mind has begun to reach higher up into the clouds. Perhaps he's beginning to have a bit of a heavenly view of things, and Philip says, "Well, Lord, if you'll just show us God now as a pledge, then we can have an assurance of all these things that you say." Philip is saying, "Lord, just show us God."

Now we see how Jesus would call them his friends, and we see something of the atmosphere of compassion and love that is shared between these disciples, and it's important as we continue through this to keep in mind the genuine compassion, the genuine love, the genuine concern that the Lord Jesus Christ has for the minds and the spirits and the lives of these disciples. It's easy for that be lost; because there's so much here to unpack and so much here to understand, it's easy to become lost and forget that the Lord is teaching in the context of a great, deep, abiding love for his own, and that's why he would call them his friends.

It's been a quest of man in every generation to see God in some fashion. People even today in worship services will strive to have some way that they can communicate, "I really felt a presence of God." You'll find those on the one extreme in the Pentecostal circles who will equate that to the Spirit. The Spirit was there as if in other congregations the Spirit of Christ is not there, and so it will be a special presence of God that they're trying to explain.

On the other hand, you'll have those who turn to icons, and they'll erect statues, or they'll erect some visual symbol that helps them to somehow feel that God is there. Candles have been used because of the flickering flame to help people feel that God is present with them, and people have been striving for some sort of concrete evidence or some sort of concrete expression of the presence of God.

The Puritans came in and they cleaned all the churches out, and the congregations in those days gathered and did nothing else at all. They gathered to hear the Word essentially read and expounded, and that was all because the presence of God was understood to be centered in the Word of God. As the Spirit of God goes out with the Word, it never returns void.

And so as we have joined in with the flow of history in church, we would say, "Yes, there has been a quest for people to understand, 'In what sense is God present with us if he is present at all?'" And we have to answer that question. Is God present, or are we simply a Christian institution teaching the precepts and teaching the moral laws of the Scripture handed down to us through the ages? If God is present, then it's an entirely different matter. If God is truly present, then there is validity to Christian worship that will be proved, certainly in the end, but even in the days in which we live.

We're not the first to ask these questions. Moses asked this on the mountain. "What would he ask of the Lord except that he would be able to see God?" And we know that God put him in a cleft of a rock and covered him so that he was only able to see God's glory as it passed by.

We believe that a view of God would convince us and the world of his power, of his immensity, of his reality. While many today sometimes wish for that same solid evidence, we have the benefit of generations who have studied the Scripture, searching them out to answer these very questions and to teach us the truth concerning God. If we have known our Shorter Catechism, certainly as we've been studying them and teaching them to our children, then we would know one of the questions there is, "What is God?" Isn't that a question that almost all people in all places would ask? What is God? And we would learn there, "God is spirit, infinite, eternal, and unchangeable."

And it continues on, but for our purposes let's limit it simply to that first part of the answer. "God is spirit, he's infinite, he's eternal, and he is unchangeable." Then we would ask, "Well then, what is spirit? You say God is spirit. That would mean that I can't see him, so then tell me, what is a spirit?" A spirit is an immaterial substance that's without flesh or bones or body parts, an immaterial substance. Our eyes are physically capable of beholding only that which is material. So if God is immaterial in the sense that he is spirit, then our eyes perhaps will not behold him.

'So we grow up understanding that God is omnipresent. He's in all places at all times. He is spirit, and he's everywhere, and he will not be limited by local and physical appearance. Isn't that really what we're asking? If we are asking for God to appear here, we are asking to see God who is everywhere present, God who is keeping creation moving by his providence and by his nature. If in fact all that is taught of God is true, then nature depends upon God in every aspect and in every place, and yet what we are asking is that God would locally restrain himself or locally confine himself to make an appearance and neglect all of the rest of creation by his presence.

It might be one thing if we just be wanted a sign, but that's not what people have been asking. They want God himself on which all creation depends to limit himself and confine himself locally that they may be able to see him with the eyes of flesh.

But let's be sympathetic to Philip. He's not expressing skepticism. He's expressing an honest expectation. There's an excitement in his voice. He wants to see God to have the assurance of all the things that Jesus is saying. He essentially wants to seal for himself all that Jesus has been teaching.

Maybe the word of the transfiguration had begun to leak out from some of the other apostles and is the source of his idea about seeing something that would validate what he was hearing. He simply can't contain his enthusiasm about all that Jesus has said, and he wants it to begin now. He wants to see it now. He wants consummation of these promises now.

I wonder if it would be enough for us if we saw God. Suppose we could see God. Suppose we were to ask that question. Philip says, after all Jesus had said, taught, and promised, "Just show us God the Father, and it will be enough."

If you could just see God and live through the experience, would it be enough? I would ask you not to answer too hastily, and don't be so self-assured because I'm convinced that the answer is no, it would not. In fact, we have seen God, and it is not enough for many. Neither we nor Philip were the first to want to see God.

The Last Sermon of Christ

I've already mentioned Moses in Exodus 33. Moses asked to see God's glory, and it was replied, "You cannot see my face, for man shall not see me and live." In Revelation 22, however, we read his servants will worship him, and they will see his face. That is, we will look into the face of Christ, and his name will be on their foreheads, which means that our characters will be transformed by his law which is written on our hearts. So the consummation of history is the accomplishment of the impossible. We will see God face to face.

These two passages, Exodus 33 and Revelation 22, can sort of set bookends on our study to help us know that first of all, in the natural state man cannot see God, and yet in the spiritual state he will see God face to face., Between these two states we have this teaching of Jesus who is saying, "If you have seen me, you have seen God." And so how is it that we are to understand that? We lack a physical manifestation and vision of God, but neither have we seen with our eyes Jesus Christ himself who has ascended to the Father and sits at the right hand in glory. Philip could see Christ in person. We have neither a vision physically of Christ present, nor of God the Father. Philip has heard Jesus teach about the Father on many occasions, yet he's saying that he's never laid eyes on him, and so he can't know him. While Jesus is talking, Philip's thoughts are beginning to wander. He's beginning to think and beginning to soar to the clouds.

When we think of wandering thoughts, usually it means that we are distracted and no longer interested in the topic at hand, but not so for Philip. His thoughts are beginning to go higher, and he wants to see God. Jesus says they have seen God, and Philip is saying, "Lord, I don't recall it. If I've seen God, I sure have no memory of it." And Jesus in a tone of disappointment says, "Philip, have you been together with me for so long and you still don't know me?" If Jesus would just show them now, it would all be settled in Philip's mind.

Martin Luther, in his comments on these verses, finds a great comfort when we consider our own immaturity and wavering as we look at these disciples. Philip had completely missed the mark with his question. Luther said, "To our great comfort however, this demonstrates how our shameful nature and reason finds it so difficult to dismiss its own notions."[1] He's saying Philip had an idea, "Lord, I want to see God." That should have been dismissed from his mind, but our fleshly nature

---

1. Martin Luther, Concordia Pub. House, 1955, p. 57.

causes us not to be able to dismiss such absurd thoughts. We cling to them and then require them to validate a faith, to desist in speculating about God and to cling to Christ alone. Even the apostles themselves who had Christ with them in person, had heard him discourse with them on the subject, could not shake off this rubbish. I love the way the Reformers simply call it like it is, this rubbish.

They had Christ with them. Jesus' own tone of disappointment betrays that they should have known this, but yet they don't. Luther's own comfort is ours, that while the disciples' thoughts wandered, and though they would stumble and be weak in their faith, they did not run away from him as Judas had. They did not betray him as Judas did, but they remained with him. They delighted to hear his Word, even though their hopes were beginning to look elsewhere beyond the cross. In himself, and in his own person, Jesus still regarded them as his own, and he judged that they did in fact know the Father even if they didn't understand it and wouldn't until later.

Their case is similar to the blind man, which we read about in Mark 8. This sometimes puzzles folks because it seems that Jesus had to take two tries at healing the blind man. You know the story. Jesus spit upon the man's eyes, and he put his hands on him, and he said, "What is it that you see?" And then he opened up his eyes. Previously, he was completely blind. He said, "Now I see men who look like trees walking around." And so Jesus again laid his hands on him, and then he asked him what he saw, and he said, "I see plainly, and I see clearly."

Here the disciples are seeing dimly, as if men look like trees. They are able to see Christ, and they hear Christ, but they don't see clearly those things which are spiritually apprehended. Many come to the Scriptures, and their view of God is simply not clear. Many read the Bible, many read the Scriptures that we have before us, many will read the verses we have before us, many will have them opened up to them, and still they walk away feeling incomplete. They walk away feeling that they just didn't quite grasp what this was all about, that it was not clear to them yet. They know that Jesus taught something, and they know it must be important, but they just can't quite apprehend what it is that our Lord is opening up to them.

Some will turn to other devices for their spiritual nourishment to give them some satisfaction or some sense of progress, but it would be best if the Spirit of Christ was to teach them the words of Christ as he delivered them to the disciples. The disciples were limited in their seeing. Jesus says to him again in that disappointed tone, "Have I been with you so long, and still you do not know me, Philip? Whoever has seen me has seen the Father. How can you say, 'Show us the Father'?"

Do you hear in Jesus' saying, "After these years, after the miracles, the healings, the raising of Lazarus from the dead, after the multiplication of the food to feed many, the stilling of a storm, after the debates with the Pharisees, and after our private teaching as I gathered with you to instruct you in the things of God, after all of that, do you still essentially not know me in the essence of who I am?" They do not know Christ except as they themselves are.

Paul acknowledges the same in 2 Corinthians 5:16. He says, "We once regarded Christ according to the flesh, but no more." The incarnation expressed in John 1, "The Word was with God, the Word was God, and the Word became flesh and dwelt among us," is elaborated in Hebrews 1. "He is the radiance of the glory of God and the exact imprint of his nature, and he upholds the universe by the power of his word."

The disciples have before them the very thing they are requesting, a "visio dei," a vision of God. They want to see God, and God stands before them. What they are looking for is an appearance that will be a manifestation of power. That's really what they're asking for. If you are not content with the teaching of the Scripture, if you're not content with the indwelling presence of the Holy Spirit, then what you really want is for God to show himself in his power. You want to see him in his majesty. You want to see him in his reign and in his power and his omnipotence.

What they couldn't grasp yet was that the Lamb of God in holiness and love standing before them was God, but they weren't looking for that. They weren't looking for the Lamb of God. As we read in the book of Revelation, there was a great sound like a lion, and then as John turned around, he beheld there a bloody Lamb.

Jesus standing before them was the moral perfection of God's character manifested in the incarnation of this Man. In the idea of moral union between Christ and between the Father is something that cannot exhaust the idea of incarnation. We who are saved can't say, for example, "If you've seen me, you've seen Christ." I can't say, "If you've seen me, you've seen Christ," because my morality is not as perfected as that of Christ. There's a unity and a spiritual union between myself and

Seeing God

Christ, but I cannot say, "If you've seen me, you've seen Christ." But the Lord Jesus Christ, because of not only the unity that he shares within the Trinity, but because of the moral perfection which he shares with the Father's own moral perfection, he can say, "If you've seen me, you've seen the Father."

There is no difference in the moral perfection of God the Father and of Christ. The idea is that Jesus, who is the Son, reveals the Father as the living Word of God. As words reveal character, as words show forth the man, Jesus shows forth the Father. Again, echoing the reading in Hebrews, chapter 1, that "he is the radiance of his glory and the exact imprint of his nature."

So just as every study of Scripture is not the same, so every seeing of "Jesus" is not the same. What do I mean by that? All who attend a particular preaching will hear the same words spoken, but many will see Christ differently because of levels of maturity, because of time spent in the study of Scripture, because of willingness to grasp and hold onto, or because of belief or unbelief, because of the indwelling of the Spirit or the lack thereof, but all hear the same, just as Christ walked before all those people and yet not all apprehended him as the Messiah.

James Montgomery Boice, in his commentary on John, brings a wonderful illustration of this difference in seeing from the post-crucifixion appearance or resurrection scene at the tomb. Here he tells very simply the story of Peter and John who are told that something has happened at the tomb. Now they're told that Christ is gone, but all they know is there's a disturbance, and they just don't know what to believe, and so they both run to the tomb.

John, being the faster runner, gets there first, stops at the door, and surveys the inside of the tomb and sees the tomb was empty. Now there are three different words for seeing used in that passage. The word that is used for "saw" is the word that would be used to describe something like a picture that is taken. He surveyed the scene in total, but had no conclusion that he was drawing on it. He was taking in this as information, and he didn't know exactly what to do with it. It was like you look up and you see a picture in its total. He saw that there were linen clothes, and he saw that the body was missing.

Peter arrives very shortly thereafter, and being as he is, doesn't say, "Excuse me," or "Pardon me." He simply pushes his way past John, and into the tomb he goes, and there we read Peter in his looking and observing the place where Jesus was laid saw the linen clothes, and this word used for "saw" is to communicate a contemplation, a thinking about it. It means that he was giving close inspection, and what he saw was that the linen clothes, if the body had been stolen, first of all, wouldn't be there. Secondly, if they were left, the body would have been unwrapped, and the clothes would have been disheveled and perhaps put to the side. But they were not. They were still in the shape of the body and in the placement where the body was with the spices still inside, and the head linen in particular was where it was supposed to be as well.

And so when we read about this, we see that Peter's mind now is puzzling over the data that he is receiving, and he's beginning to try to make sense of it. He saw it in a different way. Now he sees it like an investigator, and he's beginning to try and discern what it is that happened. Then John enters, and we come to the third and last of the words used to describe seeing. John comes in and he sees and believes. It's a seeing with understanding. This seeing and believing is the word that's used in John 14, when Jesus says that whoever has seen him has seen the Father.

That old saying that seeing is believing is reversed for the Christian. We do not see until we believe. We believe in what we cannot see. That is by definition faith. Faith is the apprehending and the believing in that which is not seen. Faith is a reaching out with assurance that we know that when our hand closes upon the object of our faith, it will in fact be there. We believe and then we see.

Because we perceive the truths that are taught in Scripture, and as we do believe, we will one day behold our Lord. The words and the works of Christ make clear who he is. I want to stress that once again. Scripture is not our textbook. It is the Word accompanied by the Spirit. Jesus Christ was the Word of God incarnate, and these are his words.

If you would see Christ at all, it will not be through some super spiritual experience apart from the Word. It will not be through meditation. It will not be through music. It will not be through some transcendental state. It will be through the Word. We open the Word to show the people Christ. Jesus told him, "Have you walked with me all this time and still I'm just words on a page, and you don't see the Father? Have you been with me all this time and still you can't commune with me here by the power of the Spirit? Have you been with me all this time and still do not see God?"

5

Doing a Great Work in the Kingdom

John 14:11–12

"Believe me that I am in the Father and the Father is in me, or else believe on account of the works themselves. Truly, truly, I say to you, whoever believes in me will also do the works that I do; and greater works than these will he do, because I am going to the Father. Whatever you ask in my name, this I will do, that the Father may be glorified in the Son."

AS WE DRIVE DEEPER and deeper into the Word of God, what are you expecting? What are your expectations? There's no hidden meaning to the question. It's not really even a redundant question. I'd like for you to answer it at least in your own mind; what is it that you expect as we go deeper and deeper into God's Word?

I pray that it would not be like the Gentile woman who, upon coming to Christ when he told her that the time was not yet come for the Gentiles, replied that she would simply be satisfied with the crumbs that fall from the table. I hope that you have heard and have received Christ's invitation, that you would not have to make do simply with crumbs falling from the table, but you have been invited to sit and to feast at the table of the Lord, and that includes partaking in his Word that you would grow more and more mature in your understanding.

The disciples themselves, having walked with Christ and listened and watched him for three years, are struggling mightily to understand what Christ is so earnestly trying to teach them now in these final hours before their separation and the crucifixion, the atoning work at the cross.

The Last Sermon of Christ

Jesus has been making an appeal for faith. He's been calling for the disciples to believe what they cannot see, and now he describes the fruit of their faith in amazing terms. Did you hear when Jesus said, "I say to you, whoever believes in me will also do the works that I do; and greater works than these will he do"? Greater works now than they had already observed in Christ. If that is not classified as amazing, I don't know that anything ever could be.

Jesus is continuing to pursue the implication of his being in union with the Father in the context of the kingdom, the establishment of the kingdom of God, and he tells them his works testify to his oneness with the Father.

Let me review the bidding, as it were, up to this point in 14. In verse 1, he said, "Believe in God, believe also in me," creating there a connection or a link. In verse 7, "If you had known me, you would have known the Father. From now on, you do know him and have seen him." We see the Father in the person in Christ. In verse 9, "Whoever has seen me has seen the Father." Again in verse 10, "The Father who dwells in me does his works." In verse 11, "Believe me that I am in the Father and the Father is in me." Is Jesus introducing some new teaching? Certainly not. Return to John Chapter 6, and read just a few verses, 53 to 58. Jesus is talking about the Bread of Life.

> "Jesus said to them, 'Truly, truly, I say to you, unless you eat the flesh of the Son of Man and drink his blood, you have no life in you. Whoever feeds on my flesh and drinks my blood has eternal life, and I will raise him up on the last day. For my flesh is true food, and my blood is true drink. Whoever feeds on my flesh and drinks my blood abides in me, and I in him. As the living Father sent me, and I live because of the Father, so whoever feeds on me, he also will live because of me. This is the bread that came down from heaven, not like the bread the fathers ate and died. Whoever feeds on this bread will live forever.'"

The unity of the Father and the Son is what Jesus is describing for the disciples. We will explore this as he unfolds it more and more in the chapters that follow. H. A. Ironside, a great commentator from many years ago, said, "The unity of the Father and the Son does not involve the thought that the Father and the Son were exactly the same person.

They were two persons, and yet one in the unity of deity with the Holy Spirit. Father, Son, and Holy Spirit."[1]

An ancient symbol for the Trinity shows in picture form that the Father, the Son, and the Holy Spirit are all one God, yet the Father is not the Son, the Son is not the Father, and the Spirit is neither Father nor Son nor are they the Spirit. This is the basic formula for the Trinity. The Father without the Son and the Holy Spirit couldn't be fully God. The Son without the Father and Holy Spirit wouldn't be God. The Spirit without Father and Son wouldn't be God, but together they are one God in three persons.

Jesus is now going back to that conciliatory tone as he's trying to unfold this for his disciples. You remember he had that initial conciliatory tone with them when they were upset and after there had been the prediction of betrayal, and he told them that he was going to a place, that they were not to be frightened because he was going to prepare a place for them, and that place was still ahead of them. It was a place they had yet to go to, and it was so much more glorious than anything they had ever known, and they wouldn't long to hold on to anything that they have now if they could but just glimpse the place that Jesus was preparing for them.

He told them, after Thomas' protest, that they knew the way to this place, and there was no need for him to disclose any further directions to them, but only that that way, which was him, would be opened up, and we know that it is through the cross. Now he wants to tell them of the work again that is still ahead of them, that will be greater than any they have ever seen, and as the work completed by Jesus testifies of his unity with the Father, so their work will testify of their unity with him, the Son.

That being said, are there any practical implications for us? Is there anything intended for us in what Jesus has said? Read this verse again. "I tell you the truth, anyone who has faith in me will do what I have been doing." The first practical implication is that there is continuity between our work and labor and the ministry of Christ. "He will be doing, the one who is a follower of Christ, that which I have been doing," that is, the work that Jesus was doing.

There's another one if we read further. "He will do even greater things than these." So first of all there's continuity between what we as

---

1. H.A. Ironside, *Addresses on the Gospel of John*, p. 615.

the church of Christ do and what Christ has done, and then there's also an increase in the ministry of the church of Christ when compared to the work that Christ has done. Finally, there is also a condition that is laid upon it. This is made possible Jesus said, because "I am going to the Father."

In the verses that follow Jesus begins to really focus the attention of the disciples upon this idea of unity culminating in his teaching of the indwelling of the Holy Spirit. Through the Spirit indwelling them, they're unified to him. It is his Spirit, but that is still ahead of us. Let's consider these verses.

Continuity: that begs the question, "Well, what sort of work are we to be involved in that has continuity with the work of Jesus?" It's continuity related to the works of Jesus. And what were those great works that Jesus did? Immediately we turn to the miracles. So he fed 5,000. He raised people from the dead. A 1991 sermon by John MacArthur on miracles cited an occasion when Oral Roberts said, "I cannot tell you about all the dead people I've raised. I've had to stop a sermon, go back, and raise a person." Now I will confess there have been a few times that I wondered if I might also have to do that, but if I wait long enough, generally the one that I thought passed will stir, and in fact it was just a little nap.

But Oral Roberts, apparently his preaching, I guess we could say, is really knocking them dead because he has had to do this a lot. In the middle of preaching, often he has to go and raise a few people in the middle of a sermon. According to John MacArthur in Charismatic Chaos Roberts said, "I can't tell you about all the dead people I've raised. I've had to stop a sermon, go back and raise a dead person."[2] John Wimber, who is of the Vineyard, teaches that raising the dead is a basic element of any reputable healing ministry. If you're in Christ, obviously you're going to be raising some people from the dead. In his book "Power Healing" he said, "In sum, raising the dead was a dramatic and infrequent event in the New Testament, but something I believe is possible still today."[3]

Are these the great works, the greater works that Jesus is describing that they're supposed to be involved in? I would contend, and I think the text certainly supports, he's not referring here to his miracles

2. John MacArthur, *Charismatic Chaos*, p. 131.
3. John Wimber and Kevin Springer, *Power Healing*, p. 166.

Doing a Great Work in the Kingdom

because he cast the miracles himself in a certain context that these were signs that pointed to the arrival of the kingdom, and the work he's called the apostles to is teaching within the kingdom. Not to continue with the signs that show the arrival of the kingdom, but the proclamation of the gospel that people could enter into the kingdom. We have the Word now which testifies to those very signs.

What we have commanded though through the rest of the New Testament Scriptures is that the people of God would take up the Word and would preach the kingdom of God to those who dwell in darkness. If we were to take it in the sense of miracles, then it would have to mean that if Jesus raised three from the dead, then we have to raise six. We have to do it greater than he did.

If Jesus cast out a legion of demons, we have to cast out two legions of demons because we have to do a greater work than he did. If he calmed the sea, I suppose we'll have to drain the sea because we have to do a greater work than he did. Surely, even the most carnal and the most uninformed mind wouldn't believe such things, and yet we hear those preachers of the airwaves, like Oral Roberts, Benny Hinn, and others. I won't go down the roll call of what I'll call the roll call of shame. We hear those who have taken captive the weak souls and the weak minds with stories of their false miracles and wonders, and people eat it, as they say, like candy.

Thankfully, we're not left to wonder, speculate, or as so many have done just simply make something up. Jesus wasn't hiding his meaning. There's no secret here that is left for us to discover on some treasure hunt of spiritualistic or allegoric meanings. All along, Jesus has made it clear his miracles were not the focus of his mission. That was not why he came. He didn't come simply to raise three people from the dead. These were signs of the kingdom.

In John 6:26, after feeding the 5,000, crowds followed him, and he said, "Truly, truly, I say to you, you are seeking me, not because you saw signs, but because you ate your fill of the loaves." They were consumers. They wanted to know what they could get out of it. They were going to eat some bread that Jesus had set before them, and they thought, "Well, if this man will feed us, then we'll join his ministry because it fills us up with what our carnal nature desires."

In 6:28, "What must we be doing to do the works of God?" Well here, we have the question. What are these works of God? We are told that we will do greater works than Christ. Here he defines by answering the question, "What must we be doing to do the works of God?" And Jesus answered them, "This is the work of God, that you believe in him whom he has sent."

"Do you not believe that I am in the Father and the Father is in me? The word that I say to you I do not speak on my own authority, but the Father who dwells in me does his works."(John 14:10). What are the works? The proclamation which Jesus was giving him, the words Jesus is speaking to them, the proclamation of the kingdom.

Jesus is not promising them some supernatural power that will give them authority over nature, authority over death, authority over the demons. He's talking about proclamation and belief. In Luke 10:17, 72 disciples return from a successful outreach adventure, and they say to him, "Lord, even the demons are subject to us in your name." And Christ's response to this remarkable revelation by them, this remarkable occurrence is in verse 20. "Do not rejoice in this, that the spirits are subject to you, but rejoice that your names are written in heaven."

Even though the 70 went out and experienced extraordinary and miraculous events, Jesus downplayed those, and said, "Don't even preoccupy yourself with thinking about that. Instead, rejoice because your names are written in the Lamb's Book of Life, your names are recorded in heaven." In Jesus' mind, the miracle of rebirth was far greater than any other miracle which we might see performed.

So the work we are called to be involved in is the proclamation of the good news for the belief of people that they would enter into the kingdom of God; then we are told that we will do it greater even than Christ, so with increase. Very few of the disciples could grasp the intent of Jesus' teaching at that point. He was revealing the Father to them. They saw a liberator. They saw a miracle-worker. They saw a teacher. But Jesus was the incarnate Word. He was and is God tabernacling with his people, God being with his people.

Notice Jesus' disappointment because the apostles don't grasp this. In 14:9, "Jesus said to him, 'Have I been with you so long, and you still don't know me, Philip? Whoever has seen me has seen the Father.'" Not until Pentecost when the Spirit of God is poured out does the increase begin to come, and here we see the first fulfillment of this promise by Jesus. On that day of Pentecost, the apostles told the people of Christ, and 3,000 believed. Within a generation, millions would believe. Cults and temples would be abandoned and destroyed and eventually an empire, Rome itself, would be declared Christian.

Jesus came and established the kingdom through his atonement, through the securing of the covenant of grace and through being the second Adam, making a way for us that we might be saved by being in union with Him. And our work which he has given us is now the proclamation of his truth, that many would come to believe.

And do they come to believe because of the power and the force of our words or because of our witty presentation or our charismatic personality? No, because of the Spirit of Christ which dwells within them, the Spirit of God which is poured out upon them that their eyes would be opened and that they would be made to see the truth of God's Word. Until then, it's foolishness. Remember the verse, "The foolishness of preaching." To the Gentile, it's foolishness, to the Jews, it's a stumbling block, but to the child of God, it is the words of salvation.

What are the conditions with which these things occur? We've been told of the work that we must do. We've been told of the extent of this, that it would be even greater than Jesus as the gospel has gone from this small band of 11 to capture the entire world by the power of the Spirit. Now as to the condition of our faith, without faith in Christ, there's no union in Christ. Without faith in Christ, there is no ability to do the works of Christ. It's always Christ who works in us, but without faith, Christ is not in us. Do you have faith to do the work of Christ?

Answer that question by exhibition, that is, by putting that work of Christ on exhibit for yourself. Reflect upon this. Inventory your own life and consider whether or not you're satisfied, that indeed the Spirit of Christ dwells within you, and you are doing the work of Christ. Do you proclaim Christ with the power of the Holy Spirit? Do you show people the Father as Christ showed them the Father? It's the condition of Christ's glorification. He said, "Because I go to the Father, these things will occur." Jesus didn't say, "When I go to the Father," but, "Because I go to the Father."

Jesus promised, "When I am lifted up from the earth, I will draw all people to myself" (John 12:32). The disciples' perspectives were limited in these two aspects. It's what D. A. Carson calls the "salvation historical realities." Now that's a fanciful way or a shorthand way of saying that their place in history and their proximity to Christ as he was incarnate in the flesh caused them to not be able to see the long view of what Jesus was teaching them.

We read the same thing in the prophet Micah, who received a word from God, that he prophesied to his people, and he could only begin to wonder at the far reaching prophecy of the coming of the Messiah. He had no idea where that would be and how that would be. He only knew that there would be deliverance, and there would be a reestablishing of God's people, but he could only marvel at the mystery of how God would accomplish it as he relayed what God had told him.

The signs and the wonders which the apostles had seen pointed to a reality which they couldn't yet understand, at least not until after the atonement and the resurrection. The kingdom Jesus showed them was not understandable until Jesus had ascended.

The second part is that the disciples couldn't understand the things of God because they had not yet been indwelled with the Spirit of God. In chapter 16:12, Christ says, "I still have many things to say to you, but you cannot bear them now. When the Spirit of truth comes, he will guide you into all truth."

Until the Spirit of Christ indwells the children of God, there is no opening of the eyes to see what the Scriptures teach. There is no illumination of the mind that we are able to understand that which Jesus teaches, and so until Jesus ascended to the Father and sent his Spirit, the disciples would not understand what Jesus was teaching them, but they reflected. They reflected, and they understood, and immediately upon understanding, they set out to do the kingdom work.

Our own Christian life is established based on our union with Christ. We have kingdom work to do. We often shrink back from kingdom work. Perhaps we imagine kingdom work is too much for us, but if you have walked with Jesus, then you must tell others about him. If you have tasted of that sweet grace of our God, then you must talk about its sweetness. If you have the assurance of faith, then you ought to testify to that peace of Christ that fills your soul. But we say, "What if they won't listen? I've tried in the past and they wouldn't hear me before." How can they believe unless they hear? How will they hear unless someone is sent?

Jesus has made us a promise. Jesus has promised to his own, "Greater works than these will you do." So with the promise of Christ, the command of God, the indwelling of the Spirit, which one of us ought to shrink back from the work of the kingdom? "Greater works than these," Jesus said, "you will do." What are the greater works? The proclamation of the gospel here and to the entire world. The expansion of the kingdom of God from its center in Jerusalem to all around the world, the expression of the ministry of Christ from 11 to millions who love the Lord God, the disenfranchisement of a few disciples that decided to follow after this man named Jesus, to the establishment and the empowerment of his church, against which the very gates of hell will not stand; history has proven this to be true.

Even for those who do not believe, if they reflect upon their history, they must wonder, "How has the church survived?" By being indwelled with the Spirit of God, by being empowered to do God's work, and by answering his calling. And where the church fails to answer his calling, the church does not survive. Where the church fails to answer, in Revelation Jesus says, "I will come there and remove my light from its midst."

The commission given to us by Christ demands that we also must rise courageously and confidently to do that which Christ has already assured us will be done, that we will proclaim and that people will believe. This is the promise of Christ, a promise which I believe, a promise which you believe too.

6

That Name

John 14:13–14

"Whatever you ask in my name, this I will do, that the Father may be glorified in the Son. If you ask me anything in my name, I will do it."

THE HEARTBEAT OF A Christian is prayer, but is there anything, perhaps with the exception of the work and the ministry in the operation of the Holy Spirit in the life of the church, that is more misunderstood than the prayer life of a Christian? If you go to any bookstore, secular or Christian, you'll find on the shelves books explaining how to pray, why to pray. There'll be patterns of prayer. There are books to teach you to pray in x-number of days. There are prescriptions for prayer. Then there are testimonies of the power of prayer to accomplish this or to accomplish that. You can pray using the names of God, which is certainly commendable, or you can pray entering into transcendental meditative states, which is not so commendable.

James Montgomery Boice said, "The doctrine of prayer according to the Bible is that there are certain people who can pray in a certain way and who will get not merely a good thing or something just as good as what they asked, or something even better than what they asked, but they will get the very thing that they asked for." What a comfort that we would actually receive what we ask for. But is it just by prescribing to a certain formula of prayer? If we utter Jesus' name, is that all that we need to do? Is that the function of prayer, to get that which we are looking for or that which we want? Christians are not the only ones interested in prayer, you know. Secular minds have adopted the whole idea of prayer as an existentially healthy experience. One doctor, Barbara Joseph, in her book *My Healing from Breast Cancer*, wrote this: "If we allow ourselves the belief in the healing power of prayer and pray for our highest good in the way that comes most naturally to us, and with the utmost compassion for ourselves, we can support our healing."

I don't want to doubt the healing effect of meditation, for example, and the way that it works with the body to lower your blood pressure and to decrease your stress, which in fact does help the body recuperate and stay healthy, but I do question the adoption of the word prayer. Why use the word prayer to describe mediation? In the same way that I object to that, I object to same-sex unions adopting the word marriage, which is clearly defined by Scripture. Same-sex union is a topic of another discussion, but it is not appropriate to rip a word from the Christian faith and the Christian Scripture and call it prayer just because the activity to which it is applied has some beneficial aspects to it.

Prayer has a certain direction. We speak to a living person in the Lord Jesus Christ. But regrettably, it's not only the secular mind that's confused. If you were to go to a website for 102.5 FM in Madison, Wisconsin, you would find there a list of 12 positive effects of prayer: To encourage; to remind you of your spiritual values; to give you hope; to help you feel better; to allow you to let go of situations; to provide you comfort; to relax your mind and relieve anxiety; to build your faith; to deepen your character; to broaden your perspective; to bring you closer to God. And then ultimately, number 12, because it works. It's difficult to find anything more profound than that. It works.

But if you take the verse, "Ask anything in my name, and I will do it," along with a couple of other verses that you can pluck out of Scripture, for example, "I can do all things through Christ who strengthens me," or perhaps 1 Corinthians 13, "If I have all faith so as to remove mountains," if you yoke these passages together and try to create a theology of prayer from them, you'll end up with a prescription for a right formula that causes your faith to be some sort of a force to accomplish your will.

So should we insist on prayer in Jesus' name? For some prayer becomes a ceremonial or a pleasant sort of way to end a meditation or a saying or a greeting that is often at the beginning of some ceremony. Still others think that a prayer has some metaphysical power of connecting us with other realities, spiritual or otherwise. Some see prayer as an act of personal piety because good people and good Christians are just supposed to pray, or a way of sealing a group to a common purpose.

The Last Sermon of Christ

You find this often in chaplain ministries of all sorts where a group will gather together and they'll use prayer to sort of seal the purpose of the group or to unify the group through the meditations of one who would offer a word in the name of God. That's still another misunderstanding of closing a prayer in Jesus' name.

But what if you have a group of believers and unbelievers? Is there really unity in that group? Shouldn't the goal of prayer be to unify believers with unbelievers? An argument is sometimes made that we should exclude Jesus' name because it unnecessarily drives a wedge of division between people. It is the nature of Christianity to divide. We read in the Scriptures that a mother will be against a daughter and a father against a son because of the gospel. We read in the Scriptures that the gospel of Jesus Christ is foolishness to Gentiles and a stumbling block to the Jews. It seems that bringing believers together using Jesus' name would be a right use of unity, rather than attempting to unify a believer with an unbeliever through the exclusion of Jesus' name.

So what prayer then would Jesus approve of? How should we pray? Is there a prescribed formula for prayer? Is there a necessity to end the prayer in Jesus' name, or is this a principle that we should follow in general? Is this only meant for Christian gatherings, or is it that every prayer we utter should be concluded in Jesus' name?

Let me point out to you in context of our passage, if we look back at verse 12, we will read there, "Whatever." Here Jesus is telling the disciples that they will be doing greater works than he has done, "because I am going to the Father." "Because I am going to the Father," is a link between the verse we have read and the words of comfort that Jesus has been giving before.

But there is a link also that follows in verse 15. "If you love me, you will keep my commandments." And so we have between these two truths, that because Jesus is going to the Father, therefore we pray in his name, and in praying in his name, we also must keep his commandments. Let's see how these work together, the prayer that Jesus approves.

Prior to this time, Jesus had been praying in front of the disciples. There were great Jewish prayers that had been drawn from the Scriptures. They were accustomed to prayer. They understood prayer. Many of them were drawn from the Psalms, such as Psalm 6:9. "The Lord has heard my supplication, and he has received my prayers."

These were prayers that the Jews knew, many of them by heart. There were prayers by Abraham in the Scripture, by Moses, there were prayers by the judges, by David, and many others that they had for them in the Scriptures that they could memorize or that they could use as a pattern for their own prayers. These prayers could be adapted in whole or in part by any Jew in prayer.

But earlier on, the disciples had already discerned in Christ an intimacy in his prayer that they did not understand and that they did not enjoy, and eventually that caused them to become dissatisfied with the older forms of prayer as evidenced in their approach to Jesus when they said, "Lord, teach us to pray." There was something about the prayers of Christ that were causing their own prayers to ring somewhat hollow.

Jesus, in Luke 11, instructed them to pray as he gave to them the Lord's Prayer. He concludes his formal instruction by stressing their union with him in the shaping of their will and their dependence on him as Advocate and Mediator. That's the importance of the links which I was showing you. He is our Advocate. He is the Intercessor for his people. He is the Mediator between God and man. There is no other.

Also, the words "In my name" stress the union that we have with him. He's not saying, "Don't bother praying. I'll do it all for you." He is telling and commanding them to pray, but to do so in his name, connecting his own name with their prayers, sealing their prayers with his name.

We can understand also in verses 13 and 14 that there is no limit that is put upon prayer. He says, "Whatever you ask." Our prayers and the response of God are limited only by the power of God, and the power of God is without limit. Therefore there is no limit placed upon God's answer to our prayer. It could, both theoretically and really, be anything, and yet there is a condition that is placed. He says, "Everything you ask, ask me anything, but do it in my name," because we are identified with the name of Christ.

The prayer Jesus hears is the Christian's prayer. He has already defined the group that he's talking to. He's speaking to those who are his followers. "Whatever you ask me in my name, I will do." He's speaking here specifically. He's not saying, "All who utter a prayer." He's not saying, "Whoever utters a prayer." He's saying, "Whatever you ask me in my name I will do."

"You" is qualified in verse 12 because it is "he who believes in me." "In my name" establishes Jesus' right to make requests of the Father, and it shows our dependence upon him. We have no personal standing to make requests of God on our own. Are we able to approach God on our own in our own righteousness and simply ask of God anything we choose? Nowhere is this made clearer than in the book of Job.

Job was provoked by his friends till he finally defended his own innocence, and he wondered aloud at God's injustice. The Lord came to Job and he said, "Will the fault finder contend with the Almighty?" And Job in chapter 42:6 responded, "I retract, and I repent in dust and ashes." In our depraved and in our fallen state, we must have a perfect Priest who will make intercession on our behalf.

I love the way John Calvin explains it. "All see and feel that they are unworthy to approach God, and yet the greater part of men burst forward as if they were out of their senses and rashly and haughtily address God."[1] If you take some time to read the Reformers, you will find that they have a good bit of humor actually in their writing. Calvin is saying that we all know that we're unworthy to approach God, but most men burst forward unto God as if they're completely out of their minds, rushing haughtily with an address to God. You get the picture here of God on his throne, and people rushing in there, screaming with their arms waving as if it's a press corps wanting to ask the President a question.

"On the other hand," Calvin continues, "when God invites us to himself, he holds out to us one Mediator only by whom he is willing to be appeased and reconciled, but men have a poor and slender perception of the power and goodness of God in Christ. To this is added a second error, that we do not consider that we are justly excluded from approaching God until he calls us, and that we are called only in the Son."[2]

Another great Reformer contemporary to Calvin was Luther who also contemplated prayer. Remember where they're coming from. At that time, the priest prayed for you. At that time, an individual believer wasn't necessarily encouraged to have such a devout prayer life, and they weren't encouraged that that would be anything that God would hear. And also they were encouraged to pray to different saints, not to

---

1. John Calvin, *Commentary on the Gospel According to John,* p. 90.
2. John Calvin, p. 91.

That Name

Christ. And so the whole idea of mediation and of Christ alone being the Intercessor was something the Reformers had to clear up.

"To pray in Jesus' name is," as Martin Luther put it, "a prayer that says, 'I have lived my best, therefore I implore thee not to regard my life and conduct.'"[3] This reflects Micah 5:1 when God told the people, "Bring out your strongest army and defend against the siege, but they will fail, and your king will be slapped on the cheek."

Luther says that when we pray we are essentially saying, "Lord God, I have given my absolute best. Please don't even look at it. Don't even look at it because it is not worthy of your sight. I implore you," he says, "not to regard my life and conduct, but your mercy and compassion promised me in Christ, and because of this to grant me the fulfillment of my prayer." That's what we say when we say, "In Jesus' name, I pray." We are saying, "Lord God, not on account of my own righteousness, but only on account of the righteousness of Christ, hear my prayer."

"He abides forever and holds his priesthood permanently. Hence, he is able to save forever those who draw near to God through him since he always lives to make intercession for them" (Hebrews 7:24). This is the work of Christ, to make intercession for us, continual intercession.

Jesus repeats this command in verse 13 and 14. He says it twice, "In my name. In my name." He says it twice, and yet we continue to seek other intercessors. We may not choose to pray through saints per se because that belongs to the Roman Church, but often we will take the avenue of either an unnamed god or a generic version of God. Isn't that what Paul encountered on Mars' Hill when he came and there were all of the temples and there was one to the god that was unknown because they didn't want to miss the true God. They simply prayed in a generic name and worshiped a generic God, but that was not the God of the Scriptures who has revealed himself through the incarnation of his Son, Jesus Christ, and has made himself known fully to people through Christ Jesus.

To pray in Jesus' name is to come as a believer, a Christian with faith in Christ, and to come in humility, recognizing we have no rights before God, but that every right is through our union with Christ, that we call on him as our High Priest, to be our Mediator and to be our Intercessor before God. The grace of salvation then is received through Christ. The grace to live out our salvation continues in Christ, not by

---

3. Martin Luther, *Luther's Works*, vol. 24, pg. 88.

the merit of our own works. What that means is that if we have any prayer at all, if we have any request of God for any operation of the Holy Spirit or for any work of his hand of providence, it is through Christ, not because I am now worthy, because I made profession of faith, but because it continues through Christ.

Christ isn't just the entryway to God; he sustains us in heaven before God. God, in the Scriptures, has plainly taught that Jesus is the Lamb of God who has borne our sins, and that those who believe in him have forgiveness solely through his name, that there is no other name under heaven by which we can be saved, and that God's children will have his own name written on their foreheads.

Often as I minister to people who are drawing near to the end of life, the name of Christ becomes more and more precious to them. As they begin to see eternity drawing closer in their view, they learn to cling to those things that give them the greatest assurance. I'll never ever forget as long as I have mind to remember visiting a relative of someone who was a member of the church who was deathly ill through a progressive sickness, being fed through the stomach with a stomach tube, barely able to speak because of loss of most muscular control of the mouth.

As we began to talk a little bit, I learned that he was a retired colonel in '06 who had commanded an artillery battery during the Cold War. He was very proud of his service, and as we spoke, I found it ironic that although he was now curled nearly in a fetal position, being fed by a nurse through a feeding tube in his stomach, barely able to speak, this man had commanded enough power in those artillery batteries to where he could have laid waste more than one city during his lifetime.

But now as he lay in the bed, there was only one thing that he wanted to talk about, and that was Jesus. I left the room, and as I often do at hospitals paused outside the door to pray, and he began to sing, and it was the clearest I had heard him the whole time I had been there. It was a Gaither hymn. "Jesus, Jesus, Jesus. Jesus, Jesus, Jesus." There is no other name by which salvation can be found.

Jesus promises that he'll answer prayer which has been sealed with his name, but which prayers? All prayers? Is it anything that we want? He says, "Whatever you ask, I will do it," but how do we know what we ought to ask? By praying in his name, we are refuting those who would deny his divinity. Isn't it interesting that he says, "Whatever you ask of the Father, I will accomplish"? Jesus is interestingly enough using language and using sentence structure to proclaim his own divinity. He's saying, "You ask of the Father, and I will answer, and you ask of the Father, but you do it in my name."

Christ's divinity is what we are denying when we refuse his name because he says, "If you pray to God, am I not one with God, and yet you would exclude me from your prayer? Whatever you ask, I will do." It is certainly a claim to be God, and so when we seal our prayer with the name of Christ, we are proclaiming Christ's divinity.

Perhaps the question is not, "Do we have to put it on the prayer?" Perhaps the real question is, "Can we dare to leave it off?" It's not so much that it's a magical formula when it's injected in, but it certainly is a profession of our view of Christ when we leave it off.

Here's the reason the disciples will do great things: Because it is God himself doing the work. "Whatever you ask, I will do." It is the Lord himself who is doing the work. The contrast in works between the Lord's work and their work which will be greater is not a contrast between the disciples' work and the work of Christ; it is the work of Christ incarnate compared to the work of Christ resurrected. Jesus is no longer limited to the finite nature of flesh, and he'll work through the disciples to glorify the Father from the arrival of the kingdom in his person through the expansion of the kingdom to the whole world through his Spirit.

And so a prayer that is in Jesus' name has God's glory as the object. There is the key to answered prayer. There is the key to what makes a valid prayer which is in Jesus' name. A Christian praying to God based on the merit and righteousness of Christ will have God's glory as their objective. This is having the mind of Christ.

Jesus words this so as to make a distinction between himself and the Father, and yet he also is identifying a unity between himself and the Father in saying that "If God's glory is your intent then you have the same intent that I have had as I was living among you on the earth." We so often think of prayer in terms of asking for our own happiness, perhaps for wealth, for opportunity, at least a break. Perhaps we are looking for justice. Maybe we just want a good night's sleep. Perhaps we're jobless and we want work, and so we're asking for work, or most anything else, but we don't think of prayer as the very means by which we glorify God in Christ.

But what if the whole objective of prayer is to glorify God in Christ? The mind of the Christian is to be so shaped by the Word of God, and we are to be so indwelled and full of the Spirit of Christ that our lives and our minds and our thoughts and our desires become patterned after and mimic his.

"Since then you have been raised with Christ, set your hearts on the things above where Christ is seated at the right hand of God. Set your mind on things above and not on earthly things. For you died, and your life is now hidden with Christ" (Colossians 2:1–3). Another verse: "Whether you eat or drink or whatever you do, do all things to the glory of God."

This concept of prayer will be revolutionary for many people because they have seen prayer as their pipeline to getting a blessing from God, but prayer is the vehicle by which we attain God's will to accomplish his purpose, and it is he who accomplishes that purpose. So the first purpose of prayer is not to have our material and earthly requests fulfilled, but to glorify God.

This is why we're mystified often in prayer, but even this has been addressed in the Scripture. "When you ask you do not receive because you ask with wrong motives that you spend what you get on your own pleasures. You adulterous people, don't you know that friendship with the world is hatred toward God?" (James 4:3). A prayer of that nature, a prayer that longs for and wants to either be established in the world or to partake of the fruits of the vine of this world is a prayer, even if it is rendered in Jesus' name, that is a mockery of the name because it is seeking after the things that God tells us not to seek after.

And so it is not a prayer sealed with Christ's name; it is a prayer mocking Christ's name because it is saying, "I'm going to ask God the Father that he would provide for me the very things which he's told me he will not," because it is God who accomplishes his will through prayer. Requests are fulfilled to the glory of God.

How does he do it? John 17:4 tells us, "I have brought you glory on earth by completing the work you gave me to do." These are the words of Jesus. How is it that we are to glorify God in our prayer? By completing the work that he has given us to do.

In conclusion, praying in Jesus' name is simple obedience to an imperative given by Christ. He says, "Pray in my name." If you are a Reformed Christian, our documents, the Westminster Confession of

Faith commands that when we pray, it is to be in Jesus' name. So we have an imperative. As a simple act of obedience, we render prayer in Jesus' name.

Secondly, prayer is a testimony to our belief that Jesus is in fact God. Thirdly, it's an acknowledgment of our need for a Mediator and an Intercessor, that we do not storm into the throne room of God and simply throw out prayers as if we are the paparazzi chasing after a movie star. We render our prayers to the glory of God through our Mediator, the One, our High Priest who makes continual intercession, the Lord Jesus Christ.

Fourthly, we glorify God by declaring that he is merciful, that he's compassionate to forgive us in the atoning work of Christ, and that our life and work remain dependent on his grace, which is renewed to us daily. Is that your prayer? Are you in your prayer testifying that you recognize that you are saved by the mercy and the grace of God in the atoning work of Jesus Christ, and you give thanks that the Lord Jesus Christ is your Priest making intercession for you before God?

For the Christian, God is glorified in the blessings he gives to his children in Christ. We might say, "Well what's in it for me? Is it all just about proclaiming the glory of God?" For the Christian, that ought to be sufficient. But then we would say, "Then how is it that we are to pray for those things that are needful in life? How is it that we render unto God all of the cares and concerns of our world, as he tells us to, all those things which distress us in life? We are supposed to cast all our burdens upon him in prayer."

It is God's glory to answer to the needs of his children. Our first aim of course is God's glory, and our confidence is that he'll be glorified in showing his love and his mercy in his provision for his people. So the Christian is one with privilege and one with hope. Privilege to pray because Jesus himself will accomplish these things that glorify God. We know that in praying for the glory of God, Jesus will accomplish that. He has accomplished it. He continues to accomplish it.

But we also know that it is through God's care for us that his name is glorified. It is testimony to a wonderful God when his people praying rightly are cared for by their God and give all praise and glory to God who cares for them. We have that kind of confidence and expectation that a prayer so sealed in Jesus' name will accomplish all that he has willed to accomplish in his people and for his glory.

7

Gospel Obedience

John 14:15

"If you love me, you will keep my commandments."

JESUS HAS BEEN COMFORTING the disciples in these last hours before he is crucified. That's what we've been reading about throughout most of 13 and certainly through 14. He's comforting them because of their angst and anxiety over his departure. He's about to announce to them the gift of the Holy Spirit. He is laying the groundwork now for the introduction to them of the coming of the Comforter, when he himself is physically removed from their presence. He is prefacing his promise of the Holy Spirit with this reminder that they are to continue to follow him in just the same way he has shown them. He's saying, "Once I am departed, you will follow me in precisely the same way that I have taught you to follow me while I have been physically present with you," and that their obedience will have their love for him as motivation.

That really is the kernel of the truth in the passage above. Jesus is saying, "Keep on following me even when I'm not with you." In the next passage, he's going to tell them how they will be able to do that. He'll grant to them the Holy Spirit, which is the Spirit of Christ remaining with them, and then he says, "And your motivation for doing this is going to be because of the quality of your love for me."

Just a little while earlier in that same night, Jesus had given them a new commandment. If we were to go back to 13:34, he says, "A new commandment I give to you, that you love one another. Just as I have loved you, you also are to love one another." He also says that it's by that love that people will know that they are Disciples of Christ. Their love will be their testimony of the authenticity of their discipleship. They were to love one another as he had loved them, and they were to love others just the same.

He commanded them in other ways too. He commanded them to keep on believing in him. He commanded them to pray in his name. He commanded them to pray to him. And now he's recapping by telling them again their obedience will be the testimony of their love.

How important is this? Is this a passing comment? Surely not. In John 15:10, we read something very similar. "If you keep my commandments, you will abide in my love, just as I have kept my Father's commandments and abide in his love." This linking of obedience to the commandments and abiding in love is repeated again in verse 17. "These things I command you so that you will love one another."

We find love being conditioned with command, but then we also find that command is conditioned by love. We're only able to obey as we love, but then love itself is only made possible because of our willingness to obey, first of all to believe, to pray in his name, and to pray to him. By making love the motive behind and in fact the goal of obedience, Jesus insists on moving from ritualism to transformed living.

This is essential for us in the days in which we live. There are many who are trying to find religion, but what they will find, although sometimes very beautiful, very well-done, is nevertheless simple ritualism, not transformed living. Transformation occurs from the inside out. It's internal character transformation rather than simply external religious observance. No matter how grand the church hall may be, no matter how eloquent the preacher may be, no matter how many voices or how beautiful the choir may be, or how new the accoutrements of a church might be, it is still ritualism unless there is a character change that comes from the heart of the individual.

He's talking about what Paul would describe later in more formal terms as being a circumcision of the heart rather than a circumcision of the flesh, a changing of the heart. The emphasis on heart and character is not a new teaching. Jesus is not introducing this for the first time. We find this throughout all of the pages of Scripture, like in Isaiah 29:13. "This people draw near with their mouth and honor me with their lips, while their hearts are far from me."

The Last Sermon of Christ

In Luke 16:15, our Lord himself said, "You are those who justify yourselves before men, but God knows your hearts." Paul in Romans 8:27 gives commentary to this when he says God searches our hearts. God observes and looks at the heart. It's the heart of a man translated as the Christlike character of a man that God is observing, not the external obedience, which is why the Pharisees could never find a place with Christ. That's why he called them "whitewashed tombs," beautiful in their external observances, and yet on the inside rotten and decaying.

No number of attendances to services could cleanse what only the Spirit of Christ can cleanse in the internal part of a man. Proverbs 4:23 commands, "Keep your heart with all vigilance for from it flows the springs of life." Human conduct will flow from the heart bearing testimony of a person's character. It flows from the heart, a person's life, and their desires, and their quest, if you will, flows from the heart. Humility. Meekness. Respect. Obedience. Love; All these flow from the heart, which is the character of a man.

Jesus has to connect authentic discipleship or translate discipleship here as obedience with authentic love for him because it's simply not natural for our hearts or actions to be inclined towards obedience to God. The problems began in the garden because we're not naturally inclined to be obedient to God. We reject at the very core of our being authority over us. We reject it outright. Oh we would love to have God's blessings on our wayward ways, but we reject authority over us. It's the natural state of fallen man and women to reject authority, and yet that's what God requires. Romans 8:7–8 teaches that the natural mind is hostile to God and will not submit to his law. One of our founding fathers, Benjamin Franklin observed rightly, "How many observe Christ's birthday? How few observe his precepts. 'Tis easier to keep holidays than commandments."[1]

In Matthew 7:21–22, Jesus describes in disturbing terms the condition of the heart in its natural self-seeking estate. He said these words, "For from within, out of the heart of man, come evil thoughts, sexual immorality, theft, murder, adultery, coveting, wickedness, deceit, sensuality, envy, slander, pride, foolishness. All these evil things come from within and they defile a person."

Our being defiled before God is not something that was splashed upon us because of Adam's sin. It comes from within us, our very selves.

---

1. Benjamin Franklin, *Encyclopedia of Christian Quotations*, p. 528.

We're not simply victims because Adam sinned and because we're born in the same genetic stream as Adam was or because his sin somehow got rubbed onto us. It comes from within the heart of every person.

What can save us from such a wretched estate? That's an apt description, isn't it? It sounds like Old English, but really is there a more appropriate word that we could use than wretched? It is a wretched estate. Such is the language we find in the hymn "Amazing Grace"—"Who saved a wretch like me." The writer there certainly had an idea of the wretched estate of man.

God's grace effects a change in the heart that changes our moral conduct from within. Morality or ethics observed without an inward change of character is hypocrisy. Morality and ethics which is observed without an inward change of character is moralism and legalism and Phariseeism, but morality and ethics that is the result of an internal change of character is a sanctified life and an obedient life and a life of a disciple.

That very thing is prophesied Ezekiel in 36:26–27. Note the prophet's words in the promise of how God would accomplish this impossible work in the heart of man. He says,

> "I will give you a new heart and a new spirit I will put within you. I will remove the heart of stone from your flesh and give you a heart of flesh, and I will put my Spirit in you and cause you to walk in my statutes and be careful to obey my rules."

And so obedience comes only from rebirth, and that rebirth is brought about only by the work and the operation of the Holy Spirit, a miraculous work of the Holy Spirit, and that's of God's initiative, proving that we love him only because he first loved us.

In stating something that might appear so obvious, Jesus is acknowledging that it is difficult and unnatural. What happens to us once we resolve to obey Christ, as we do when we first come to faith? Or if we are raised in the faith and we finally come before the church because we know that we belong to Christ, and we have the zeal and enthusiasm to take up the Scriptures and study them? In that first love, we speak to our neighbors and our friends and our family about the love of God and the grace of Christ and the gospel of Jesus. But what happens to that zeal and that enthusiasm, that commitment to observe our duties and to be obedient even to the Great Commission? What happens?

The Last Sermon of Christ

It's not uncommon to us. If we read in Revelation 2:4–5, we discover that the church in Ephesus also struggled with the same issue that we do. Many began their Christian life well, but soon they faltered in their obedience to his commands. "But I have this against you, that you have abandoned the love you had at first. Remember therefore from where you have fallen; repent, and do the works you did at first. If not, I will come to you and remove your lampstand from its place, unless you repent."

The lack of obedience, which some will erroneously label as mere works, is a lack of love for God. The two are yoked together. An observance and a sense of willingness to do that which God has commanded, our Christian duties, is a result of the love which we have for God. Consequently, a resistance to completion of the duties which God has given to us as disciples must also bear evidence of a lack of love for God.

Some will cry, "You're preaching works! You're preaching legalism. You're preaching Phariseeism," to which John replies in 1 John 2:3, "By this we know that we have come to know him, if we keep his commandments." You see, Scripture doesn't give obedience as a condition of salvation, but it does hold it out as evidence of our rebirth, as the natural consequence that flows from one who is born again. It's the inevitable outcome. There is no other way. There is no other fruit that we would bear except the natural consequence of conversion which is obedience, following after God, living a life as Christ lived his life.

Drifting from our love for Christ is natural to man just as swimming in water is natural for a fish. We live in a fallen world, we work for material rewards, and we're concerned to keep the affections of others around us. Anything that causes us to be exalted in our own mind, we love and we are drawn to like a moth to the flame. Yet 1 John 2:15–17 teaches that love given to such things is in fact adultery against God, and if anyone does love such things, the love of God simply is not in him.

And so through this short sentence, "If you love me, you will keep my commandments," we learn that our Lord says that unqualified love results in obedience. His love is unqualified and without end. His infinite love that results in obedience is for us a matter of spiritual life and death.

What are the commands that he gives then? What is it that Jesus has commanded that's so vital? If our spiritual life and death, our

Gospel Obedience

spiritual health at the very least depends on these, then what is it that the Lord has commanded? In John 13, he simply says, "Love one another as I have loved you." And so we would ask, "How is your love towards others? How is your love towards other people?"

Before you answer, I want you to consider these characteristics of love. Firstly, service to others. Jesus had just demonstrated this in action. He humbled himself to act as a servant when he took the towel and he wrapped it around his waist, when he took the basin and he washed their feet. Peter protested against that, and he said that the work was beneath Christ. This is not work becoming of the Lord! And Christ said, however, the work fit him very well, and it demonstrated meekness, power that is controlled, authority that is ruled. "Blessed are the meek, for they shall inherit the earth." Isn't that fulfilled in Christ Jesus himself? Christian service is selfless. It forfeits time, it forfeits resources, it forfeits its own rights, and it gives for the good and the progress and the happiness of others.

Secondly, it's sacrifice. Serving and loving others is not scheduled at our convenience. It is responsive. Serving others isn't without cost. It ALWAYS costs. It's the nature of service. Jesus took the bread and he said, "This is my body which is given for you." How do we measure the cost of service? We measure it against the service of Christ himself who took upon himself the sins of all mankind, serving man by dying in our stead.

If it's service and it's sacrifice, it's also a sharing with one another. Our life was not given for us to use it up on ourselves, to burn it up on our own pleasure, on our own work, on our own deeds, on our own joy, our own happiness, which ultimately is not even accessible unless we receive our happiness through Christ. The chief end of man is to glorify God. The Scriptures teach us how that is to happen. Like clay in a potter's hands, so are we in God's hands, created for his purposes, to live and show forth his grace and testify of his love, to be obedient to the Great Commission.

And finally, in verse 23, we read something similar, but phrased differently. It reads, "If anyone loves me, he'll keep my Word." I believe the expositor H. A. Ironside is correct in his 1942 commentary where he rightly sees a subtle but an important difference in the way these things are expressed. Verse 15 says, "If you love me, you'll keep my commandments," and in verse 23, "If anyone loves me, he'll keep my

Word." And so we have here two different words that are used. One, we keep his commandments, and in the other, we keep his Word.

A command is easy to find. There's a list of ten of them that we could turn to right away. If we were to do a textual study of all of the Scripture and write down all of the commands, there's a finite number. We would eventually arrive at the last word of Scripture and our list of commands would be complete. However, even though there is a finite number, some are all encompassing of life, which is what I believe John is teaching.

A man keeping a list of external expressions of commandments might be tempted to never deal with the internal disposition of the heart, but when Jesus says to keep his Word, that's a broader application of the idea of love and obedience.

Ironside gives an illustration of the young girl simply named Mary. Mary is the only daughter of a widowed mother. Mary goes to school, and her mother asks very little of her, knowing the demands of life and of family where there is only mother and daughter.

The only thing that she asks of Mary is that she take care of her own space, that she keep her room clean, and she keep it straight, and so every morning as Mary prepares to go to school, she does in fact tidy up her room and clean it up and make it all prepared so that her mother has no concern over that part of all of the responsibilities the widowed mother has to keep in order.

Mary loves her mother, and she keeps that commandment. She keeps it to the letter with a glad heart. No matter where she is going, no matter how much of a hurry she is in, she always stops to make sure that she has managed her own room according to her mother's wishes.

One day after school, Mary plans on playing tennis with friends, and she gets home, and she hears her mother tell a neighbor that there's a large company coming that night and she has a meal to prepare, but she hasn't been feeling very well at all, and that she's not looking forward to the labor. Mary goes to her mother though she has plans of her own, and she tells her to lie down, that she'll peel the potatoes, she'll prepare the meat, and she will get everything ready for the guests to arrive.

Her mother of course protests, but Mary insists that she couldn't be happy knowing that her mother was ill and had this need of her. In the morning, Mary kept the commandment. In the afternoon, she kept her mother's word by counting it a duty and a privilege to honor her mother by sharing in her mother's work. One is obedience and the other is devotion, but devotion is also obedience.

The Christian journey to obedience and devotion begins and ends with Christ. The family is the work ground. It is the workshop where children learn the lessons that are later applied to their own walk with Christ. The Christian journey in obedience and devotion beginning and ending with Christ begins with a listening to his Word, observing his work, learning of his expression of love and service on the cross of atonement. As we grow in our love for him, as life becomes ours, it becomes our life to obey his commands out of our love for him.

8

A Very Real Comforter

John 14:16–18

"And I will ask the Father, and he will give you another Helper, to be with you forever, even the Spirit of truth, whom the world cannot receive, because it neither sees him nor knows him. You know him, for he dwells with you and will be in you. I will not leave you as orphans; I will come to you."

CHRIST HAS BEEN INTRODUCING to his disciples all they are to do in his absence. Their work will not be in their own power, nor their own energy or their own efforts. The coming of the Holy Spirit will enable them to accomplish these things which he has been instructing them in.

There are many controversies in the church. Should we sprinkle, pour, or dunk for baptism, for instance? Is the presence of Christ physical, spiritual, or is the Lord's Supper just a memorial? Should we serve wine or juice when we serve the Lord's Supper? Should we sing psalms only, or psalms and hymns, or hymns only, or psalms and hymns and spiritual songs, and if we are, then are all those describing one song or are there in fact a variety of songs the church could sing? Or perhaps we should sing nothing at all and avoid any opportunity for error. Should we sing to soundtracks if we don't have musicians? Or perhaps we should just sing a cappella. After all, there were no baby grands in the New Testament.

Should we have stained glass, plain glass, or no glass at all in the church windows? Or even more important issues like should we have white rocks or pine barks, or should we drink regular or decaf at our fellowships? There are important controversies in the church today, but

A Very Real Comforter

more important than any of these is how do we know, how do we understand, and how do we talk of the Holy Spirit? How do we know of the Holy Spirit? How are we to understand the Holy Spirit, and in our conversation, in our teaching, in our prayers, how do we speak of the Holy Spirit?

Robert Murray M'Cheyne said this: "The unconverted don't like to hear much about the Holy Spirit."[1] Why is that do you imagine? If you had to answer the question why the unconverted don't like to hear much about the Holy Spirit, you probably would deduce it is because first of all they're not indwelled by the Holy Spirit. Secondly, the Holy Spirit seems to be intangible because he's immaterial. Not immaterial in significance, but immaterial to the touch. We can't grab hold of the Holy Spirit.

Only the fool has said in his heart, "There is no God." The very creation testifies there must be a Creator. Even those who are agnostic and are not giving any thought to Christianity acknowledge there does seem to be intelligent design in creation. There must be a first cause in all of creation. Things can't simply appear out of nothing. There had to be something, and if there was something, there must be something that is eternal, and that thing that was eternal seems to have had a creative process and a master design in mind.

Now they can go no further to explain it, but they acknowledge that all roads and all inquiry seem to point that there is an intelligent designer behind all creation. So in essence, they are acknowledging that there is a God. Historians can find evidence, and they can find proof of Christian traditions and of the teaching of Christ certainly going back as far as the Dead Sea Scrolls. Now we can acknowledge that there was a historical figure named Jesus of Nazareth who was crucified and whom Christians have embraced as an atoning sacrifice for their sins.

But the Spirit, the Holy Spirit, where does the Holy Spirit enter into any sort of tangible or evidential history that we can look to and say, "Well, there you go! There is where the Holy Spirit made his appearance. There's where the Holy Spirit touched down"? And we can point to that, and we may choose to disregard the meaning of it, but we can know that that is when it all occurred.

No, for an unbeliever, the Holy Spirit is a concept that they can't even find a good way to rebut or argue against. Some assemblies never

---

1. Mark Waters, ed, *The New Encyclopedia of Christian Quotations*, p. 487.

speak of the Holy Spirit at all, and I'm speaking here of Christian assemblies. They speak mightily of God, they speak wonderfully of Christ, but the Holy Spirit only receives occasional mention, and that only as transitions in prayer or in other teachings.

Then there are other assemblies who speak of nothing but the Holy Spirit. It's all about Holy Spirit power. It's all about Holy Spirit dwelling. It's all about Holy Spirit gifts, and all they do is speak of the Holy Spirit as if God the Father and the Lord Jesus Christ are now nearly inconsequential, and it's all about the Holy Spirit.

And then there are still others who would be able to summarize their understanding of the Holy Spirit based upon a cheer we heard in high school that went something like, "Have you got the spirit?" To which we would reply, "Yeah, man!" And if we were quite honest, we would say that at least at some point in our life that might be about all we could actually say we know about the Holy Spirit, that we have the Spirit.

In the Apostles' Creed, all we simply do is say we believe in the Holy Spirit. The Nicene Creed says a bit more. We say that he is the Lord and the Giver of life, a testimony to the deity of the Holy Spirit, a member of the Trinity, and that life comes through the Holy Spirit.

We also say there that the Holy Spirit proceeds from the Father and the Son together, and that he is to be worshiped as a person within the Trinity. We say in that creed that it was the Holy Spirit who spoke by the prophets. These brief statements are meant to testify of what we know, but often they are the sum of all that we know.

If we were to be pressed to explain these affirmations from the Nicene Creed, we might be pressed beyond our ability to explain in particular detail how it is that the Spirit proceeds from the Father and the Son together. How is it that the Spirit is a member of the Trinity, and that we ought to be worshiping the Spirit?

Is it proper to pray specifically to the Spirit? Is it proper to speak specifically of the Spirit without reference to God the Father or to the Lord Jesus Christ? To know so little, it seems when it comes to the Holy Spirit, we assume much. When we turn away from these principles that are contained in our Nicene Creed regarding the person of the Holy Spirit, and turn the conversation to other issues regarding the Spirit, we find ourselves speaking of spiritual gifts, of speaking in tongues, of the strengthening that comes through the Holy Spirit, or the enriching of

A Very Real Comforter

the Spirit, or filling by the Spirit, or indwelling by the Spirit, the sanctifying of a life by the Spirit, or even the presence of the Spirit in our worship.

Isn't that where we hear people talk about the Spirit mostly? If we did something right and we enjoy it, the Spirit, we presume shows up, and we say, "Well, the Spirit was really there." Is it the Holy Spirit that was really there, or was it simply our spirit of enthusiasm that we're talking about. Were we so filled with joy over the particular organization or expression of worship that we were excited to be there, and therefore presumed the Spirit must have been excited about the same things that we were.

So we would simply ask, "What do you really know about the Holy Spirit?" We have many assumptions, but what do you really know about the Holy Spirit? When we think of God the Father, we can quantify that fairly easily. We might not be able to say everything the Scripture teaches about God the Father, but we certainly think of creation. We think of sovereignty. We think of providence and power. We think of judgment, grace, and mercy.

We do the same with Christ. When we think of the Lord Jesus Christ, we think of the incarnation. We think of the cross, the atonement, his mediation and intercession for us, the resurrection and salvation, his coming again in glory to judge the quick and the dead. These are things that we can understand, and we can latch onto and describe, but when we think of the Spirit, what comes to mind? A feeling? Inspiration?

In Romans 8:9–10, 16, and 27, Paul himself was dealing with issues concerning the Spirit and the right understanding of the Spirit. Note some of these affirmations of the role and the wok of the Holy Spirit in Romans 8.

"You, however, are not in the flesh but in the Spirit," (so here we have the idea of being in the Spirit) "if in fact," Paul says, "the Spirit of God dwells in you." So we are in the Spirit if the Spirit of God dwells in us. "Anyone," he continues,

> "Who does not have the Spirit of Christ does not belong to him. But if Christ is in you, although the body is dead because of sin, the Spirit is life because of righteousness. If the Spirit of him who raised Jesus from the dead dwells in you, he who raised

The Last Sermon of Christ

Christ Jesus from the dead will also give life to your mortal bodies through his Spirit who dwells in you."

Did you pick up on yet one other aspect of this teaching? Here the Spirit is called a Spirit that would dwell in us, but it's also called the Spirit of God. It is also called Spirit of Christ, Christ's Spirit that dwells in us. So this Holy Spirit stands alone as a third person in the Trinity, but also there is a divine connection. It is God's Spirit, and it is the Spirit of Christ which dwells in us.

Verse 16: "The Spirit himself bears witness with our spirit that we are children of God." Here we have an inward testimony of the Spirit that bears witness to our own spirit that we in fact are the children of God.

Verse 27: "And he who searches hearts knows the mind of the Spirit, because the Spirit intercedes for the saints according to the will of God." So the Spirit is divine. The Spirit indwells us, and brings testimony to us that we know that we are children of God, and the Spirit intercedes on our behalf before God.

Now we're beginning to form a working definition. Abraham Kuyper said, "We know not what spirits are nor what our own spirit is. How much less capable are we of comprehending the Spirit of God?"[2] We're most likely to echo the words of the disciples Paul met at Ephesus who said in Acts 19: "We have not so much as heard whether there is a Holy Spirit." So Paul teaches them, those saints in Ephesus.

In Ephesians 5:18, "Do not get drunk with wine for that is debauchery, but be filled with the Spirit." The great preacher D. L. Moody said, to be filled with the spirit is "not experience to be enjoyed, but a command to be obeyed."[3]

Jesus will spend a great deal of his time in these next chapters dealing with the teachings on the Holy Spirit. Over and over again, he'll mention the Spirit. Often he will repeat that which he has already told and expand and elaborate on it. He has been leading the disciples up to this very point, especially as he described to them the greater things that they will do. These things will depend upon their being indwelled by the Holy Spirit. They'll need to understand the Holy Spirit and depend on him if they are going to do these greater things.

2. Ferguson, "The Holy Spirit," p 15.
3. D. L. Moody, p. 489.

A Very Real Comforter

And we likewise need to understand if in fact we are going to depend upon him and do those greater things. Jesus has gone to prepare a place for us, and the Holy Spirit has been sent to prepare us for that place. So the first matter before us is to determine whether the Holy Spirit is a person or a power. Fundamentally, is the Holy Spirit just the power of God, or is the Holy Spirit a person in the Trinity? Even in the title "Holy Spirit," we are affirming the Spirit is holy. That means separated, belonging to God. Like God, the Spirit is high and exalted, infinite and eternal. In short, divine. And we'll leave that there simply saying when we utter the words, "Holy Spirit," we are testifying that the Spirit is a divine person.

Secondly, the Holy Spirit is spirit, Holy Spirit. Now this may be a little bit more difficult for us to grasp. The Spirit is not visible, but yet it's real. In your high school English class, your teacher may have taught you about onomatopoeia. It is a figure of speech in which a word sounds like the concept it describes. Words like "pow" sound like what they describe, a strike or a hit. Other words like "clunk" or "snap" or "roar," all sound in the saying of the word something like what you are to understand by their meaning. They convey a concept. They speaker wants you to feel what is being said.

The Greek words for spirit did the same thing, but that sense has gotten lost in the process of translation. In the New Testament Greek, it's pneuma, and in the Hebrew, it's ruach. And if you were to put your hand in front of your mouth when you say both of those, you'll hear a rush of air that comes out of your mouth when you speak the words. When they're properly spoken, you'll feel that air coming out as you were exhaling motion. These words are associated not only with motion, but also with the breath of life, with energy, and with force and power.

A couple of verses that help elaborate on this are Job 1:19. There that very word "ruach" is used to describe a powerful wind or a storm, not the Holy Spirit but rather something like a tornado or a cyclone. The emphasis there in Job is on an overwhelming power, and so we attach to our understanding of the Spirit this idea of motion and life and overwhelming power.

Micah 3:8 captures this in a very simple verse. "But as for me, I am filled with power, with the Spirit of the Lord," here equating power and the Spirit of the Lord. So whether it was through the judges, whether it was through kings or prophets, the Spirit of God describes God's personal activity in creation, a powerful moving in creation by the Holy Spirit.

But if we leave our study here with only these ideas as a backdrop, we have an impersonal force that's really nothing more and nothing less than God's activity, and the idea of Trinity is lost. If we just end with this idea of wind and power and force of change, we have no person of the Holy Spirit. We only have a force of the Holy Spirit.

Reuben Torrey, in his work on the Holy Spirit, warns of yet another danger. The conception of the Holy Spirit as a divine influence or power that we are somehow to get hold of and use leads to self-exaltation and self-sufficiency. There's a great danger here that is practiced by many people. They'll talk of the Holy Spirit as something they need to grasp and get more of to accomplish their goals and their ambitions and their work. They need to get a little bit more as if it were a water fountain and they could drink deeper to get filled with more of it to accomplish their own work.

We have an example of that very misunderstanding in Acts 8. Simon the magician believed in Christ, but he lacked any depth of understanding regarding the Christian teaching and the background of the testimony of the Scriptures, and so when it came to issues of the Holy Spirit, he misunderstood precisely this point and interpreted Holy Spirit as an agent of power, something that could be harnessed and channeled, much like he was accustomed to doing with his magic.

Simon asked the disciples if he could have more of the Spirit and even made them a monetary offer for the Spirit, to which Peter replied that if he were to repent of that thought, repent of that offer, God may in fact forgive him, so egregious was the error. So we want to affirm first that the Spirit is powerful and the Spirit is personal. In John 14:16, Jesus said, "I will ask the Father, and he will give you another Counselor." The Father gives him; the Son sends him.

I can recall, by way of illustration, just before I was deployed to go overseas. It was a very short notice, and there was not a lot of opportunity to prepare the family, and so instinctively I wanted to give each member of the family some token of my own. I don't know to what end, this thing to remember, something to hold, some idea that they would have a sense of my presence remaining with them even as I departed. I gave different things to different ones. I gave a dog tag to

A Very Real Comforter

one, or whatever it was that I could hand and say, you know, "Hold this until I return." Now those were just material objects. They were not me. I did not remain with them, but it was this desire of wanting to be there to comfort, be there to sustain and to hold, be there to encourage, be there to protect even though I knew that I would be far away.

Jesus refers to another Comforter. Have you thought about that word another? Jesus is referring to *another* Comforter. This mean that Jesus is not only the first Comforter, but also that the Spirit will do the same work for the disciples that he has been doing while he has been present with them. He says, "I will pray to the Father to send you another Comforter" in his place. He's describing to them his departure and that there will be one to come who will take his position in their life. There are two words in Greek that are translated as another. One means just like the first. The second one means one that is coming but different. It's the first sense that's used here, the one that will be like the first.

Jesus is also called a Paraclete in Scripture just as the Holy Spirit is a Helper in the sense of being our Advocate. If you were to look in 1 John 2:1, you would read there that Jesus is our Advocate, the Paraclete. The same word is used to describe the Holy Spirit. The first Helper is leaving the disciples, but while he is physically absent, he remains a Helper in heaven; the second Helper is here on earth. The first pleads our case with God; the second pleads God's case with man. This second Helper will never depart from them though Jesus physically has ascended to the Father.

So the Spirit is a person, he's like Christ, and not just a power. The Spirit will come and take the place of Jesus. That's in the first place. Jesus says he will send another Comforter. In the second place, the Holy Spirit is described as a Comforter or a Paraclete. Not only is he coming like Christ, the Spirit of Christ to be with the disciples in the place of Christ, but he is also to be their Comforter, their Advocate, their Paraclete.

The term describes one who strengthens and encourages, but strengthens and encourages with a purpose. The disciples are being called to witness to Christ, and the Spirit will also bear witness to Christ. In John 15:27, we read that they'll testify for they have been with him since the beginning. The disciples were with Jesus from the beginning of his ministry, but the Spirit has been with Christ since the beginning of time. This qualification for bearing witness is shared with the Holy Spirit because he too was with Jesus from the beginning.

In the gospel of John, Jesus is on trial from the beginning to the end. From chapter 1 through chapter 12, various testimonies, various witnesses to Christ are presented. In John 20:31, we're told why. "These are written so that you will believe, and we know that that testimony is ongoing even today." The idea of being a witness in Christ's time, though, is different from ours. There were trials that weren't centered on the lawyers and weren't centered on codes and loopholes and letters of the law, but on a judge simply hearing from witnesses. And important witnesses were those that were eyewitnesses or character witnesses, those who had known the defendant, as it were, for his whole life.

A judge wanted to hear from someone who had a relationship, someone that knew what this person was all about. Who has known Christ longer and can bear greater testimony and witness to him than the Holy Spirit? So we ask then, how does he testify? How does the Holy Spirit testify of the Lord?

John 16:12–13 teaches us that he guides us into all truth. He also inspired the writing of the New Testament. He presented to us the truth. Second Peter 1:21: "For prophecy never had its origin in the will of man, but men spoke from God as they were carried along by the Holy Spirit."

Let me close this introduction to the Holy Spirit with a question. Does it really matter that we know that the Holy Spirit is divine and that the Holy Spirit is personable, that is, a person with a personality, a uniqueness from the Father and the Son? Yes. If we know the truth of the person of the Holy Spirit, then we will know the power and testimony in our witness. The disciples would be powerless to witness except they trusted in the power of the Holy Spirit to effect change through their witness in those whom they witnessed to. Because of an understanding of the Holy Spirit, we will know that we are not relying on our own strength, but we will be bold in our witness, relying on the work of the Spirit rather than our own ability, and that he will minister to us in our time of distress as well.

In Martin Luther's commentary, he said, "The world lives freely, smugly, and riotously," not righteously, but riotously, "without fear and anxiety and heeds neither God's wrath nor his grace. Besides it is giddy and reckless and does not stand in need of comfort, but the few who were called to believe are baptized in Christ and remain loyal to him are in dire need of a Comforter to strengthen and preserve them that they may be able to endure and bear all things."[4]

The Father and the Son have given the Holy Spirit to be our comfort in times of trouble to teach, to guide, to be an inspiration for truth, and to give whatever help is necessary. We must be encouraged and emboldened in our testimony when we know that the one whom Christ has promised, the one who has known Christ from the beginning is behind and in our witness and our testimony of him even today.

---

4. Martin Luther, vol 24, p 110.

9

Four Promises

John 14:19–24

"'Yet a little while and the world will see me no more, but you will see me. Because I live, you also will live. In that day you will know that I am in my Father, and you in me, and I in you. Whoever has my commandments and keeps them, he it is who loves me. And he who loves me will be loved by my Father, and I will love him and manifest myself to him.' Judas (not Iscariot) said to him, 'Lord, how is it that you will manifest yourself to us, and not to the world?' Jesus answered him, 'If anyone loves me, he will keep my word, and my Father will love him, and we will come to him and make our home with him. Whoever does not love me does not keep my words. And the word that you hear is not mine but the Father's who sent me.'"

CHRIST, IN SPEAKING TO the disciples, has been considering them in his language and in his mood as being his own children. Jesus is giving them lessons and he's giving them comforting words to assure them that they will not be left to face the world on their own. The verse just before this says, "I will not leave you as orphans; I will come to you." You see, an orphan is one that is just left to roam the street, to fend for himself, one whose life hangs in the balance from one meal to the next, from one season to the next, in the heat, in the cold, begging for help along the way.

Jesus says, "My children will not be as orphans whose parent has left them to fend for themselves. No, I will return to you, and I will come to you." Fathers or mothers, if you've gone on a journey or on a trip, and you can see that troubled look in your children's eye, don't you speak to them the same way? Don't you turn to them and say, "Honey, I won't be gone forever. I'm going to be back at the end of the day," or, "I will be back later. It's going to be okay"?

We can't speak that way to our pets. When you leave, they think that you're gone forever. And then when they see you again, they act as if they thought you would never return, and they're always so excited to see you. But we can reason with our own children, and we can reason with one another that it's not the end of the world as we know it. We will return. These are soft and gentle words of comfort and of reassurance.

Imagine how cynical these fisherman could have become, these fisherman and tax collectors after the crucifixion if in fact this was not the case. They had given their lives to following Jesus, had divested themselves of their livelihoods to follow him, and now at the end when they should have been getting established and getting the great reward for their devotion, instead they were learning that their leader was going to leave them. Cynicism could have very easily set in.

Back in 2003, when I deployed to Iraq, there was an individual that went along with me. He was a public affairs officer, and he was in business for himself in Little Rock, Arkansas. How could I possibly forget Little Rock, Arkansas? He was a plumber. He was a contractor. He had developed a customer base that he went back to all the time. They were his livelihood. I sometimes would joke with him a little bit about not completely fixing his plumbing so that he knew that he could have a return job. I've got a mechanic I'm convinced does that for me. I go in to have one thing fixed, and he gives me a list of other things, and somehow they don't work as well when I left as they did when I went, and so I continue to have to see my mechanic.

When Roy deployed with me, however, he lost his customer base because all of the plumbing needs and all of those other issues had to be serviced by someone else, and so as we were deployed for a time, he kept getting word back of someone who thought a lot of him, but they were having to switch over, and they were developing a relationship with someone else. So this man now who was near 50 when we deployed was watching an entire adult lifetime of a carefully established and serviced customer base begin to melt away, and he was going to be left with all of his tools and all of his ability, his truck and his home, but no livelihood when he returned.

The Last Sermon of Christ

Can you imagine the cynicism that he began to feel towards his being called into the mission he was doing, his service to his country which was costing him his livelihood? Of course, it was a time of war, and everyone was having to serve as they had volunteered to serve, and he knew that going in, but now he was watching his livelihood melt away. Here he was at a point in life where he was not just starting out, and it was all crumbling around him. He had to start over.

The disciples are being told that such is not going to be the case with them. Jesus is telling them, "This is not a start over for you." Now we know that after the resurrection they still didn't quite understand because some of them returned to their fishing nets, and they wandered a bit even while they still clung together. There was a little cynicism. There was a tendency to give up, even just after three days.

But that was not what they were being told that they would be doing. They were not going back to the old way of life. Jesus had called them into a new life, and that's what they were to be engaged in. They were not to revert back to the old ways because he was not leaving them as orphans to fend for themselves, but he would come to them.

He's assuring them that his departure is not abandonment. To children, your presence is just as important as what you do when you're there. Just being there is a comfort. One of the great tragedies of our age of divorce is that children do not have much of that comfort available to them.

When a child is afraid of a monster under the bed at night, they don't ask that you go and flip over the bed or climb under the bed. They just want you there. They don't even ask to leave the room if you're there with them. They just want you to be there with them. They don't necessarily want you to leave the light on if you're there. They don't want you to come in and just toss them a walkie-talkie so they can call you if there's a problem. They don't want you to teach them that martial arts can take care of any animal that happens to be under there. They want the loving parent's presence to be with them in a time when they are afraid. No matter how terrible the storm that rages outside, when dad says, "It's going to be okay," that reassurance is enough.

Jesus was giving his disciples reassurances and promises. He was going to prepare a place for them, he had already told them. They would continue his work. His departure was not the end of their calling. There was a work to continue in their walk as disciples. He would hear their prayers, and he would answer their prayers. He would send them the Holy Spirit, and by virtue of the Spirit, the Spirit of Christ, which he sends, he would abide with them forever. These are promises that he had already made to them.

In the verses for this chapter, he adds four more promises, that he would be resurrected, and more particularly, that they will be resurrected too. That, number two, they will have a great and full understanding of him, that they're going to see what it is that he's talking about. And third, that he'll continue to teach them even more in the church age by virtue of the Word and the Spirit. And finally, that he will dwell in them, and they will dwell in him—unity with Christ.

Regarding resurrection, the first of these promises, he says it will occur "before long." "Yet a little while," he says. "Yet in a little while" places it in history. He doesn't say, "In generations to come," or, "Sometime," or even, "In the fullness of time." He doesn't use that more ambiguous language.

He says, "In a little while," or, "Before long," as it's translated in some versions." It places it in the near term. It places it as something that is imminent, about to occur. He says, "The world is not going to see me, but you will. You will see me." He's not lining these up necessarily in concert with one another. This is after the grave, and when he is ascended. And he's saying, "The world won't see me, but you will see me." He is referring to his resurrection and ours because we all will be resurrected.

"But they will still be on the earth," we say. We're talking here about the first resurrection, when we see with and not through the eyes, when we see Christ with the eyes of faith. This promise was particularly important to those who were standing there on the Mount of Olives, when Jesus ascended to the Father, because they were standing there watching, and they can hear it ringing in their ears, "The world is not going to see me any longer, but you will see me."

It would have been easy to lose heart, wouldn't it? Remember the disciples who were on the road to Emmaus? They said, "We had hoped that he was the one to redeem Israel." You can hear those hopes beginning to thin out and to evaporate. "We had hoped," as in, "We do no longer hope." And while the Scripture doesn't have these words, it's almost as if they're saying, "But he is gone. We see him no more, and so we're going home."

The Last Sermon of Christ

Remember the disheartened and unbelieving Thomas who said, "Unless I myself see the wounds in his hands, I just won't believe. I must see the nail marks for myself if I am to believe." The disciples were disillusioned, but the promise is that there is a resurrection, the first of which is near term—before long, in a little while.

He also promises them understanding. When we start talking about the first resurrection, what are we talking about? That we'll be born again. That our dead hearts will be quickened and made alive by the Spirit of Christ. That requires some understanding. That's the second promise.

He says, "I'm telling you that there's going to be a resurrection. You will see me." And you can see some begin to scratch their heads, and then he says, "You're going to be able to understand what I just told you." This understanding is based on the resurrection promise.

Donald Grey Barnhouse used to hold an open forum on Sunday nights. He would stand before the congregation, which was mostly students, with just the Scripture, and they would ask questions. One evening, a student in the balcony stood up, and said, "Dr. Barnhouse, why is it, or how is it that the Hebrews were able to wander in the wilderness for 40 years and never wear their shoes out?"

Sometimes you wonder why people would ask such simplistic questions of a man who's able to answer profound questions, but they do, which is why we don't have those sessions here.

Dr. Barnhouse blinked, and he looked up at the man, and there was a moment of silence, and all he said in reply was, "God." The young man sat down, and he said, "Oh, now I understand." To which Barnhouse gave a longer answer, "No, you don't. Nobody does."

Saying we understand doesn't remove complexity or mystery. It doesn't remove the complexity or the mysteries around creation. We understand God spoke into chaos and nothingness and created from nothing something by the power of his voice. We believe it, but we don't understand it. We can profess it, but do we really understand how that was? It's the quest of science always to be trying to explore into these mysteries and to explain them, but the answer is God, and we don't understand necessarily.

So understanding that God created doesn't remove mystery. Understanding that the Hebrew people were in the wilderness for 40 years doesn't remove the mystery of their footgear. We understand God can sustain and we have to leave it at that.

I don't mind telling you by way of testimony to God's grace and God's supply, while we were in seminary—I say we because everyone suffers when someone goes to seminary—and money was tight. We ate Corn Flakes quite often, and we would get free bread from a bread company who was very gracious to bring it to the seminary, and they would stack the shelves, and we would all go down like locusts on the field and take bread back to our rooms.

Every morning, I would get the Corn Flakes, and pour myself a bowl, and then suddenly it dawned on me that we had had this box of Corn Flakes for an awfully long time, and so I took the box, and said, "I must have just had the last bowl," but the box was still nearly full.

If you eat Corn Flakes often, you know it doesn't take many weeks to feel like you've been eating them forever. I'd been eating these Corn Flakes forever, and I couldn't get rid of the box because the Corn Flakes continued to go on and on and on. I don't remember throwing them away. Someone probably is still eating out of that box today. Could I explain what I knew to be true? No. I can't explain the mysteries. I can only observe and acknowledge and profess that they are true, but I can't always explain the mystery.

So Christ tells us that we will understand, but we can't always explain things such as the incarnation, the foreknowledge and the predestinating work of God. There's a long list of only-God-can-do-that subjects, but it does remove the cross as a stumbling block of offense. It does make us to see that there is sin that needs and requires atonement. It helps us to understand the parables and many other teachings in the Scripture that we take and apply to our lives. It helps us understand the covenant and God's offer of salvation. It opens our eyes to the issues of salvation, although many other issues remain a mystery.

Jesus promises to give them understanding. That understanding is because they have been raised to life. The Scripture teaches that unless a man is born again, he'll never see the kingdom of God, and the truth about God is spiritually discerned, remaining foolishness to Gentiles and a stumbling block to the Jews. It's like this: If you've ever been to a hydroelectric dam or some sort of a power plant, even those that are sub stations, you can see huge transformers and large, thick wires going in with "Danger! High Voltage!" signs all around. Hundreds of thousands of volts are pouring out of these power production facilities. Who can use that? Who can use 100,000 volts? I know that I can't use 100,000 volts, so on our poles, we see step down transformers, big round transformers that always blow up in the middle of the night. These transformers are scattered all through neighborhoods to take the power and to reduce it down so that it can go into your home, and you can plug in your television and watch it 24/7.

But it goes even further than that because we have mp3 players and all sorts of other little small electronic devices that require as little as 12 volts or less, and so there are even smaller transformers that take that 100,000 volts of raw energy and continue to reduce it down to something we can use.

In the Christian life, the Spirit of God does the same thing for us. It is a fact that 12 volts is electricity just as 100,000 volts is electricity. But the Spirit of God opens up for us and gives us understanding as we are able to understand, and as we grow, and as we continue to mature, God continues to reveal the Scriptures.

That's why when you read Scriptures or hear a sermon series, and then you return to it five years later, you say, "You know, I went through this thoroughly, and I never saw that before," or, "I never really understood that before, but now it's so clear to me, and I don't know how I missed it." That's growth and it's maturity, and it's the work of the Spirit in the life of one who has been raised to life. We see him in his Word. In John 17, I keep referring to this because it is so profound to me. Jesus prayed that we would see the Father through the testimony of the Scriptures.

The third promise relates to our knowing him. The disciples saw Jesus, they heard Jesus, they walked with Jesus, but we, without the benefit of his physical presence, also need to believe. They saw, they heard, they walked. We have distance, historically as well as geographically, but we need to believe just as they believed without that visual sight. Jesus promises that he will be revealed to us. This knowledge of Jesus is passed down in terms of a personal relationship.

But how are we, so far removed from the cross and from the first century, supposed to know Christ personally rather than just historically as we would know any other historic figure, like Napoleon or George Washington, or Caesar? Jesus isn't manifested to us physically, is he? He doesn't come to us and show himself to us physically, nor does he suggest that he'll come in a vision. That's not the way the New Testament tells us that it will be. In fact, it says explicitly in Hebrews that will not be the way that we come to know Jesus.

There's a vital theology in Christian experience called a theology of Word and Spirit. It's an area of study of the mystery of Word and Spirit that goes beyond the physical existence of a bound book with printed words on the page which can be explained objectively in terms of their connotative or dictionary meaning. We can explain the text. We can read it. It's in English. We can parse the sentences. We can diagram them. You don't have to be a believer to handle the Scriptures, even to preach the Scriptures, unfortunately. But is that all there is to the Bible, that we just simply would study it as a body of literature, that we'd be able to explain it as a book?

The Word is preached, and Isaiah says when the Word goes out, the Spirit goes with it, and it doesn't return void. What does that mean? It means that the Word goes—somewhere. In the economy of God, the Word must go, and the Spirit takes and works with the hearts of the hearers to change their hearts through the means and the medium of the preaching of the Word.

Paul said, "People must be made to believe, and they must be made to hear, and how can they hear unless someone goes to preach?" And so the Word is preached, but it's not the preacher that changes the heart no matter how charismatic. A preacher can be exciting. In fact, there's a danger in an exciting preacher because you can get distracted by the charisma of the preacher and feel as if you're getting it and you're excited about the Scripture when you're excited about the presentation of the passage and the message. It's the Spirit that applies the Word to the heart.

Christ is revealed through the preaching of the Word and through the inner work and testimony of the Holy Spirit. The disciples come to not only know about Jesus, but come to know Jesus personally because the Spirit is alive, and the Spirit is within us, and within us the Spirit makes the Word come to life and bear fruit.

Notice the conditions however that Jesus put on this revelation of himself. He said, "It's given to those who keep his commandments and those who love him and love the Father."

Mark Twain was speaking to a ruthless businessman from Boston once who bragged that nobody ever got in his way once he had decided to do something. He told Twain that he was going to go to the Holy Land one day, he was going to climb Mt. Sinai, get to the top, and at the top of his lungs, he was going to shout out the Ten Commandments as loud as he possibly could. Twain, with the wit that only Twain seems to have been blessed with, looked at him, and he said, "I've got a better idea. Why don't you just stay in Boston and keep them?"

Keep his commandments and love the Lord. When James wrote that faith without works is dead, and John wrote in 1 John, "This is love for God, to obey his commands," we hear the echo of the same instruction that those who love the Lord obey the Lord.

A. W. Pink wrote, "This manifestation of Christ is made only to the one who really loves him, and the proof of love to him is not by emotional displays, but by submission to his will."[1] You know what Pink is talking about? He's saying it's not by going to the worship service and showing a tremendous amount of emotion; it's by keeping his commands.

"The Lord will give no direct and special revelation of himself to those who are in the path of disobedience. 'He that hath my commandments' means hath them at heart and keeps them. That's the real test," Pink says.[2] We hear, but do we heed? We know, but are we doing his will?

If you want a closer walk with Christ, if you desire to see God in the Scriptures, then obey in the light of the truth you have already been given. Don't aspire to emulate someone that you see as a super Christian who's getting 100,000 volts. Take what you understand and obey, and to the one that has much more will be given.

The final promise that is foundational to all the others that we've looked at is in verse 23, and it is the promise that Christ will dwell within us. The disciples understood the Spirit of God could be with his people. Throughout the Old Testament, we read that the Spirit was with his people. It was with Saul and it was removed from Saul.

But the idea that the Spirit of God would be *within* his people was something new. The union of the Spirit of Christ with the people of God in the church of Jesus Christ, that union is mystical, and it's compared to marriage in Paul's teaching in Ephesians 5. There two are described as becoming one. It's made clear in perhaps one of the most profound

---

1. James Boice, *Commentary on The Gospel of John*, p. 1145.
2. Ibid, p 1145

statements in Scripture by Paul in Galatians 2:20. "It's no longer I who live, but Christ who lives in me."

Jesus compares our union with him to the union he shares with the Father. It's from that vital union that we draw our spiritual life. Jesus declares to the apostles and to us that the Spirit of God that has been with them will now be in them as he returns to them.

We have these four great promises: that we'll be made spiritually alive by being resurrected in Jesus, the first of those resurrections coming at your conversion; that we'll know him as God; that we will receive a greater revelation and knowledge of Jesus given when we obey him and we love him; and he will come to us, and he'll dwell in us, never leaving nor forsaking us.

Do you have the comforting words of promise and assurance as Jesus gave them to his disciples and to us? For we don't see Jesus with the eyes of flesh, but we do see him in his Word. Christ loves you, and he has not left you alone in the world. He died, but has risen, and has come to you that you may also live in him. The world is not for the Christian. We have been called in Christ. Don't walk alone. Don't journey in the dark.

Hear the kind words of our Savior who desires your heart to be given to him, as he says, "Beloved in the Lord, hear the gracious words of our Savior, Jesus Christ, who says unto all who truly turn to him, 'Come unto me all you that labor and are heavy laden, and I will give you rest. Take my yoke upon you and learn of me, for I am meek and lowly in heart, and you shall find rest unto your souls. I am the Bread of Life. He that comes to me shall never hunger, and he that believes on me shall never thirst. Him that comes to me, I shall in no wise cast out. Blessed are they which do hunger and thirst after righteousness, for they shall be filled.'"

10

Class Is In Session

John 14:25–26

"These things I have spoken to you while I am still with you. But the Helper, the Holy Spirit, whom the Father will send in my name, he will teach you all things and bring to your remembrance all that I have said to you."

ONE OF THE FACTORS that makes a study of the Holy Spirit complicated for the Church today is that we don't talk about it very much in the context of biblical theology. So it seems that whenever we do want to discuss the Holy Spirit, it's all new to us. It's not that we don't mention the Holy Spirit. We'll talk about the Spirit in the sense of a feeling that we might have in worship, or we'll mention the Spirit sometimes in prayer, particularly in being empowered for work in the kingdom, and those are not necessarily wrong concepts of the Spirit, but they are those extras that are added to the foundational knowledge of the Spirit.

They are works of the Spirit, but it would be like going to the supermarket, and as you purchase vegetables or fruit in the supermarket, you never consider the vine or the tree from which the fruit came. You simply believe that grapes just are, that they don't come as part of the growth of anything else. Or if you ask a child where a pineapple grows, they might even say it grows in a tree, and those of us who have asked the question in the past learned, usually to our embarrassment, that they actually grow in the ground looking more like a bush would with the pineapple in the middle.

And so we go about our lives often speaking of what we might observe about the Holy Spirit, but yet never really focusing on the person of the Holy Spirit much to our chagrin and much to our own deficit in understanding. The work of the Holy Spirit, as we'll examine in this chapter, is one particularly of teaching. But teaching what and to whom and to what end, that's what we will explore here.

There isn't just a single aspect to the work and ministry of the Holy Spirit. We can't summarize the person of the Holy Spirit or the work of the Holy Spirit in a single sentence. To do so would be to rob ourselves of a wonderful understanding, and it would be to rob the Spirit of the glory which the Spirit of God is due. When we speak of the Holy Spirit in the New Testament, we're speaking of that same Holy Spirit that hovered over the deep at the beginning as God created the heavens and the earth. It's the same Spirit that was present at all of God's great works and with all of those works accomplished with his people.

It's the same Spirit that was with the judges and the prophets, the same Spirit that was with the kings that led Israel, the same Spirit that inspired the New Testament writers, which was the same Spirit that descended on Jesus as a dove at his baptism. It's the same Spirit that our theology and our doctrine teaches us that regenerates a dead man and makes him alive, that sanctifies us in Christ, and it is the same Spirit that teaches us.

As Jesus had been speaking to the Disciples, he was talking about leaving them, departing from them, going to heaven to prepare a place for them, and that they would follow, that they knew the way, that he was the way and the truth and the life. Now, however there seems to be a shift in the flow of the conversation, where he is not talking about his going from them, but of his coming to them, of his coming to them and joining them in the work. Whereas before he was leaving and they would be going to join him, now he is coming to join them where they are.

In the context of his announcing their departure, we might be able to empathize a bit with the Disciples, for they were being given a mission that depended on Jesus himself. Imagine that you're the Disciples gathered near Christ, and you've been going out as commanded to do great and marvelous works in the name of Christ, establishing the kingdom among the people. And so you have come to understand that your success in your ministry is only effective as you are tethered to Christ, that independently you have nothing to offer. It's only as you are empowered by the Lord that you are able to do great and wonderful things, and only as you are empowered by the Lord that you have anything to say at all.

Everything else would be worthless if it wasn't for Christ, but now Jesus has just said he's leaving. It would naturally follow then that it's all over. The work is completed, or the work has come to an end, but Jesus says, "No, you will continue that work."

You would naturally begin to think, "Well, Lord, I can't do that work without you. The work depends upon you. I can't accomplish the work if you're gone." And now Jesus is telling them, "But don't you see? I'm not going to be gone. I'm going to come to you in the person of the Holy Spirit."

I think we could sympathize with their anxieties about the departure of Jesus, and then we might also come to understand the comfort that these words are intended to bring. One thing is clear, that their future communion with Christ depends on their keeping his Word, and all of that is expressed in chapter 14.

Note verse 15. Let's survey just a couple of these verses. "If you love me," Jesus says, "you'll keep my commandments. On down to verse 21, "Whoever has my commandments and keeps them, he it is who loves me, and he who loves me will be loved by my Father, and I will love him and manifest myself to him."

All of these rewards seemed to be based upon the keeping of commandments. In verse 23 and 24, Jesus answered him, "If any one loves me, he will keep my Word, and my Father will love him, and we will come to him and make our home with him," but there's a condition. If a person will "keep my word," then I will come to him, and the Father will come to him and make our abode and our home with him." Again, "If you keep my Word."

Verse 24 continues, "Whoever does not love me doesn't keep my words, and the word that you hear is not mine but the Father's who sent me." So the condition for receiving the Holy Spirit is that they love the Lord and that love would be manifest in their keeping his Word, in remaining true to what Jesus had taught them.

Now put yourself in the apostles' shoes. That means you have to remember all Jesus has commanded. If you're to keep the commandments, you have to know what it is that you are to keep.

Have you ever given instructions to a child, and you thought you were perfectly clear, and then they went off to do the task only to come back frustrated because they couldn't understand the concept which you were trying to communicate to them? Here, our Lord has said, "I'll come to you if you keep my Word." Now you, as an apostle, would be wondering, "What exactly was that Word—all of it? How are we going to keep all that you told us over these three years of teaching? We have to keep all of that in order to have continued communion with you?"

Even if they had applied all of their energies to understanding, the concepts Jesus had introduced to them were so vast and so foreign to them as he talked about going and preparing a place for them, that they had trouble understanding. When Jesus said, "I will destroy this temple and in three days I'll rebuild it," how were they to understand these things? And yet, Jesus said that they must understand them if they were to commune with him.

These concepts, vast and foreign to them, are not easily grasped, and what's more, their future success depends on them receiving and remembering what they had been taught. They must receive, they must remember, they must abide by the Word of Christ if they are going to continue the work which Jesus has been accomplishing.

You see, that was their calling, to take this ministry that Jesus was now handing to them and say, "What I have been doing, this proclamation that the kingdom of God is at hand, you are to continue to do. You're not to abandon the work or to take off in a different direction. You are to continue in the same stream of ministry that I have established you in." They were to remember what they had been taught.

I was pondering this, the sheer amount of teaching Jesus had given to them in all of the parables, in all of the miracles, and that doesn't even count all of the dialogue as he simply was teaching them about himself, about the Father, about prayer, about the kingdom, about spiritual healing, about rebirth, and these are only what we have recorded. The Scriptures tell us there were many more things that he said to them, more than could possibly be contained in all the pages of all the Scriptures, and yet we have these, and even what we have is so vast that we struggle to comprehend it all.

In pondering the sheer scope of the teaching of Christ, I remembered back when I was first married with Bevalie, and we were of course broke like most folks when they first get married, and so we sat around twiddling our thumbs most of the time, hoping that the paycheck arrived before the food ran out. And what are you to do for entertainment?

Well, we saved our pennies a little while, and one day we bought a jigsaw puzzle, and so we decided we would sit and do that, but we didn't want it to be very quick, so our first jigsaw puzzle was of bagels, a lot of bagels, and we spent a lot of time putting the jigsaw puzzle together. We were so proud of it that we framed it and hung it on the wall.

After that one, we thought we were pretty good at puzzles, and so we wanted something more challenging. We found another puzzle that was nothing but nails. I barely even remember this, so horrific was the experience. It was nothing but nails that had apparently been poured out, and they were all the same. Somebody took a picture and thought this would make a nice puzzle. I don't know what sort of madness comes into people's minds.

We spent long, long hours on that puzzle, and I'll be honest with you, I have no recollection that it was ever complete. Why was it so hard? Because there was no way to distinguish between the pieces. In a regular puzzle, you have blue skies and green grass and borders. There was nothing really to give any guidance here. It was all the same. All the pieces were the same. You had to just take each individual piece and begin to put it together. I'm sure it was 20,000 pieces, or something ridiculous.

It took us forever to work on that puzzle because there was so much there, and we couldn't distinguish between the parts. We couldn't put it together, and I believe that it was much like this in the mind of the apostles.

They had all of this teaching before them, but we know that there was confusion because Peter himself, in talking with Jesus about the cross, said, "Lord, let's just avoid it. Let's don't go to Jerusalem. Let's not go to the cross." And Jesus rebuked him with, "Get thee behind me, Satan."

And so we know that even in the most essential part of Christ's ministry, the most basic understanding of Christ's ministry, the apostles struggled to put it together. We also know that while they should have anticipated three days and the resurrection, they were all shocked, and even when all the other Disciples believed, Thomas himself wouldn't believe till he saw it with his own eyes.

And so we know that these truths which we take for granted as being so evident and so basic were still a jumble in the apostles' minds. They were struggling to put it all together. They didn't have a formula.

They didn't have an outline. They didn't have parameters. They didn't have the church. They didn't have tradition. They had none of the things which we enjoy, and they didn't have the Holy Spirit which teaches and brings things to remembrance.

Many of us stand just like the Disciples wondering about these teachings of Jesus, but no new words are needed. No new teaching is needed. Nothing needs to be added. There is nothing in the epistles which is not already in the Gospels, but something is needed to bring these truths to the human heart.

Dr. Martyn Lloyd-Jones, in his little book titled *Authority*, says, "We can study the authority of the Lord and of the Scriptures in a purely intellectual manner. We may have intellectual convictions even, but they do not of necessity affect our lives and our work. Only when the authority of the Holy Spirit comes to bear upon us do all these things become real and living and powerful to us."[1]

God names it as punishment to his people when he shuts up the Book and makes it incomprehensible. In Isaiah 29:11, "And the vision of all this has become to you like the words of a book that is sealed." For his people, God desires to open up the Book and to give them understanding. When Isaiah prophesied about the book being sealed, there wasn't a physical seal on it. It meant that they would not understand the prophecies.

So how will we know? How will we understand the teaching of Scripture? Jesus promises the Disciples a Teacher. And the first thing that he says about this Teacher is that he is holy. He calls him the Holy Spirit. He's holy because he shares a nature with the Father. He is sinless, and he possesses all of the divine attributes.

Note the words in Romans 8:9–10. "You, however, are not in the flesh but in the Spirit, if in fact the Spirit of God dwells in you." The first point here: The Holy Spirit is called the Spirit of God. So the Holy Spirit, unique in his own personhood, is also the Spirit of God and the Spirit of Christ. Verse 10: "But if Christ is in you. . . ." When we are indwelled by the Holy Spirit, it can be said that it is Christ who dwells in us. "Although the body is dead because of sin, the Spirit is alive because of righteousness." Now we're referring to the Spirit of Christ, Christ who dwells in us as the Spirit, the Holy Spirit.

---

1. Martin Lloyd-Jones, *Authority,* The Banner of Truth Trust Carlisle, p. 62.

Verse 11: "If the Spirit of him who raised Jesus from the dead dwells in you, he who raised Christ Jesus from the dead will also give life to your mortal bodies through his Spirit who dwells in you." Who is the one who raised Jesus from the dead but God the Father? And the Spirit of God the Father raised Christ from the dead, and then that same Spirit of God the Father is said to dwell in us.

What's the purpose of all of this? This Holy Spirit is divine just as the Father is divine, just as the Son is divine, and yet the uniqueness of the Holy Spirit is in his work. By our association with the Spirit, we're also called holy. Verses 17 marks a deep separation between the world and the Spirit and the Disciples and the world.

Verse 17: "Even the Spirit of truth, whom the world cannot receive, because it neither sees him nor knows him, you know him, for he dwells with you and will be in you." We are given the promise of the Holy Spirit, and there is a clear separation between the Holy Spirit and the spirit of this world.

Here, we're going to take advantage of an opportunity for reflection. In 1 John 5:19, we read, "We know that we are from God and the whole world lies in the power of the evil one." As we consider the holiness of the Holy Spirit, the separateness of the Spirit of Christ from the spirit that is the world, and we are reminded that the world lies in the power of the evil one, our point of reflection is this: What is your view of the world, and what is your view of your own place in the world? How do you see yourself in the world as one living in the world yet not belonging to the world? Are you a participant more in the world than you are in the kingdom of God?

If you have to weigh the bulk of your work, are you working for the world, or are you working for Christ? There is a distinct separation between the two. It's easy to work for the world because the world frankly has ownership of our time and of our physical body for six days. We praise God for the Lord's Day as a time of refreshment and remembrance when we rejoice in the Lord on the Lord's Day. And so it is a struggle for God's people to make sure that our lives are not so invested in the world that we have little to show for our walk in the kingdom.

In our creeds we confess that we love the Holy Spirit and the holy catholic church. We're saying that the catholic, that is the universal church, is holy, made so because the Spirit dwells in it. We're affirming our belief in the presence and work of the Spirit in the church. The function of the Spirit in the church is to unify men and women with Christ, that is, to simply connect men with Christ through the gospel. That union with Christ is what makes men holy.

How specifically is that work accomplished? How is it that men are made holy by the work of the Spirit in the holy catholic church? By faith, through the hearing of God's Word, and through the observation of the sacraments, the means of grace established by God. Not magically, not by some mystic formula, not by the power of a priest or of a minister, but by faith and by hearing and by participating in Christ. Ephesians 5 calls this union a great mystery, and indeed it is, but it is a mystery that is revealed to us and that we receive by faith.

In monastic times of the Medieval Age, monks sought to make themselves holy by rigorous disciplines, by attending and by becoming members of monasteries, but they were not made holy through this. They were not found to be in Christ despite their great excess in practice and despite their great efforts.

And so this brings us another opportunity for reflection. Do you use your church membership in the same way that the monks would have used their monastic orders? Is your membership basically where you feel that you are becoming holy by association, that is, that just as they found their acceptance in the Lord by their being a Franciscan or by their being an Augustinian monk, do you rely on official membership in the visible church to make you acceptable before God?

Membership is important. I would never disqualify that because that marks our public profession of faith, that we in fact are following after Christ. But if the public profession of faith doesn't call us also to rely on the means of grace which God has appointed for our continued sanctification and spiritual growth, if in fact we have come to feel that because we're members we're somehow accepted by God even though we would neglect obedience to his commandments and obedience to his Word which Jesus said was required, then of what value is our membership at all? We are to be counted just as the Franciscans and just as the Augustinians because our name is on a roll book in an office rather than in the Lamb's Book of Life.

Then Jesus calls the Spirit a Teacher. He says, "He will teach and remind." One important linguistic point here: it's a pronoun, and it's not neuter. He! It doesn't say, "It." It says, "He will teach and remind." The Spirit will accomplish his teaching as an individual person of the

Trinity, not a power, not a force of God. We'll find this further attested in Scripture when we hear the benediction in the name of the Father and the Son and Holy Spirit, for example, which is the baptism formula as well. The Spirit is listed separately as one person in the Trinity.

The specific reference here by Jesus is clearly to the apostles however. "All things." What things? All that Jesus had taught them, all of it. Now we get a sense of their panic. "All things that I have spoken while still with you." He meant that the Holy Spirit would reveal to them the fullness of understanding associated with Jesus' incarnation, with his life, with his teaching, with his death, with his resurrection. This is the idea behind inspiration, where we get the rest of our New Testament epistles. The inspiration of the Scriptures came because the Holy Spirit brought remembrance and taught the Disciples what Jesus had intended them to know.

The specific instruction to the apostles who were contemporary to Jesus made all of their memories and all of their reflections of their time with Christ align with the truth of God. The Bible itself is evidence that this happened. It can well be said there's nothing in the epistles which is not also represented in the Gospels. There's no new teaching in the epistles, that is, the letters of Galatians, and Ephesians, and Philippians, and Hebrews, and 1, 2 John, 1, 2 Peter, and all the rest. There's nothing new there that hasn't been intimated and alluded to or taught directly by Christ.

There's some expansion on themes and explanation of doctrine. There's connection with Old Testament Scriptures to New Testament fulfillment. All of that is in there, but the priesthood of Christ, the electing power of God, salvation in the gospel itself, the church itself as it is growing out of the nation of Israel, all of these are in the Scriptures before the epistles.

The inspiration of the apostles was that they would remember all things that Jesus had taught them, and that they would be able through the agency of the apostles which each of their unique backgrounds and training and understanding to record those for us as they addressed the church to be established in Christ.

We also understand it applying to us as well. Paul writes about this clearly in 1 Corinthians 2:9–13.

> "But, as it is written, 'What no eye has seen, nor ear heard, nor the heart of man imagined, what God has prepared for those

who love him'—these things God has revealed to us through the Spirit. For the Spirit searches everything, even the depths of God. For who knows a person's thoughts except the spirit of that person, which is in him? So also no one comprehends the thoughts of God except the Spirit of God."

Only by the Spirit of God can the mind of God be known. The same thing is repeated in 1 John 2:20, 27 and 1 Peter 1:12, which I encourage you to reflect on and study as well. These passages, 1 John 2, 1 Corinthians 2, and the others, teach us that the work of the Holy Spirit as our Teacher is essential if we are to understand the mind of God.

Here's an important principle regarding revelation: The Reformers were adamant about these two principles in particular, when Jesus says, "In my name," and "What I have said to you." The Holy Spirit is sent by the Father in Jesus' name and also to bring to their remembrance what he said to them. This disqualifies any continuing revelation or any new revelation from God. The Spirit is to teach us the meaning of what Jesus has taught. What is required of us is the same as what was required of the Disciples. We must first hear what Jesus has taught.

Dr. John Peter Lange says, "In performing this, his office, he shall unfetter the Word, break down the barriers of individualization, misunderstanding, thus causing it to develop into an ever living organism of doctrine, the specific soul and character of which does nevertheless remain the Word of Christ."[2]

We are limited by what the Spirit teaches us concerning what Christ has delivered. The Father sends the Holy Spirit in Jesus' name. The Holy Spirit is sent to represent the character of Christ as an ambassador of Christ sent in Jesus' name and in no other. He is not sent in his own accord to bring another epic of revelation, but sent to represent the teaching of Christ to his people.

If we've not heard what Jesus has said, however, that is, if we have not been in the Scriptures, if we have not been reading and studying the Scriptures, then how will an explanation of its meaning mean anything to us at all? How will we have any idea what God is intending if we have not read the Scriptures?

Here is a good case for the teaching of children in the doctrines of the Scripture. We might make an argument, "You know, children do not have the intellectual capacity to grasp these serious doctrines

---

2. John Peter Lange, *Commentary on the Holy Scriptures*, 445.

in the teaching of Scripture," but didn't we just read that the apostles themselves misunderstood the most basic explanations and ideas concerning Christ? Didn't we just read that those who are the founders of our church and of our faith, who were the ones who delivered to us the Word of God, they themselves couldn't understand it even with Jesus himself speaking in their midst until the Holy Spirit came and clarified it in their mind by teaching them and bringing them remembrance?

Whether it's a child or whether it's an adult, it is all the Spirit who does the teaching. But in addition to the ministry of teaching, the Holy Spirit has one other ministry. Those who have spent many years in an organization love to say to those who are new, "I've probably forgotten more than you'll ever know about this subject." In their own mind, I'm sure that they think that that is true, but that would mean that they have attained the maximum of learning in any particular area.

Nevertheless, it is true that we have all forgotten a lot. We have studied the Scriptures. We've sat through sermons. Before going into the ministry, how many sermons have I sat through in my lifetime? And some of you, being older and wiser than I am, have sat through two or three times as many as I have, and sometimes you might say the right word is endured three or four times as many, but nevertheless, you've been there as the Word of God was opened and read and preached. How much have we forgotten?

Where would we be if we recalled every single word that was preached, and our life at every single point was changed and conformed, and we were continuously made more? How much peace of Christ would we have? What rancor and tension would there be in Christ's church if we were able to retain and be shaped by every word of Christ that has ever been preached to us?

If we could only remember it, but from the emphasis on remembrance in the ministry of the Spirit, we learn that Christianity and the gospel doesn't depend on novelty. It doesn't depend on us coming up with something new. It doesn't depend on us reinventing Christ to present him to a new generation. Theology and doctrine are not something that evolves for a people who are always evolving themselves to a greater maturity and understanding.

We do grow in our knowledge. We do certainly do that as we study, but we are not having to reinvent or become novel in our presentation. The Spirit is not building on these new revelations or novelties.

In a sense, there really isn't any new sermon at all. Hasn't it all been preached before? Haven't you studied many of the cardinal doctrines in Bible studies yourself?

The Spirit ensures that every one of Christ's words lives on in the fullness of their purpose. Not one word of the Lord Jesus Christ is lost. He brings the together to form a coherent whole. Here's the great objected testimony to the skeptic: Jesus' words continue to teach, shape, and transform men.

The skeptic would say, "Dead words of a dead prophet," and we would say, "Words that by the power of the Holy Spirit are still today shaping and changing and transforming men." We do in fact forget important truths and doctrines over time, and we must revisit them. That's one reason we value our creeds and confessions so much because they are summaries of the Spirit's ministry of remembrance in the life of the church. They stand as testimonies to a time when men were taught and reminded of great truths of Scripture, and they set these down that they might be passed along because in the finiteness and the carelessness of our own minds we forget these great truths.

So what are we to make of this ministry of the Holy Spirit? Let me summarize in these three short concluding points. First of all, the Spirit is holy. We are made holy by our association and union with Christ in the Spirit and through his church, and we are to be separated out from a profane world. We learned that the Spirit is divine. He's personal and he's distinct from the Father and the Son, and yet he is equal to the Father and the Son.

Secondly, we also know that we are to study the words and life of Christ with confidence because the Spirit will teach us the meaning of the words of Christ, and the meaning must be accompanied with our actually reading the words of Christ. The apostles had to hear Christ speaking, and the Teacher, that is, the Holy Spirit, instructing them to the meaning of the words. It's as if I walked into a math lab and found an incredible math equation on the board that meant nothing to me until the teacher came and instructed me, but the teacher could not instruct me with a blank board, so we must also be in the Word of God if the Holy Spirit is to teach us its meaning.

And then finally, that we are to trust the Spirit of Christ that it will cause us to remember those truths that we might have an assurance that becomes our testimony in Christ. We are a people, just as the apostles, given the Great Commission, given the command to be obedient to the Word of God, and just like the apostles, if we stand alone and separated from Christ, we are ill equipped to the task. And we struggle with even what to say. How many times do we say, "Oh, I would share my testimony, I just don't know what to say. I just don't know how to put it"? But the Spirit teaches us when we've been in the Word of God how we are to share the good news of the kingdom of God.

Jesus didn't leave his Disciples ill equipped for the task, and he doesn't leave us ill equipped for the task either. He comes to us in his Spirit. The same promise that they received that would enable them to continue their work through the empowering of the Spirit, the self-same Spirit is given to you and to me this very day. We are equipped as the Disciples to go and to be obedient to Christ, to take the words of Christ and to preach them. We are not inspired writers of Scripture, but we are inspired servants of God that we are able to give by testimony in the power of the Spirit the gospel of Jesus Christ.

11

The Peace Dividend

John 14:27–31

"Peace I leave with you; my peace I give to you. Not as the world gives do I give to you. Let not your hearts be troubled, neither let them be afraid. You heard me say to you, 'I am going away, and I will come to you.' If you loved me, you would have rejoiced, because I am going to the Father, for the Father is greater than I. And now I have told you before it takes place, so that when it does take place you may believe. I will no longer talk much with you, for the ruler of this world is coming. He has no claim on me, but I do as the Father has commanded me, so that the world may know that I love the Father. Rise, let us go from here."

PEACE. "PEACE I LEAVE with you; my peace I give to you." Jesus is now changing the tone and the subject of his discourse with his disciples, nearing the end of their time. Since he says, "Rise, let us go from here," it would seem that they are still in the upper room. In any case, they are still together, and Jesus is in the same conversation that he had begun when they first entered the upper room where he had begun by washing their feed and talking to them about the servanthood disposition of a believer.

Jesus has been dealing with their anxieties. Remember, first, it was the disturbing scene to them where he took the basin of water to wash their feet. Then prior to celebrating the Lord's Supper, he had predicted that one would betray him. As they began to eat, he announced that the bread would be as his body and that the drink was his blood which was to be poured out, and then he predicted Peter's denial of him and the scattering of the rest of the disciples. Followed was his announcement that he would be leaving them and that they would no longer be able to commune with him, so you can see how anxiety was building upon anxiety, and we are now coming to the conclusion where Jesus was telling them, "Peace. Peace I give to you; my peace I give to you."

This is basically what Martin Luther called a "good night blessing." It's a legacy that he's leaving behind and a treasure which he is giving. "Peace I leave with you," is the legacy that he's leaving behind. "My peace I give to you," is the promised treasure that is still ahead.

So the question before us as we begin an examination of this passage is whether it is a theoretical peace. Is it a utopian peace? Is it a peace that we would look forward to post-resurrection of our own bodies when the Lord returns and all sin is eradicated and Satan has been thrown into the pit and every tear has been wiped from every eye? Is that when we will know this peace, or is there peace which is available to us now, a peace which perhaps in your Christian walk thus far has escaped you? Is there in fact a peace now as well as a peace that we look forward to in the future?

Is it simply a horizontal dimension, a peace between peoples? Is it peace with God? Is it peace or subjugation to some feeling that we might have inside, a peaceful feeling? What is it that we are to experience in the Christian life? What sort of peace should we expect?

Christ here is actually giving them peace in the presence tense, a peace. Is this a hope for peace only in this life or the one to come? Here it seems it is a peace in the present as well as in the life to come. The answer really should have come to us rather quickly. We've already studied together the work of the Holy Spirit. Jesus has been discussing the promise and the work of the Holy Spirit with them, and we know from Paul's teaching in Galatians 5:22 that peace is a promise of that coming of the Holy Spirit. "The fruit of the Spirit is love, joy, peace, patience, kindness, goodness, faithfulness, gentleness, self-control."

For those who are in possession of the Holy Spirit, or should we say are possessed by God through the Holy Spirit, peace is a fruit of the Spirit. And so the absence of peace in our lives should disturb us because the presence of the Holy Spirit will have peace as one of its fruits. In Micah 7, we find that the prophet goes out and he looks for fruit in the people's lives, and he says, "I find nothing but leaves."

We need to consider in our lives the fruit of the Spirit as being evidence of the presence of the Spirit. Not necessarily that we would question that we have the Spirit, but that we might wonder, "What is it about our understanding of the work of the Spirit and of our place in life that causes us to neglect those gifts and to take advantage of those fruits of the Holy Spirit?"

James Montgomery Boice illustrates peace wonderfully when he talks about a contest in which artists were to offer paintings for competition, and in those paintings they were to represent peace. There were beautiful paintings that were submitted. Paintings of sunsets. Paintings of tranquil lakes. Paintings of mountains.

The winner of the contest was unusual in that it was the painting of a bird's nest on a limb which was protruding from the middle of a raging waterfall. A bird's nest with tiny birds hatched waiting for a mother to come and feed them, protruding from a raging waterfall. Why would that be the picture of peace? Because as chaos and as destructive forces raged all around, there was complete peace as that nest sat firmly and stable on the limb protruding from the midst of the waterfall.

It's one thing to acknowledge that the Scripture teaches that we should have peace, which we would all affirm. It's one thing to acknowledge the Scripture teaching and that Jesus himself teaches it and quite another thing all together to find it in our own lives.

We look at the world. We see division, strife, plotting, politics, schism, war, but in the church, what do we see there? We see division, strife, plotting, politics, schism, war. No matter how large, no matter how small the church, even in the household of faith, even in the household of God, we see the way of the world more often than we see the way of Christ.

As Jesus tells his disciples he's leaving them peace, he does so with a bit of an air of a bequest, almost as if in leaving he's going to bequeath them peace. Again, Martin Luther said, "It is a very comforting and pleasing bequest that he leaves them. It does not consist of cities or castles or of silver or gold. It is peace, the greatest treasure on earth."[1]

As Jesus leaves his disciples, he's not promising them those things that usually are accompanied with a last will and testament. He's promising them peace, and in leaving them peace, he was identifying a fundamental character trait of the Christian life. I use the word

---

1. Martin Luther, Luther's Works vol. 24, p 177–178.

"fundamental" in the fullest and most exclusive sense of the term. It is a fundamental characteristic of an authentic Christian life. It's what Christ left his people, peace.

In his parting comments to the disciples, he said to them, "I give you my peace." Our tendency to be disturbed, bitter, and at war with Christ's own people is distinctively uncharacteristic of a Christian. In other words, it is not characteristic of a Christian to be going after one another or to pursue vengeance with one another, but it is characteristic of a Christian to be at peace with one another. We should leave the politics, the strife, the schism, and the warring to the world because Jesus said, "My peace I leave with you," and it is not the peace of the world. It is something entirely different.

Rather than sinning in order that grace may abound in continuing our ways, we should, every one of us, seek the peace of Christ. Colossians 3:15: "Let the peace of Christ rule in your hearts, to which indeed you were called in one body, and be thankful." I would repeat it again, but instead let me just emphasize the word "rule." "Let the peace of Christ rule in your heart."

It's not simply some add-on or some footnote or something that the really mature Christian who has learned not to care so much about the things of the world has. It is a command of Scripture that peace will be indicative, or peace will be descriptive of the Christian life, and where it is absent, we do not have to go to seminary to understand the implications. We must be careful to make close examination of peace.

Jesus says to them, "Peace I leave with you; my peace I give to you." After the resurrection, in John 20, Jesus again addresses the issue of peace. In John 20:19, Jesus appeared to the disciples, saying again, "Peace be with you." In verse 21, Jesus said to them again, "Peace be with you." In verse 26, eight days later, when Thomas was in the room, Jesus again appeared to them, and he was among them, and he said, "Peace be with you."

What is the significance of that? Isn't it just a cultural greeting? Actually it's much more than that because there is a thread that runs through the Old Testament where peace is characteristic of the kingdom of God. It's what the Jews were longing for. They were a people in a hostile land. Remember the wilderness. Remember as they came into the Promised Land the wars they had to fight. Remember the time of the judges and the Philistines. Remember how they were always at war, even being carried off and dispersed away from their land. They longed to be a people at peace, and they wanted God to bring them peace. Peace is an eternal, fundamental expectation of the kingdom of God. When we talk about the kingdom of God, don't we expect peace with the kingdom of God?

In the Old Testament times, they longed for the establishment of the kingdom, and it was seen as a kingdom of righteousness and peace.

> "For to us a child is born, to us a son is given; and the government shall be upon his shoulder, and his name shall be called Wonderful Counselor, Mighty God, Everlasting Father, Prince of Peace. Of the increase of his government and of peace there will be no end." (Isaiah 9:6–7)

> In Isaiah 52, "How beautiful upon the mountains are the feet of him who brings good news, who publishes peace, who brings good news of happiness, who publishes salvation, who says to Zion, 'Your God reigns.'"
>
> "All your children shall be taught by the LORD, and great shall be the peace of your children."(Isaiah 54:13)

> "I will make a covenant of peace with them. It shall be an everlasting covenant with them." (Ezekiel 37:26)

> And lastly finally, "The latter glory of this house shall be greater than the former, says the LORD of hosts, and in this place I will give peace, declares the LORD of hosts." (Haggai 2:9)

It was this prophecy of the kingdom of peace that Jesus signaled as fulfilled after the resurrection. When he arrived with the disciples and announced to them peace, saying, "I'm going to give you my peace," he was declaring these prophecies are fulfilled in him. He is the Prince of Peace and the kingdom has been inaugurated. The peace of Christ is available just as it is promised.

Isn't this what Luke is explaining in Acts 10:36 when he talks about preaching the good news of peace through Jesus Christ and which Paul continues to elaborate on in Romans 14:17, "For the kingdom of God is not a matter of eating and drinking, but of righteousness, peace, and joy in the Holy Spirit. So then let us pursue what makes for peace and for mutual upbuilding."

If we want to know something of the flavor of the kingdom of God, if we want to know something experientially of the kingdom of God, then all of our ministries and all of our efforts and every word that comes from our mouth should be according to righteousness, peace, and joy. It should be that we are pursuing peace with one another and mutual upbuilding because those are the characteristics of the kingdom and of the kingdom people, and if they're not the characteristics of the ministries of a church, then the ministries of the church are not conducive to the building of the kingdom of God.

If we desire to be used of God in the building up of the kingdom, then we ought to be aligning ourselves to those ministries and those expressions which are complementary to the kingdom itself. So we've established by the Scriptures that peace is an indispensible fruit of those who are in the kingdom, who have belonged to the kingdom because it is an indispensible fruit of the kingdom itself. The kingdom people will share the characteristics of the kingdom. That peace is founded in the finished work of Christ to give us peace with God in eternity and granted by the indwelling of the Spirit to give peace in our soul now. Peace in eternity; peace in our soul now.

I love the way D. A. Carson puts this. "Jesus displays transcendent peace. His own peace." Transcendent, meaning above all the peace of this world. "A transcendent peace throughout his perilous hour of suffering and death."[2] As Jesus was facing the cross and his own spirit was anxious because of the weight of the cross which was falling upon him and the weight of the sin of man which would be upon his shoulders, he was still able to say to his disciples, "Peace I leave with you; my peace I give to you."

In the face of all that Jesus had before him, he was a man at peace. We're not to say that he was carefree about the cross as we know that he sweat drops of blood in the garden, but he understood the suffering that was before him, and his soul was at peace because it was in harmony with God's will, and he himself was the perfect manifestation of the kingdom.

Carson says, "And by that death he absorbs in himself the malice of others, the sin of the world, and introduces the promised messianic peace in a way none of his contemporaries had envisaged."[3] The malice of others is absorbed in Christ. What's left to express but peace in the kingdom of God, for all that is not at peace and all that is not edifying

---

2. D.A. Carson. *The Gospel According to John*, p 506.
3. D.A. Carson, p 506.

The Peace Dividend

and all that is not uplifting has been absorbed by Christ at the cross. So where those expressions are manifest, they are not indicative of the presence of the kingdom because those have been absorbed by Christ at the cross.

What sort of peace, what sort of messianic peace did his contemporaries envisage? As Carson says, "The Pax Romana, that is, the peace of Rome, was won and maintained by a brutal sword. Not a few Jews thought that the messianic peace would involve conquest by a larger sword, secured by a still mightier sword. Instead, it was secured by an innocent Man who suffered and died at the hands of the Romans, of the Jews, and all of us, and by his death he effected for his own followers peace with God, and therefore the peace of God which surpasses all understanding."[4]

What does this mean? This means that there is a way of the world in which the world seeks to produce peace. It seeks to produce peace either by the might of the sword or by political maneuvering. It seeks to enforce peace by force, but that's not peace as Christ would give peace. That's not the peace of Christ which surpasses understanding, and it is not the peace of the kingdom. It is an enforced will, which means a lack of war.

The Pax Romana was peace in the land, but it was peace over a conquered people. It was not the peace of Christ. So then let's ask, what is the practical, that is, this worldly nature of peace? If we are not to know peace as the world has its peace, then while we are living in this world, what does this peace look like for us? What is our experience of the peace of Christ?

There's a wonderful story in the Scriptures of Jesus. He came to the disciples in the midst of a storm, walking on the water as they were out in the boat afraid for their lives. Jesus is walking across the water to them. Peter calls out to him, and he wants to go to Christ, and Christ offers him the opportunity to come out of the boat and to come, and Peter begins by walking on the water, keeping his eyes upon Christ, but then as the sea billows rise up around him, and as the waves crash in the unabated storm, Peter becomes distracted, and he begins to sink into the water.

A peace is a stable balance between two opposing forces for us in this life. For the world still exists, and we still must live in the world,

4. Ibid, p. 506.

and like the storm and the sea billows raging around Peter, it will continue around us unabated until the end of time. There will always be wars and rumors of wars. There will always be plots and schemes and whispers. There will always be these things that go on around us at all times. There will be financial insecurities. There will be vocational insecurities. There will be splits and divisions among people, tragically even among God's people. And yet, if we keep our eyes upon Christ and Christ alone, we will not sink.

How do we do that? How do we keep our eyes on Christ? Is it through a personal devotional life? Certainly personal devotional life is a significant part of keeping our eyes on Christ, but the Lord has not left us without devices. He gave us his Word. He has given us the sacraments. He has given us the church itself. And through these means of God's grace and through personal devotional life translated as prayer, through the celebration of the sacraments, through mediation and study of God's Word, we keep our eyes on Christ, and the peace of Christ which surpasses understanding is made to be ours.

It's not the absence of threat or discomfort, but the strength to check it which gives us peace because just when we eliminate one thorn in our side, another one will appear. As long as we are in this life, there will always be a thorn in our side, always. Whether it's here, whether it's in your work, whether it's driving in 5:00 traffic, whether it's in your home, there will always be an issue. As soon as you eliminate one, there will be another.

The quest for happiness does not begin through the eradication of those around us. It begins with the possession of Christ in our soul, and if we keep our mind on Christ, and we keep our eye on Christ, we won't be so concerned about the destruction of the waves around us. The waves will always be there. One wave will be replaced by another wave. It's the absence of Christ which disquiets our soul.

A Christian knows the tension of peace in this life and the difference between peace and paradise. We long for paradise, but we understand peace now. A Christian knows what it means to live in a bird's nest on a limb protruding from a thundering waterfall because that's where we always remain as the world rages around us. A Christian knows that the peace of this world is temporary and deceptive. Every time there's an election and a particular party wins the election, there's a day or a week or a month or a hundred days of celebration, and then

The Peace Dividend

the reality sinks in that no, it's not perfect, and no, things are not going to always go the way we thought that they would go.

Even when it's a charismatic leader or a soft touch or financial gain or smooth handshakes or a wink with the eye, none of those things give you peace because hatred, divisions, plotting, envy, selfishness, and the sin of the world will trump world peace every time.

There is no guarantee of world peace because this world is dying, and the Christian knows that God condemns every prophet or every priest that would lead people to look anywhere but to him for peace. Anyone who would preach or teach that there is another place to fix your gaze, that that will give you peace is indicted by the Scriptures in Jeremiah 6. "For from the least to the greatest of them, everyone is greedy for unjust gain; and from prophet to priest, everyone deals falsely. They have healed the wound of my people lightly, saying, 'Peace, peace,' when there is no peace."

The indictment is that where a prophet or a priest has opportunity to train the people's vision on Christ, instead he has deflected it to something else. For his own reputation, he has told them, "There'll be peace if you just do this," when there is no peace by doing that. And lost is the opportunity to say, "Turn your eyes upon Jesus. Look full in his wonderful face."

So what's the ground then for real peace? Jesus told the disciples, "Let not your heart be troubled." In other words, "Do not be terrified. Do not shrink back in the day in which you live," because he had reminded them all of the proof of his ability to make peace. That's what he's reflecting on. That's what he's reminding them of. He's saying, "I'm telling you to have peace, but it's not empty. I've already proven to you that I can give you peace."

They could shake off their fear and timidity because he was making many mansions for them. He would call them to himself because he himself is the way to the Father, because they know God as they know him, because their work will have continuity with his own work. They will labor in the power of the Holy Spirit, because the Spirit will come and teach them all things. In the giving of the Spirit, the Father and his Son will reside in the heart of every believer.

Harry Ironside tells this story. At the end of the Civil War, the federal cavalry were riding on a road between Richmond and Washington. Suddenly, from out of the bushes came a Confederate soldier. He was

The Last Sermon of Christ

ragged and starving, and he called out to the captain of the Union cavalry. The soldier approached, essentially surrendering to the captain, and he said, "I'm starving to death. Do you have any food?"

The Union captain was perplexed, and he said, "Why don't you just go to Richmond and eat? Why don't you go there and get what you need?" And the Confederate soldier explained to him, "I can't because I'll be arrested. You see, three weeks ago, I deserted from the army, and if I'm caught, I'll be shot as a deserter."

The captain asked him, "Well, haven't you heard the news? The war is over. Peace was made at Appomattox two weeks ago. The Confederacy is ended and there's no longer a conflict between us." The Confederate looked at him in amazement. "What?" he said, "I've been starving and hiding for two weeks just because I didn't know it."

Jesus has bequeathed to us a great legacy of peace. He has given to us a peace and promised us a perfect peace in eternity, but have we entered into that peace? Has unbelief, rebellion, vice, hatred, ignorance, willful sins, have these things kept us from that peace? This is a good picture of our peace with God as we contemplate the condition of that soldier. Peace was available. Peace was there, but for two weeks he had been starving to death.

Christ went to Calvary and accepted our surrender. The war is over. Rebellion is ended. Peace is available for those who have an ear to hear it, and this has been the love and the treasure of the church through the ages. We have hymns which speak of the people's love and understanding of this peace of Christ. They've even named their children words for peace, such as Irene, which means simply peace.

During services, people used to greet one another with, "Peace be with you." If you go to the catacombs in Rome, you'll still find inscribed there on many of the tombs simply, "In peace." And if you go to many of the cemeteries, you will find there tombstones with the epitaph, "Rest In Peace." Do we simply mean that when we put you in the ground it should be quiet? No, we are saying, "May your soul be at peace."

And then finally there are hymns which we sing that give great expression to the theology concerning peace. You know them. "When peace like a river attendeth my way, when sorrows like sea billows roll, whatever my lot thou hast taught me to say, 'It is well, it is well with my soul.'"

Another hymn says, "Like a river glorious is God's perfect peace, over all victorious in its bright increase. Perfect yet it floweth, fuller every day. Perfect yet it growth, deeper all the way. Stayed upon Jehovah, hearts are fully blessed. Finding as he promised perfect peace and rest."

How has this idea of peace escaped us? How is it that we have been so focused on all things and missed peace, the peace of Christ which surpasses understanding? As he finished teaching, what did Jesus want for his disciples? Peace, and through peace, strength not timidity. Through peace, unity not division. Through peace, hope not despair. Through peace, possession of Christ in his Holy Spirit rather than a belonging to the world.

Peace is the way of the kingdom. Peace will be the defining mark of the kingdom when we're in the presence of God. Peace should be a character of God's people now.

12

The Gospel of Unity

John 15:1–7

"Rise, let us go from here. I am the true vine, and My Father is the vinedresser. Every branch in Me that does not bear fruit he takes away, and every branch that does bear fruit he prunes, that it may bear more fruit. Already you are clean because of the word that I have spoken to you. Abide in Me, and I in you. As the branch cannot bear fruit by itself, unless it abides in the vine, neither can you, unless you abide in Me. I am the vine; you are the branches. Whoever abides in Me and I in him, he it is that bears much fruit, for apart from Me you can do nothing. If anyone does not abide in Me he is thrown away like a branch and withers; and the branches are gathered, thrown into the fire, and burned. If you abide in Me, and My words abide in you, ask whatever you wish, and it will be done for you."

THE LAST VERSE OF chapter 14 suggests that our Lord was on the move with the Disciples. Many commentators think that as they journeyed through Jerusalem, through the city gates and out of the city, they would have passed the Temple. As they were passing the Temple, as was often the habit of Jesus, he would look at what was around him and then draw a spiritual truth by telling a story based upon what he was able to see.

On the Temple, there would be in an ornamental type of structure a golden vine sculpted on the Temple gates. Vines grew everywhere in Jerusalem, so it didn't have to be the one that was on the Temple, but we do know the vine represented the people of God, the Israel of God, and that it was very frequently found sculpted onto something to communicate that this was representative of the people of God. In fact, on the Maccabean coin, Israel is represented on the reverse side by a vine. And so it was a common understanding that the Israel of God was represented by a vine.

We also find it in the Scripture, Psalm 80, verse 8: "You brought a vine out of Egypt." You brought a people out of Egypt, and he calls them a vine. It's frequently used in the Old Testament to represent Israel as a people who are separated from the world, a people who are a testimony of God, bearing fruit for his glory. You see, that is the purpose of a vine. It's to bear fruit. A vine really is of no other use if it's not to bear fruit. It won't provide shade. It can't be used for construction. It's really good for nothing else but to bear fruit. And so God's people are called a vine, and their purpose is to bear fruit for God's glory.

A song in Isaiah 5 tells of God's love for his people in calling them a vine and establishing it. It's a wonderful place to enter into the whole idea of a vineyard and of God's relation to that vineyard. And it forms the background in the Disciples' minds as Jesus teaches them about the vine.

In Isaiah, chapter 5, the prophet says, "Let me sing for my beloved my love song concerning his vineyard. . . on a very fertile hill. He dug it and cleared it." Who is *he*? God. God himself prepared the place for his people. "He dug it and cleared it of stones, and planted it with choice vines." What place is he talking about? He brought his people into the Promised Land, and it was by *his* hand that the walls of Jericho fell. It was by his hand he sanctified the land through the people Israel, and established them, and created a place that can be described as a land of milk and honey, a wonderful place to plant his vineyard to grow luscious fruit.

"He built a watchtower in the midst of it. . . and he looked for it to yield grapes." This represents God's presence. He is watching out for his people. And in this watchtower, he is now observing his field. He is never apart. He is never away. He is always watching his people, watching the fruit of their lives, watching what they produce.

"He built a watchtower in the midst of it. . . and he looked for it to yield grapes, but it yielded wild grapes." In other words, the vineyard was given the most beautiful circumstances, and the best opportunity to grow. God himself cleared and tilled the land, and planted the vines, and cared for them. And yet even then, the vineyard produced sour grapes, or no fruit at all. God's preparation and planning of the vineyard of his people only resulted in a yield of corrupted fruit.

The same is reported by Jeremiah in chapter 2:21. "I planted you a choice vine, wholly of pure seed. How then have you turned degenerate and become a wild vine?" While a vine was well-established as a symbol for Israel, even today grapes on a vine symbolize the nation of Israel. But whenever the Scriptures mention the vine, it's a symbol of Israel's failure and degeneracy rather than their fruitfulness. It's a wonder they retained the image of a vine for they had never fulfilled God's design for yielding of fruit from that vine. It had turned wild in Israel, producing only sour grapes. In Jeremiah, Israel turned degenerate and strange. In Hosea the vine is described as empty and producing no fruit at all.

And so as we begin to understand Jesus' teaching on the vine, we need to understand when he says, "I am the vine," he is saying, *I am the true vine, and this vine which we have been calling Israel has not produced the fruit which God has called Israel to produce.*

Augustine of Hippo, one of our ancient Church fathers, sees the teaching of this similitude to be that the mediator between God and men, the man Christ Jesus, is the Head of the Church, and we are his members. He became man that in him human nature might be the vine, and we who are also men might become the branches. In other words, the incarnation itself was so Jesus would become the vine, and that we could be grafted into that to become the branches. Otherwise, no vine of man could reach to God. Only through the incarnation was man made able to be in unity with the Lord Jesus Christ.

So we have a people of God established and prepared by God to be fruitful, but they are producing nothing because a vine is not used for building. It's not used for anything except to bear fruit, and so without fruit, it's good for nothing. It's called an empty vine. This is our starting point. We have to know this before we can even begin to unfold and untangle the similitude which Jesus has presented.

It's a picture of life without the Spirit of God when we see a vine that produces no fruit. In previous studies, we have discussed the fruit of the Spirit. When the Spirit indwells us, the evidence of that is fruit, and the fruit of the Spirit is described for us in Galatians. And now Jesus is going to say to his people, "I am the true vine." He is the vine that will be all God wants his people to be.

The Gospel of Unity

That very night at Passover as Jesus was instituting the Lord's Supper, they had bread and the fruit of the vine before them in wine. It was the fruit of the vine, and they shared in that together. Jesus said, "This is My body. This is My blood." In other words, "This bread and this cup of the vine have no significance unless they are found in Me." No longer would the meal mean anything to them unless it was done in remembrance of him. The bread and the cup are empty unless they have their meaning in Christ.

And so it is with the vine that is Israel. Unless it has meaning in Christ, it bears no fruit at all, and it is empty because Jesus is the One who will bring forth good fruit. Not only will Jesus supersede the Temple with its sacrifices, the feasts of the Jews, and Moses himself, but he will supersede Israel as God's vine, as his chosen people. The true vine is not an apostate people, but Jesus himself who alone is righteous and faithful. And so our turning point, as it were, in this first unfolding is that where Israel has been unfaithful, and has not produced fruit, and has not brought people into unity with God, but instead has brought a people under God's judgment, Christ is faithful, and Christ will fulfill the idea and the hope and the prophecy of the vine bearing spiritual fruit.

Jesus says, "I am the true vine." The true vine. I'm not a false. I'm not an apostate. I'm not anything but the true vine. There is only one true vine. There is only one place where we find ourselves unified with anything that would truly give us hope, and that is with the true vine.

So of Jesus, who is the true vine, we would ask, do branches have unity anywhere except in the vine? Do any of us have any relation with one another except in the vine? When we bow our heads, and we pray together, do we have anything in common or any reason to join together in prayer except as we are found to be brothers and sisters in Christ and Christ alone? Is life given and sustained outside of the vine? Can we have any hope for spiritual life except as it is found in Christ? Can any fruit be born on the branch without the vine? Surely not.

In a higher degree, the Church, like the branch, finds its unity, its life, and its fertility in Jesus. I would repeat that because often I know these terms can slip by us. So we find our unity together as brothers and sisters in Christ; we find our life—that is, life and hope which is eternal—and we find our fertility— that is, the fruits which we produce, those things in life which bear testimony of the Spirit dwells in us— we only find those as we are in Christ.

They cannot be faked. They cannot be made in any other way. We simply are in Christ, and find them, or we have them not at all. As amazing and true as an organic union of vine and branch is, how much more amazing is it to find the oneness of believers united to Christ, bearing spiritual fruit in the Body from Christ as the Head? The vine can only sustain a branch for a time, but the true vine, the living Christ, sustains his people in eternity, giving them love, joy, peace, patience, kindness, goodness, faithfulness, gentleness, and self-control—the fruit of the Spirit.

Jesus concludes this first lesson on the vine to teach his Disciples what their position is. Their position is that they are in him. They are unified in him, and on the basis of that, they will accomplish their mission, the mission he gives to the Church. They will be in him. So when Jesus says, "I am the true vine," he is saying to them, "You will find no blessings that you have anticipated from the nation of Israel except as you are found in Me. There is no people of God except as you are found in Me." It is not Israel that is the vine, except as Israel is the people of God, and they're only the people of God as they are found to be unified to Christ.

Then Jesus turns to the second lesson in verses 4 and 5.

> "Abide in Me, and I in you. As the branch cannot bear fruit by itself, unless it abides in the vine, neither can you, unless you abide in Me. I am the vine; you are the branches. Whoever abides in Me and I in him, he it is that bears much fruit, for apart from Me you can do nothing."

Did you pick up the key word which very clearly would make Jesus' second point? *Abiding.* Abiding in Christ. He is saying it is the duty of their position as they are now united as branches to the vine, the true vine. They must abide in Christ, remain in him.

I am the unhappy owner of a very healthy wisteria vine, a wisteria vine that produces a purple flower that frankly smells wonderful. But a wisteria vine grows and takes over everything. It takes over the trees that are nearby. It takes over the fences that it grows near. It has even begun to take over the lawn itself as it begins to creep and to crawl across the lawn.

The Gospel of Unity

We've taken machetes and chain saws, and we've hacked, and we've sawed, and we've cut. And just when we believe we have found success by leaving shreds of vine all over the place, we return in the next season only to find that it has begun to grow again. It is as close to immortal as anything I have ever seen in this life. No amount of destructive force seems to be able to destroy this vine.

A branch left attached to the vine will reestablish it again. Even though the ones we cut quickly die and stop producing, any that is left takes over and multiplies because it still has life flowing from the vine to the branch. So however much we do destruction, however much we make it look unsightly, if there is but one that remains, just one, the strength of the life that flows through the vine to the branch is enough to reestablish it and cause it to grow again.

And there I think we have a picture of Christ's Church? How many times and how many persecutions have been brought against the Church? How often has it been hacked? How often has it been persecuted? How often has it been drug? And how often has it been beaten? How often have the saints been carried out and crucified or burned or persecuted for their testimony in Christ? But if there is one who remains, if there is one, then from the vine flows the living Word of life to the branch, and that branch continues to produce fruit, and the fruit continue to multiply, and the Church continues to grow.

Verse 7 teaches how we abide in Christ. "If you abide in Me, and My words abide in you, ask whatever you wish, and it will be done for you." The fundamental means of our abiding in Christ is by his Word. Not by a hyper-spiritual approach, not by some sort of an imaginary approach of abiding and remaining in him simply as a matter of the will, but through his Word. Any other way may give us a feeling of abiding, but it's artificial. It's not truly the life of Christ flowing from the vine to the branch. It's in his Word.

As we abide in him, and his Word abides in us, the Christian continually, not just once, but continually sets aside all things that would draw us away from that narrow gate that is set before us that we would stay in his Word. Whatever strength we may imagine that we have in our own wisdom, whatever we believe we draw from our relationships, our education, our own charisma, perhaps our influence by position or simply by power, all of those will prove to be empty and leave us longing for the life-giving power of Christ.

The Last Sermon of Christ

Verse 7 gives us the only condition that gives us Christ to abide in us. "If you abide in Me, and My words abide in you." Without this abiding in his Word, there will be unfruitfulness, and we will be cut off from the root. We have to abide in his Word if Christ is to abide in us for where else will the life of Christ flow if we do not abide in his Word.

Will it flow simply by our saying and demanding that it flow? Where will we connect with Christ except by the means of grace which God has provided? Did he provide them only for those who desire to take part of them? Only those who are studious and desire to study his Word? Only those who have a higher Church sense of the sacraments, and so they feel that we ought to observe the sacraments regularly? No! He gave them that his Church might be unified with Christ, and that the love and the life of Christ would flow to his people through the living Word.

So the second teaching is our duty to abide in Christ. . . our duty. So first of all, we have our position which is in Christ. We're unified in Christ who is the true vine, and by that we have life, and we produce fruit, and then we remain in that state as we abide in him. And that is our duty—to abide in him. It's not our option. It is our duty. Otherwise, we will cease to bear fruit, and we'll be cut off from the vine.

The third point Jesus teaches them is the consequences of all of this. What does all this mean then? How are we to draw this together and make something practical of it? Most translations that you'll read would indicate that the vines producing no fruit are cut, gathered, cast off, and burned.

Maybe it is as John Laing, an ancient commentator, suggests that Jesus is, instead of passing by the Temple, on a hill on the outside of Jerusalem. Perhaps it is the season where the vineyards are being worked and indeed dead vines are being cut off and carried, and there would be fires all around the hillside from the growers who are clearing out those unproductive vines and burning them. Maybe Jesus is looking, and he is seeing these fires around, and he is using that as an illustration.

The commentator and the pastor, Dr. James Montgomery Boice, prefers to translate this *cast away* or *remove* as a concept of lifting up. . . as a way of lifting up, which is part of the translations. There are about four different meanings for this word. Three of them are fairly consistent with the idea of carrying off and disposing, but there is one which remains that has the idea of lifting up. In fact, it's the primary use of this word. It's the idea of lifting up as in to repair.

Boice gives us the picture of a vineyard owner who comes, and he sees his vineyards in need of care. When I lived in Germany, I noticed they were all very neat. Perhaps you haven't seen a vineyard. Just very briefly, a vine can't grow on the ground and produce fruit. It has to be suspended. And so you'll find poles, sometimes with nets, sometimes with wires. And a gardener who keeps a vineyard will very carefully attach the vines to those poles and to those lines that are strung across them.

In Germany—and I love the way the German mind works—everything is, as we would say, "Dress right dress." Everything is in line and in proper order, and the grass around it is all cut nice and neat, and the vineyards are beautiful. We crossed over into Italy, and the countryside looked more like a 5:00 shadow. The vineyards were there, but what was the order and why where they placed there, I could never figure out. They were unkempt, and yet the Italians are known for producing wonderful wine. And so there must be a large enough crop to produce a wine.

In Germany, it was such a beautiful scene. What made it so beautiful? The vineyard keepers would go and take those vines which were on the ground, and they would lift them up, and they would clean them off. And then they would reattach them so once again they're exposed to sunlight, so once again they are able to receive those nutrients that are required for the production of fruit. No vine lying on the ground is going to produce fruit.

And so Boice prefers the idea of a vineyard owner going through and lifting up and placing a branch where it can once again be nourished and produce fruit. Certainly, restoration and strengthening are vital themes in Christian teaching. In fact, the objective of church discipline is restoration. In Hebrews, chapter 12, verse 12, we read these verses of encouragement actually. "Therefore lift your drooping hands and strengthen your weak knees, and make straight paths for your feet, so that what is lame may not be put out of joint but rather be healed."

And so it's a perfectly legitimate theme in the Scripture to say we are about the business of restoring those who have drifted, those who are struggling, those who are crippled in the faith. But is that what the sense of the context contains for us here? It's important that we not become focused on being an arbiter of justice, discerning the heart of men, because only God can do that. Boice does avoid that because of his concern of unfruitful Christians being lost, but I don't feel that is really the proper interpretation here.

But what most have traditionally decided is the one that I have settled on myself. It's not a reference to restoration in this context. It's not a reference to judgment in this context where we would judge the hearts of men and decide whom the Lord is dwelling in and whom he is not. It's not a reference necessarily even to backsliding and then followed by restoration. It's a reference to sanctification. It's a reference to the life here of the Disciples and what they are to expect as they are indwelled by the Spirit and united to Christ to undertake the mission he is giving them. Jesus is addressing the purification of the branches.

There is a corporate as well as an individual application. Let's deal with the corporate first. Christ is talking about purification and sanctification of individual lives. We also know that the Church is also purified and strengthened. We should remember well the passage from Ephesians 5, verses 26 and 27, where Jesus, in talking about the Church, says that he has loved her. He has given himself for her, "that he might sanctify her, having cleansed her by the washing of water with the word." Here again we see this emphasis on the Spirit and the Word and the work of the Word in sanctification. "So that he might present the church to himself in splendor, without spot or wrinkle or any such thing, that she might be holy and without blemish."

There is a purification and a cleansing of the Church, a making holy of the whole Church. Martin Luther, with his pastoral expressions which I have grown to love so much, says this: "He shows that there are false Christians. Some are called suckers, or wild branches." And I couldn't help but chuckle at that. I think what he means by *suckers* are those who suck the life out of the Church without producing any fruit. But in our modern parlance, it simply was entertaining. "They bear no fruit, but only consume sap which the truly faithful branches should have."

So here, Luther is saying that there are those in the body of the Church who instead of producing fruit and strengthening the Church are sucking the life and energy of the Church out so that those who ought to be producing fruit can't produce because so much of the energy of the Church is being sucked out by these unproductive branches.

The Gospel of Unity

"To our sorrow we see in Christendom," Luther continues, "there are always wild and useless branches that bear nothing but immature fruit which must be rejected. They develop into large branches, and they want to be honored and acclaimed as the best of Christians, and they put it on display outdoing the rest. But it is a sham, and they will be exposed for what they are. It's all make believe. We call them schismatic spirits and false brethren."

So even though they may grow because of age into large branches, if there is not the fruit to bear evidence of the indwelling of the Holy Spirit, then they're simply there sucking life out of the Church that the Church itself would be handicapped in producing its fruit.

All farmers who have any crop want every branch to produce and to produce more and more fruit. If a branch is to produce fruit, a farmer is not going to cut it off. My grandfather used to prune peach trees after his retirement. He would not go out and cut off branches that had the potential for producing good fruit. He would only cut those which were clearly dead and would never produce fruit. And so in the lives of individual believers, just like the Church, do we think that God will cast off those who have the potential to produce fruit because they are truly indwelt with the Spirit, or will he sanctify them so that they might be able to produce fruit in the future?

Another great commentator, Frederick Godet, sees the purification in the life of every believer a natural consequence of abiding in Christ is the mortification of sin. If you abide in Christ, and his Word richly dwells within you, then sin will die in your life. It will not grow and prosper. It will die. Godet says, "It is intended to cut off all the shoots of their own life which may manifest themselves in them and would paralyze the power of the Spirit. And it's the Word that is sharper than a two-edged sword that cuts to the very marrow that will prune the shoots."[1]

So with the mouths we confess that Jesus is Lord. With the heart we believe he is Christ. And God is not satisfied until not only with mouth and with heart but with our whole bodies we offer ourselves a spiritual sacrifice unto him. Only then will our whole person be given to producing spiritual fruit.

In verse 3, Jesus tells them that they already abide in him, and it is a pruning they will now expect as a consequence. We already heard this

---

1. Frederick Godet, *Commentary on the Gospel of John*.

at the foot washing. He says, "You're clean already." He is telling them, "You already abide in me, and yet you will experience the effect of this pruning I'm telling you of." The old man has received a mortal strike, and he is even now withering away. They are no longer on the vine of the world. We are grafted into Christ, and we'll show his fruit.

Let me wrap up by answering two questions; *How does this happens?* And then, *What fruit are we to produce?*

How? How is it that we will be made to produce fruit? How is it that the sin in our life will be pushed out and pushed away? Again, Godet: "By the moral education which they have received from Jesus, the principle of perfect purity has been deposited in them. For the Word of Christ is the instrument of a daily judgment, of a constant and austere discipline which God exercises on the soul which remains attached to him."[2]

Here we see this working of the Word. As the teaching of Christ is deposited within us, joined there with the sanctifying power of the Holy Spirit to cause life, we see lives changed. We see sin instead of cherished. And we see people being transformed more and more into the character of Christ, imitators of God.

What fruit? What fruit is it that we would be required to produce? They are worth repeating. Love, joy, peace, patience, kindness, goodness, faith, meekness, and self-control. H. A. Ironside said, "If you profess you've been saved through faith in the Lord Jesus, is the fruit of the Spirit in your life? It will be if you are living in fellowship with him."[3]

He continues, "If the contrary to these is manifest, then you may be sure of this, that even though you have trusted Christ for salvation, you are not living in fellowship with God." And here is why I have retained this quote. "If instead of love, there is bitterness, malice, unkindness, if instead of joy, there is gloom, if instead of peace, there is unrest, if instead of longsuffering, there is impatience, if instead of gentleness, there is harshness, if instead of goodness, there is a moral evil beginning to be manifested, if instead of faith, worry and a lack of confidence, if instead of meekness, pride and haughtiness, if instead of temperance or self-control, you are subject to the lusts of the flesh, then that tells the

---

2. Frederick Godet, 294.
3. H.A. Ironside, *Addresses on the Gospel of John*.

story that no matter what you profess you are not living in fellowship with God."[4]

Shouldn't we stop and examine not only our hearts, but our lives? Am I abiding in Christ? Are there the evidences of the fruit of the Spirit being manifest in my own life? Am I united as a branch to a vine? Am I filled with his Word, and is it having a pruning effect in my life? Can I see sin dying daily in my life as I learn to cherish Christ more and as I grow in knowledge and understanding of his Word, or do I resist the very means by which Christ would accomplish these things?

Does my life show more and more the fruit of the Spirit to assure me that the Spirit of Christ dwells in me? Because apart from him, we can do nothing. If so, then all of our hearts will be blessed and encouraged. And if not, then may God do with us what we cannot do on our own. May he indeed repair us and restore us and remove from us those things which would keep us from him.

---

4. Ibid.

13

Love that Bears Fruit to God's Glory: Part 1

John 15:8–11

"If you abide in me, and my words abide in you, ask whatever you wish, and it will be done for you. By this my Father is glorified, that you bear much fruit and so prove to be my disciples. As the Father has loved me, so have I loved you. Abide in my love. If you keep my commandments, you will abide in my love, just as I have kept my Father's commandments and abide in his love. These things I have spoken to you, that my joy may be in you, and that your joy may be full."

WHERE IS CHRISTIAN JOY really? Is the Church a joyous place? There are many preoccupations in the Church, many distractions in the Church. There are many types of relations in the Church. There are many sub-organizations within a church. Can we say that all of those are typified by an expression of joy?

What about the individual Christian's life? Do we see Christians as a whole as a joyful people? Is the voice of the Church one of joy, or is it one of despair? Do we seek to explain away our despair by saying that we're just sober-minded and serious about our faith? While we can be sober-minded and serious, would you say within the heart of each Christian, there is true joy? Or are we distracted with troubles and concerns as every detail of life brings something that causes us to stumble? Do we focus on the minutiae of life? Or overall do we say, "Our God is in control. He has loved me and saved me, and I'm full of joy as a result"?

Love that Bears Fruit to God's Glory: Part 1

Does joy superintend all other issues of life? If not, why? I'm not here talking about a superficial joy. We see a lot of that, and in my comings and goings in the chaplaincy, running across all sorts of denominational backgrounds, there are some who frankly seem to major in an artificial atmosphere of joy. They certainly don't think it's artificial, but there seems to be this demand for expressions of joy and an intolerance that you would ever express anything else. But I have found that many times they do that in the assemblies together, but then their life outside of the assembly is a stark contrast.

At least we might say our expressions in the church are consistent with our expressions outside of the church, so then our challenge is, *How can we have joy across the board so that we don't engage in superficial or an artificial expression of joy. We are supposed to be happy as Christians here, but then we go out to the real world where we carry the burdens around, and we look very weary from our toils and travels?* How can we have joy in both places and it be authentic? Authentic joy.

It's evasive, isn't it? It's hard, we believe, to attain an authentic joy. I'm convinced our passage here ties our joy to the glory of God. In glorifying God, there and only there will we find joy. Think of the glory of God as a well, and going to this well is the only place you will drink the waters which quench your thirst and give you joy. In no other place will you find joy.

How do we glorify God? We talk about it a lot, don't we? We sing of it every Sunday in the *Gloria Patri*, "Glory be to the Father, and to the Son, and the Holy Ghost." We sing of it every week. We ascribe him glory verbally, that is, with our mouth. We affirm it in the first and probably the most often quoted of the catechisms that our children memorize. We ask them, What is the chief end of man? What is the primary purpose of man? It is to glorify God and enjoy him forever.

So we recognize and we affirm that our primary occupation is to glorify God and enjoy him forever. So even in our catechism, we find a linking of glorifying God and joy. Where is the linkage between joy and the glory of God in our life?

Jonathan Edwards, great theologian, said, "The great end of God's work, which is variously expressed in Scripture, is indeed but one; and this one end is most properly and comprehensively called the glory of God."[1] What he is saying is that all we do, and all we study, and all we

---

1. Henry Rogers, *Jonathan Edwards*, p 119.

preach, whether the application of a sermon is pronounced and clear, or whether it's ambiguous, and it's more of a rambling through the Scriptures, whether it's well preached or poorly preached, the Scriptures themselves, however presented and however read, have but one end in mind, and that is the glory of God.

And so whatever benefit we would seek to draw from it, to include salvation itself, is attached to the one overarching head, which is the glorifying of God. That is the Christian's ambition. That is the Church's ambition. That is the ambition of our ordering of worship. The glorifying of God.

And so everything we do has as the first question, *how do the Scriptures teach us we are to glorify God in every activity or in our thinking, or in our conversation, or in our study, or in our journeys, or in our projects?* Whatever it may be, all is done to the glory of God.

I look forward to many more years of studying and dwelling in God's Word myself. At a very personal level, I have been noticing an evolution of my relationship to the Word over the years. When I first began to study, I was intrigued with the meanings behind the words, the language, and the structure. It was so alien to me. Outlining a book of the Bible seemed foreign to me. It was like a whole world I had never explored, as if I had gone on a journey, and had entered into a city where I had never been. There was a familiarity because I know the language, but then there was a disconnect and an unfamiliarity.

If you're moving into a town, you almost at once begin to explore, and you want to learn the roads, and the networks, and the transportation, and the people, and the places to go, and the things to see in those places that are important, and the things are important, and those things which are not so important.

And so in the early days of study, you have the whole Scriptures which are opened to you like a vast city to study. But as time goes on, and as you come to grips with the language, and you're more familiar with the flow of Scripture and what the purpose is, we come to know that its primary focus is always the glory of God.

And so when you read a passage, you're putting it within that framework instead of starting with, *I wonder what in the world it's talking about.* As Scripture begins to come together for you, you begin to ask questions like, "What does this mean? How do I find a right application

Love that Bears Fruit to God's Glory: Part 1

to this?" Gradually your study develops into asking the right question instead of knowing the question and finding the right answer.

In 1 Corinthians 10:31, Paul says, "So, whether you eat or drink, or whatever you do, do all to the glory of God." We think of glorifying as testifying, but it's more. It's all-encompassing. It's all of life. So the Scriptures may be clear to us, but our minds are not. We need to learn the question to ask. Rather than simply assuming we know the question, and groping about in the darkness for an answer, we need to first learn the question.

And the question before us here is, *how do we glorify God?* How does this teaching show us how we glorify God? And then some would say, "But of what benefit is that to me?" The benefit is that there is no salvation that doesn't glorify God. There is no joy in the Christian life that doesn't glorify God. There is no unity in the Christian Church that doesn't glorify God.

And so the starting point *always* is, *how does this glorify God?* And then finding how we glorify God, we fulfill all of those other issues, and desires, and functions that we turn to the Scriptures for. The Scriptures are not like other religious books that are nothing but commandments for our lives. The Scriptures teach us how to glorify God—by obedience, by love, by profession, by confession. All of these things function to glorify God. And if it is not our purpose to glorify God, then whether it's the liturgy in our bulletin, or whether it's the way we go through life, or the sermons we listen to, it's all disconnected, and none of it really seems to make sense. We might enjoy one part and have no use for another. But when we connect them all to the whole, which is the purpose of glorifying God, then it all comes together, and it all works to bring us all of these wonderful gifts God has for us.

Paul adds to 1 Corinthians 10:31 that it's not only in the eating and drinking and all we do that is to glorify God, but he adds this, "Be imitators of me, as I am of Christ." He is saying, "Don't simply speak as I speak, but live as I live."

So a reflective and a conscientious Christian is going to understand his focus in life to be God's glory, to rejoice in it and live for it. So I ask, how do you glorify God? I asked myself the same question, of course. But more pointedly, how do you glorify God? I know you speak of it. I know you sing of it. We affirm it, but how do we do it?

The Last Sermon of Christ

The Scripture is clear, our worship liturgy is clear, but is our mind clear on how we glorify God? Jesus tells us how. He instructs us very simply and very plainly in the passage for this chapter. He says, "This is my Father's glory. This is how you will glorify my Father, that you bear much fruit and so prove to be my disciples."

Are they then to become disciples through works? we ask. Are they to achieve discipleship by performing acts of obedience? Jesus has already disqualified the moralist who would seek discipleship through action by saying that apart from Christ you can do nothing. None of the good works you would do amount to anything apart from him.

Jesus' meaning is this: The world is full of religious people. It's full of ethical people. But you will be known differently as disciples of Jesus by the unique quality of the fruit you bear. There is a difference in the fruitfulness of a Christian from the ethical living and lifestyle of those who are not Christian.

The world is full of priests in every religion, but in 1 Peter 2:9, we're taught that we are a royal priesthood. We are a holy nation. And then in 1 Peter 2:12, when the Gentiles see your good deeds, they will glorify God on the day of visitation. Christianity has a creed, but is Christianity really your life? We must be more than simply professors of the faith; we must be living disciples.

As we talk about fruitfulness, it will benefit us to be reminded again in Galatians 5, verses 16 through 26, of those fruits of the Spirit. The Christian who is indwelled by the Spirit is in possession of these fruits. And where we find ourselves out of harmony with these fruits, we need to address it.

We can't be content to not be in possession of the fruits because these are the fruits of the Spirit, not the fruits of ethical, Christian living. They are the fruits of the Spirit of God who dwells within man. In the absence of the fruits, the Spirit frightens us.

Here, in verses 16 through 26, we find a contrast between the fruits of the Spirit and those of the world, the flesh. "But I say," Paul writes, "walk by the Spirit, and you will not gratify the desires of the flesh. For the desires of the flesh are against the Spirit, and the desires of the Spirit are against the flesh, for these are opposed to each other, to keep you from doing the things you want to do." Paul assumes that our desires are influenced by the Spirit, and that we lack the discipline to walk according to the unction of the Spirit in our life. We lack the discipline and

Love that Bears Fruit to God's Glory: Part 1

perhaps the courage to live according to God's Word empowered by the Spirit of God, and instead are being swept along by the whitewaters of the world.

He says these two are in opposition to one another. You can't simply be swept along by the world and assume all is well. For the Christian, this is an intolerable position. You cannot continue to swim in the streams of life that the heathen swim in and consider that to be God's will for you. He says, what you want if you are indwelt by the Holy Spirit is something different.

Verse 18: "But if you are led by the Spirit, you are not under the law. Now the works of the flesh are evident: sexual immorality, impurity, sensuality, idolatry, sorcery, enmity, strife, jealousy, fits of anger, rivalries, dissensions, divisions, envy, drunkenness, orgies, and things like these." In other words, this isn't all. This isn't a complete list. If you're not involved in one of these, that doesn't mean that everything is okay. It does mean that you still need to ask yourself if you are living according to the Spirit? He is saying, I can't begin to give you an exhaustive list of the deeds of the flesh. For as many days as there are in life, there is creativity in the flesh of new ways to offend God. He says, "I can't tell you all of them."

"I warn you, as I warned you before, that those who do such things will not inherit the kingdom of God." There is no conditional clause in that statement. There is no *but* in that statement. It's simply, factually rendered. If you walk with the world, and your conscience is not bound by the Spirit of God, and the fruits of the Spirit are not being manifest, then you are not in the position of inheriting the kingdom of God.

"The fruit of the Spirit is love, joy, peace, patience, kindness, goodness, faithfulness, gentleness, self-control; against such things there is no law. And those who belong to Christ Jesus have crucified the flesh with its passions and desires. If we live by the Spirit, let us also walk by the Spirit. Let us not become conceited, provoking one another, envying one another."

We sometimes read through these fruits of the Spirit as if they are some sort of a goal to be achieved. They are not a goal to be achieved. They are the fruits of the Spirit that indwells each believer.

Now it's true that maturity of expression comes in time as we mortify the sins of the flesh, and we learn to hate the deeds of the flesh, and love the things of God. We can accept that for a new believer or for an immature believer, these fruits are manifest imperfectly. In fact, they're imperfect in all of our lives. There are times when we have fits of the flesh, and those sins that are condemned. But in the course of our lives, we should not see more of a tendency towards the flesh than we do the Spirit.

Not only is there a contrast with the world because of our profession of faith in Christ, but there is also a contrast in the fruit of our lives. No one has a doctrine like ours in all the world. Christians are a people who hold to the incarnation, the atonement, the resurrection, and nobody has a joy like ours because joy is given to us by God. We don't have to conjure it up. We don't have to create it out of nothing. We don't have to pretend to be joyful in situations where there is no joy. We don't have to look at the despair of the world and be indifferent to it so that we might have joy. The joy is given to us because of our possession of the Spirit of Christ.

And so we would go with a *how*? How, because I just simply don't feel joyful? How is it that joy evades me since I believe I truly have called out to Christ, and I believe I truly belong to him? But yet as I'm looking at my own life, I'm having to realize I'm not really all that full of joy. Should I be afraid? Should I doubt my own profession of faith? Should I stop going to church altogether? Am I an offense to God? Why is it that I don't have joy?

There is a unique quality of the Christian life that if we don't attend to, it will cause our joy to be lost. Jesus said to his disciples, "You'll glorify God because you will bear much fruit." Now this is taken in connection with the passage in the previous chapter where we talked about the vine and the branches. And it shows us that Christian discipleship is not static.

Our Christian lives do not begin and end with our profession of faith. There is a progression, a movement. We call it sanctification. There is a growth in Christ. Discipleship is something that grows. It produces a greater harvest each and every year. What brings more joy to the vine-dresser, or the farmer if you will, than for his crop to produce with increasing abundance year after year?

It grows as it is fed from the branch. Jesus identifies the nourishment as his own Word. The Word coursing through the life of the disciples produces a fruit of obedience, which proves the love of God, and that is what glories the Father.

Love that Bears Fruit to God's Glory: Part 1

We see the vital connection between verses 7 and 8. "If you abide in me, and my words abide in you, ask whatever you wish, and it will be done for you. By this my Father is glorified, that you bear much fruit and so prove to be my disciples."

Frederick Godet sees what is called a parallelism here. We would expect when we read, "If anyone abides in me, then I will abide in you." That would be a parallelism properly constructed. But that is not what we read.

He says, "If you abide in me, and my words abide in you." It's an awkward construct. It's not a "If you abide in me, I abide in you." It's "If you abide in me . . . my words abide in you." Godet says this: "Jesus wishes to make known to his own by this change of expression that it is the constant remembrance of and habitual mediation upon his Words which is the condition on which he will be able continually to make his strength dwell in them and act through them."[2]

I don't want that to get lost because in many respects that is almost the main point of the passage. The habitual meditation upon the Word of God is the strength of the believer through which the Spirit, working with the Word, causes us to bear much fruit. Think back to the vine and the branch. Using that simple illustration, the vine and the sap that runs from the vine feeds the branch which then produces fruit.

What is the sap that flows through? What drives that sap up through? The sap is the very Word of God. What drives that sap? The power and the work of the Holy Spirit. And what is the result? The branch produces fruit.

But what if there is no sap? You can tie all the branches you want to the vine, but if there is no sap, if the Word is not dwelling in you, according to Jesus' own teaching, then there will be no fruit. But if you are habitually dwelling and meditating upon God's Word, and you are growing in your understanding of God's Word—in other words, if you're not three miles wide and one inch deep—then you produce much fruit. And that glorifies God.

Saint Augustine makes a similar connection between obedience and love. And I'll paraphrase this. "It is love that produces the fruit of obedience and so serves as a testimony to love. But obedience never

---

2. Frederick Godet, 297.

produces love. Obedience performed with a love that only testifies of self-righteousness will never bring glory to God."[3]

In John 15, Jesus describes three qualities of fruitfulness as in Galatians 5. They do more than describe a character and quality of a Christian. They are telling us what it is we ought to do. It is correct to say that the fruit of the Spirit is to possess the character of Christ as our own character. James Boice said, "It is the indispensable heart of Christian witness, the divine character."[4]

Those fruits of the Spirit that Jesus describes are love and obedience and joy. And they form somewhat of a formula for us. Obedience before love produces legalism, which saps joy. But true love for God results naturally in obedience, which is a transformed life that brings joy. If it's not followed in that formula if you will—and I hate to use the word *formula* for we don't reduce Scripture to formula—but nevertheless, if love does not precede obedience, you're left with obedience, and that is legalism or moralism. And there is no joy there. There is only condemnation for we can never be perfect enough.

But if there is a true love for God, a true and genuine love, then that results naturally in a desire to obey. And in that obedience, we then produce fruit which glorifies God, and in that glorifying of God, being in union with Christ, living as Christ, and having the character of Christ in us, we find joy. Joy comes to us.

We can't reach and take joy. We can't fake joy. We can't convince ourselves to be joyful when there is no foundation for joy. The foundation of joy is love for God, obedience to Christ, the glorification of God, resulting in joy.

---

3. St. Augustine, Vol 7, 347.
4. James Boice, p 1172.

14

Love that Bears Fruit to God's Glory: Part 2

John 15:8–11

Let the word of Christ dwell in you richly, teaching and admonishing one another in all wisdom, singing psalms and hymns and spiritual songs, with thankfulness in your hearts to God. (Colossians 3:16)

"If you abide in me, and my words abide in you, ask whatever you wish, and it will be done for you. By this my Father is glorified, that you bear much fruit and so prove to be my disciples. As the Father has loved me, so have I loved you. Abide in my love. If you keep my commandments, you will abide in my love, just as I have kept my Father's commandments and abide in his love. These things I have spoken to you, that my joy may be in you, and that your joy may be full."(John 15:7–11)

OBVIOUSLY, THE EMPHASIS, AS we reflect on the reading from the previous chapter, is "Let the word of Christ dwell in you richly." Just by way of reminder, I showed you in John 15 that John was setting up for us what we anticipated to be a parallelism. That is, where Jesus says, "Abide in me," and we would expect him to say, "And I will abide in you," instead, he changes that subject to say, "And the Word will abide in you."

The significance was of the unexpected words. Why not say, "I will dwell in you," for certainly we know he teaches that in his Spirit he does come to dwell with his people? But why here would he say, "The Word. The Word dwells in you and abides in you"?

The Last Sermon of Christ

In the fruits of the Spirit, we discovered what the Christian ought to be. If we are indwelled by the Holy Spirit, the Christian, shall we say, *will* be in possession of the fruits of the Spirit because they belong to the Holy Spirit, and the Holy Spirit dwelling in the Christian does not lose those fruits, those expressions of his own divinity, but they come to be a part of the believer.

And so we have to reflect on our own lives to see first of all, are there any fruits at all present, these fruits of the Spirit? And if they are not, that gives us serious reason to pause and to reflect upon our understanding of the gospel itself, and on our relation with Christ, and our walk with Christ. We must to seek to develop those fruits more and more, knowing it's not through the strength of the flesh or the will that we will possess these fruits, but only because of the power of the Spirit.

And to what end? This actually was our very beginning point. The glory of God. We sing of it every Sunday in the *Gloria Patri*, "Glory be to the Father." We sing of it each and every week. We teach it to our children in the catechisms. What is the chief end of man? To glorify God and enjoy him forever.

How wise were those who wrote the catechisms to capture this because we have to glorify God as our chief end, and the result of the glorification of God is that we will experience joy. And that is the teaching of this chapter—that our end is to have joy, and that joy is to be complete, and that joy is the result of glorifying God.

And if we don't glorify God, we will not know that joy that is complete in Christ. We might have passing pleasure. We might have enjoyment, but we will not have joy complete in Christ, the peace of Christ—as Jesus has put it before—that peace of Christ which surpasses understanding. Is that not also a part of joy?

But if there is a love of God, then it's a natural outflowing that obedience would be the result. And in love plus obedience, God is glorified because it's by our obedience we are known to be lovers of God, and in that glory we find joy.

We can't seek joy first because joy will remain elusive. We have to first love God, resulting in a life of obedience, which then results in joy because it is the overarching theme to which everything in the Christian life is connected. How can we say that it's our chief end to glorify God? And in glorifying God, we will enjoy him forever. So if the glory of God is our whole purpose, then everything else we do and study, all of our study of Christian obedience, the gospel itself, is connected to God's glory.

Isn't the gospel to God's glory? Isn't the incarnation to God's glory? Isn't the atonement to God's glory? Aren't the people of God to his own glory? Isn't creation itself a testimony of God's glory?

So if our Christian life is so ordered, and our minds, if you will, are so ordered that we understand that God's glory is the focal point for everything we do, then all of the rest will fall into its proper place. Otherwise, we will struggle like someone with armloads of groceries who never got the basket, but thinking they would only grab one or two things. And now they're overloaded, trying to balance the Christian life and Christian walk as they walk around with all these disconnected parts of a Christian life. But if they are united in the whole, and that is to the glory of God, what a perfect tapestry they will form.

In John 15, Jesus describes three qualities of fruitfulness because he says that we are to be fruitful in our life. We must dwell on that Word, and ponder that Word, and meditate upon that Word, and in so doing, we will know God's will in our life so that we know how to be obedient. And we do that out of a motivation of love. That sap being pushed through our lives by the power of the Holy Spirit, our lives then become fruitful.

As in Galatians 5, these qualities of fruitfulness we are about to explore—love, obedience, and joy, which are listed also as fruits of the Spirit—these qualities do more than describe simply a character or a quality of the Christian life. They are characters and qualities of the Christian person. They are, if you will, our character, who we are. Not simply what we do. Not just habits we use to express ourselves. They are who we are.

It's correct to say the fruit of the Spirit is to possess the character of Christ as our own. In the words of James Montgomery Boice, "These are the indispensable heart of the Christian witness, and in this we find the divine character."[1]

The first of the named fruits is *love*. Love can be called the highest order of fruits or gifts. In 1 Corinthians 13, Paul even names the gifts, and he says these are the gifts granted by God to the Church, and he calls the greatest of all of them *love*.

---

1. James Boice, *The Gospel of John*, 1172.

In fact, Paul said if he has all the others, but he doesn't have love, he actually has nothing at all. So it's not a matter of how many qualities, or how many gifts you have, or how many talents you may possess. The whole issue is, if you have not love, none of them work to the glory of God. Paul says of himself that he is nothing more than a noisy gong or a cymbal if he doesn't possess love.

But love doesn't and it can't begin with us. We can't conjure it up. We can't make ourselves love. We can't say we love God until we acknowledge he first loved us. That is the teaching of Scripture in 1 John 4. It says very simply, "We love because he first loved us."

I like Boice's distinguishing of the three loves shown to us there. He calls it first an electing love, where God knows us in all eternity past. And then he says there is a love that is shown in the incarnation, as Christ humbled himself and became a servant for our benefit because of love. And then there is love that is expressed at the atonement where he loves his Bride so much that he would give his own life for her. And so he sees these as three expressions of love.

The Scripture would teach us these as well. Concerning the electing love of God, Deuteronomy 7:6 and 8, the writer says of Israel: "God has chosen you to be a people for his treasured possession. . . it is because the LORD loves you."

God did not choose the people of Israel because they were greater than all the other nations nor because they had so much to bring to the table to accomplish God's will on the earth. They had absolutely nothing to bring to the table. They had nothing to offer. They had nothing to give. They had no reputation. They had no armies. And yet, God said, "I chose you because I love you, and I elected you as my own because I love you. I adopted you as mine because I love you."

In Ephesians 1:4, speaking of the Church, "He chose us in him before the foundation of the world." When did God love you? Before you were born. Did he love you because you have amounted to so much? No. He loved you because God is love. Did he love you because you have such high ambitions? No. He loved you because he is love.

Did he love you because you haven't amounted to anything, and he looks for the weak? He does indeed use the weak for his own glory, but that is not why he loved you. He loves you because he himself is love. Psalm 33:18: "Behold, the eye of the LORD is on those who fear him, on those who hope in his steadfast love."

Love that Bears Fruit to God's Glory: Part 2

This electing love of God is steadfast. It's everlasting. God's sovereign decree of election is not based on anything arbitrary. It's not based on anything random. It's not based on good works. It's based on nothing but the love of God.

God's eternal and perfect love is shown in the election of his people to salvation, and it's also shown in the incarnation. 1 John 4:9: "In this the love of God was made manifest among us, that God sent his only Son into the world, so that we might live through him." Isn't this echoed in one of those favorite verses of Scripture, John 3:16: "For God so loved the world, that he gave his only Son."

So this is the measure of the love Christ had for us. "As the Father has loved me, so have I loved you." How much did Christ love us? As much as the Father has loved him, and as much as he has loved the Father, so he has loved us. It's an infinite love.

In Jesus, we have a picture of a bridegroom coming for his bride, and expressing love in beautiful, often pictorial language that we might be made to understand, such as in Song of Solomon, chapter 1:15, "Behold, you are beautiful, my love; behold, you are beautiful; your eyes are doves." Or in chapter 2, verse 2, "As a lily among brambles, so is my love among the young women."

As the Lord looks at his people, he sees us as beautiful, not because of physical attributes, but because of the contrast with that world which is fallen. What is the extent of his love? In Revelation 21:9, "Come, I will show you the Bride, the wife of the Lamb." And in Ephesians 5, we understand the depth and the quality of Christ's love for his Bride. "Husbands," he says by way of analogy, "love your wives, as Christ loved the church and gave himself up for her."

He died, in obedience to God, yes, but because of love. God loved and sent his Son. Christ, showing forth that same love, died for those who could not die to save themselves. Our only hope was in the Lord. And so he died that we might live.

The incarnation of Christ—Christ becoming flesh—was the unmerited, voluntary, condescension and humiliation of Christ to rescue his Bride because of his love. He heard the cries of his people, and he came to save.

An expression of this love is contained in the words of the hymn, "O Love of God, How Strong and True." Here is just this one verse.

"O Love of God, how strong and true,

Eternal and yet ever new;
Uncomprehended and unbought,
Beyond all knowledge and all thought.
O love of God, how deep and great!
Far deeper than man's deepest hate;
Self-fed, self-kindled like the light,
Changeless, eternal, infinite."

If we had hymns such as this treasured up in our hearts, wouldn't we have some way of expressing and understanding God's love? But even hymns are no replacement for the Word itself.

God's love is expressed in the atonement, which is why Jesus said, "No greater love has man than he would lay down his life for his brother." Man may give diamonds to those he loves. He may give rings and necklaces as tokens, as symbols of love. But there is no greater symbol that has stood before men as a testimony of true love than the Cross.

Saint Augustine said, "Love is the fullness of the law." We know from Romans 8:10 that love is the fulfillment of the law. And so where there is love, what can be wanted?

Because the quality and the measure of this love is the same as God has for his own Son, it's a precious love and one to be cherished. And we should give all of our energy to abide, that is, remain in it.

Jesus tells us how we are to abide in his love. In verse 7, he says to abide in his love, we are to have his Word abiding in us. And again, we find ourselves returning to that theme of that constant consideration and meditation upon the Word. And so the second fruit we are to bear is obedience. That second characteristic that a disciple possesses is obedience. And God is glorified in that obedience that springs forth from love.

Again, Jesus emphasizes this is the very pattern he himself set for them in his own obedience to the Father. It's important that obedience is second. It's not superior to love, and obedience cannot produce love, but love cannot be true love without obedience to follow.

In chapter 15, verse 14, "You are my friends if you do what I command you." Or in chapter 14, verse 15, "If you love me, you will keep my commandments." And then in verse 21, "Whoever has my commandments and keeps them, he it is who loves me." So we see there is a vital connection between an expression of love and obedience.

Jesus brings obedience back up to teach them that only in this loving response can they truly abide in his love. We say we want to know the love of God. Jesus says, "You'll know the love of God if my Word is in you, and you have a life that is typified by obedience." With the Word within informing our actions, we know we rest securely in his love.

It's so simple a concept, and yet it's so often misunderstood. People get wrapped up in the obedience, but lacking love, they then become legalists. And so they begin to decry the law because they feel the weight of the law upon them, and they decide the law itself is bad and is against the very grace of God. They run away from the law as an expression of glorifying God for his grace, but in running away from obedience, they're actually demonstrating a lack of love, not an appreciation for grace.

Martin Luther was adamant that these two doctrines of Christian life should be taught DAILY. So simple are they conceptually, and yet so easily lost to us. No sooner do we have them in our hands then they are lost. So easily are they lost that even now you're wondering, *What two is he describing?* Love and obedience.

Luther says, "These two items of Christian instruction must be inculcated daily in Christendom. Neither one dare be neglected."[2] He exhorts us after we have become his branches and now abide in him to hold together in love as his true branches and parts of his vine lest we be misled by alien doctrine, and thus be cut off from him. Wherever love and unity are destroyed, and schism and discord take root, there agreement in doctrine disappears and defection from Christ ensues.

What a consequence there is of neglecting these two simple, cardinal doctrines, of neglecting to foster a love for God. Not out of our own strength do we love God, but by abiding in the Word. A neglect of the Word will cause us to not love the Lord, for his Word is where we commune with God. The means of grace, the Word and the sacrament, that is where by the power of the Holy Spirit we find our communion with the Lord. Then as the Holy Spirit causes this truth to transform our lives, we naturally live out the very character of Christ.

The third of the fruits that Jesus taught is joy. Christians should manifest joy. Ask any young person whether their joy will come from following their own passions and their own dreams or obeying their parents, and you're almost sure to hear that their joy comes from doing

---

2. Martin Luther, *Luther's Works*, 249.

their own heart's desire. They may obey parents out of respect, but if you were to ask them, "Which would you rather do?" most of them would say, "I'm truly happy when I'm doing what I want to do." It's human nature. Spontaneity, rather than habits that have been trained and a commitment to a disciplined life, seems to bring them happiness. And so we would answer, those of us who have learned by our own folly in that regard, "If only ignorance truly was bliss." But Jesus is here teaching that a lover of God is filled with the Word of Christ, and lives to manifest the same obedience Christ had for the Father, and that obedience in love leads to real joy.

Joy is the flag that flies over the Christian heart, announcing that the King is in residence. Joy is that mark of true Christian fellowship with the Lord. A joyless Christian is one who is not walking with the Lord, for those who have known the Lord even in the deepest, darkest persecutions, when they're being starved or thrown to the lions, we read in history that they still expressed joy even in their death.

As the martyrs were burned at the stake, they sang hymns of love for God. Were they mad? No! They had joy and peace because they had the Word of Christ stored up in them, abiding in them, and they had such an assurance, and they had lived such a life of obedience that their joy was complete.

A Christian's joy discovered and made complete by following the pattern and example of joy given by Christ is a complete joy, one that complements the peace of Christ. The supposed joy of the world is carnal. It's temporary, shallow, incomplete, and eventually—and this is key—eventually it consumes.

That joy of the world will eventually consume the one who is seeking it, or it will consume the one who is used by the one seeking it to try to attain it. To try to attain some sense of human euphoria or human peace in even the most virtuous sense will consume. Such worldly pleasure is an antithesis for what we were created to find, for there is nothing in it that glorifies God.

It's the deception of the serpent in the Garden at the very beginning. "Do you really need to abide in God's Word and obey God? Surely not! Take and eat this, and find true joy." Wasn't it the initial deception of man to seek joy in some other way than to abide in God's Word, to be nourished by God's Word, and to live in obedience to him? The promise

Love that Bears Fruit to God's Glory: Part 2

of obedience born from love is true joy, and that joy is only found in complete fulfillment.

We were created to glorify God. When we misuse our lives, when we are not being sanctified in lives, when we spend our days in disobedience, we may be in perpetual motion, but we will never find joy. If you lack joy, it's not a lacking in Christ's provision. Joy is available. It's a lack of love for God that is expressed in obedience.

We can sum it up with terms we've used historically, such as Christian piety, but piety must result from love that gives birth to obedience. Otherwise, it becomes pietism, which is nothing but obedience absent love, which will never render joy as a result. But Jesus is saying, "If you abide in me, and make my Word the very words of your own heart and mind, if you make it your life to glorify me by bearing the fruit of a converted and consecrated life, by being obedient to my command, then I will give you my joy." That joy that will fill your life makes you complete because of your peace with God.

And so we ask then, if we are to obey the commandment, and the commandment brings us joy, then what commandment is it we are to obey that brings us such great returns? And we conclude with this. Jesus says, "That you love one another as I have loved you."

That simple commandment lived truly is a fulfillment of all that is necessary to have joy, for we are not able to love one another unless it is also true that we love God and are living in obedience to him. If we do that, we find love for one another to be a simple thing to follow. And in doing that in Christian community and unity and communion of the saints, then we come to know the love of Christ and the joy that is ours.

15

Friendship

John 15:12–15

"These things I have spoken to you, that my joy may be in you, and that your joy may be full. This is my commandment, that you love one another as I have loved you. Greater love has no one than this, that someone lay down his life for his friends. You are my friends if you do what I command you. No longer do I call you servants, for the servant does not know what his master is doing; but I have called you friends, for all that I have heard from my Father I have made known to you."

REMEMBER HOW IMPORTANT FRIENDSHIP was when you were a child? It really was everything. Having a friend was to a child one of the most important elements of life. Without a friend, there was depression and a real sense of aloneness. No matter how large your family was, we all wanted a best friend. Girls would even often sign their letters "best friends forever."

Guys would undertake ceremonies such as pricking their thumbs and pushing them together when they bled so that they could be blood brothers, showing how close and inseparable they were in friendship. Little girls would often cry when their best friend would play with someone else on the playground. They would come home devastated because their friend chose to play with somebody else.

As boys enter into the teenage years, they get jealous when their best friend has a girlfriend and begins to spend time with her instead of with him. They are jealous because they want their friend with them all the time.

But friendship doesn't end with childhood. In the day in which we live, where friends number in the hundreds online and you get friendship requests from people whom you don't even know, I sometimes fear we may have lost the sense of what a true friend actually is.

In the 1700's, Samuel Johnson said, "True happiness consists not in the multitude of friends, but in their worth and choice."[1] The careful choosing of a friend is a stewardship of our own selves that we seem to pay little attention to today. On line, we click Okay for anyone who asks to be a friend. "Oh sure! I'll be a friend. Why not?" Have we lost somewhere along the way the definition of friendship, and in having a multitude of friends, are we finding ourselves really more alone than we've ever been?

On the value of friendship, Henry Adams said, "One friend in a lifetime is much. Two are many. Three is hardly possible."[2] Aristotle said, "What is a friend? A single soul dwelling in two bodies, and without friends no one would choose to live though he had all other goods."[3]

Is there any way for us to measure the true importance of genuine friendship? So important is genuine friendship that a husband and a wife often consider, in fact, we would say *ought* to consider one another their best friend. They who share in all things spiritual together would find in one another best friends. And at the end of our life, as we grow old in years, we will often lose our will to live not because of the infirmities of our body, but because so often we hear our last friend has died. And with the passing of friends, there seems to be a passing of our own history and our own reason to be. So important is friendship.

So when Jesus says, "You are my friends," he is using an understandable language. He is using an example that the disciples would be able to understand. He was using a metaphor, yet there is a reality in it as well so that the disciples would know the nature of the relationship to which he was speaking.

But Jesus doesn't leave the word to their subjective interpretation even though they probably would have had a narrow definition. We, in our day, have very broad definitions of what makes a friend. If we meet people once, often we like to claim they're now our friends even though we know very little of them.

1. Mark Waters, *Encyclopedia of Quotations*.
2. Ibid.
3. Ibid.

The Last Sermon of Christ

We know some are capable of deep and lasting friendships in the Scripture, such as David and Jonathan. And while others aren't able to be selfless enough even to understand that sort of relationship, we have to admit there is a limitation to the Scripture's teaching on friendship. There are rare examples in the Scripture of the kinds of friendship that the Lord is speaking of. Here, again, I would hold Jonathan and David up, but even that is not going to be a perfect example because there was a reciprocal relationship there between David and Jonathan.

There are places in the Scripture where God calls people his friend. He calls Moses a friend. He calls Abraham his friend. Jesus calls the disciples his friend. But did you know there is not one place in Scripture—not a *single* place—where man calls God his friend. Not one. God calls man his friend, but there is no reciprocal relationship based on the friendship metaphor. That probably escapes most of us, and we would include that analogy in our description of our relationship with Christ, or even our relationship with God the Father.

There is no peer relationship with Christ, and there is no peer relationship with God the Father. His extending of friendship to us finds in our human living an imperfect metaphor, yet it's the closest we're able to come to understanding what Jesus is instructing them here.

Jesus is defining his friendship as a relation of love. And more than that, it is a love that is the foundation of their discipleship. Notice that Jesus commands to obey, and then tells them obedience is summed up in one word, *love*. This idea, this principle, this precept of love is the foundation of the relationship which Jesus is now explaining to them.

In 1 Corinthians 13, verse 13, Paul lists the fruits of our union with Christ as faith, hope, and love, but he points out that the greatest of these is love. Without love, there is no faith, and there is no hope. Where there is love, there is faith and hope. In fact, in Romans 13, verse 10, he teaches that love is the fulfillment of the entire law. All of the law can be summed up in this word *love*. Where there is love, nothing is lacking. And when there is no love, nothing can be attained.

Jesus had already taught them in John 13:35 that love would be the evidence of discipleship. It was to be their strongest testimony. Not their rhetoric, not their apologetics, not their great strength in the building up of physical structures of church, but love would be their strongest testimony to the world. It would be the defining characteristic. That

Friendship

which distinguishes them from any other religious cult would be love. Love for one another. Love for Christ.

This is made abundantly clear in a story that is told by H. A. Ironside, a great commentator and expositor of Scripture. He tells of a missionary to China who was working on a Chinese translation of the Bible. He wanted this translation to be as nearly perfect as it could possibly be. He employed a Chinese academic, a linguist. And this Chinese academic worked with him diligently in the translation of the Scriptures. They spent days and months together going verse by verse and word by word.

As the Chinese linguist would tell him the translation of the passage, the missionary would then work to place that in the context and make sure it was nuanced as perfectly as possible to communicate the real meaning of the text. As they began to near the end, the missionary began to anticipate the moment and the translation was finished when he would speak with the translator about the gospel.

He had held off doing so out of respect for the work the translator was doing, not wanting to offend him, or not wanting to overplay his hand. He was waiting until the translation was finished, hoping the Word itself would have its work upon the Chinese man, and that then as he simply opened himself up to share the gospel, that it would flow quite naturally.

As the missionary and the translator finished, the missionary asked him whether there was anything about Christianity that appealed to him, after they had finished their work. And the Chinese translator said, "Yes. In fact, it does. It's a wonderful system of ethics and philosophy. The best probably I've ever known. I think if I were to ever see a Christian, I might in fact become interested."

The missionary protested, "But I am a Christian!" And the Chinese translator looked at him, and said, "You? Oh no. And don't be offended, but I've observed you and listened to you all along. If I understand Jesus, he gave a commandment that you are to love one another. But I've listened to you talk about others that aren't present, saying unkind things about them. No, you're not a Christian. Not at all. But I think if I ever did see a Christian, I might like to be one."

A true story, but what a testimony of that unique, defining characteristic of Christianity—love. And how disqualifying it is when we fail to show it. How disqualified are our words when our posture betrays a lack of love? John 13:35: "By this all people will know that you are my Disciples."

What is the law? Love the Lord your God with all your heart, soul, and mind, and love your neighbor as yourself. Now Christ identifies this love as the same as his love for them, as he tells them, "You are my friends."

But we protest, "You don't know what folks have been doing to me. You don't know what they've been saying about me. You don't know what they've cost me. You don't know the sleepless nights I've had because of their carrying on in the way they do. You don't know the struggles I've had. You don't know the time I've had to spend explaining things because of all of the antics of this person, or this crowd, or this group. How terribly I am offended! How disappointed I am in them!"

Ephesians 4:1 and 2: "Walk in a manner worthy of the calling to which you have been called, with all humility and gentleness, with patience. . ." and here, ". . . bearing with one another in love." "How can we do that?" we say. How can we bear up under such belligerent action of people who are so unnerving in the way they carry on. We have all the excuses. We have all of the justification for our posturing and self-defense against those who would assail us.

But yet we know from the Scriptures, the standard is that while we were yet sinners, Christ died for us. By qualifying the love of a Christian as being like the love of Christ, he is commanding us to a selfless rather than a reciprocal love. We don't love because people are lovable; we love because Christ loved us. We don't love because they have earned it by their high standard of communication and their self-discipline in speech, but because it is the result of the fruit of the Spirit in us.

As commendable as all of those are, and as healthy as they are for the Body, we don't love because of that. We love because Christ loved us. To be giving rather than gaining love is our goal, and to a biblical rather than a worldly love is what we point ourselves.

By reflecting the love of Jesus in our love for one another, love becomes the testimony of the Church. It becomes the testimony of the gospel. So vital and central to the testimony of the gospel is love that Luther himself is confident that here is where the devil will work his greatest cunning against God's people. He said that trifles can lead to such quarreling and enmity that great harm results to many. The blood soon begins to boil, and the devil shoots his venomous darts into the

Friendship

heart by means of evil tongues, and finally, no one says or thinks anything good about the other person at all.

But this is not the way of Christ. We can't give way to the devil, to the world, or to the flesh and become schismatic, vindictive, or loveless, and even assault those who are members of Christ, branches of the same vine which we claim to grow from. But we are to remember not only *that* Jesus loved us but *how* Jesus loved us. Christ loved the Church, and he gave himself up for her. Greater love, we are taught, has no man than this that he would give his own life for his friends.

"How far," we ask, "do I have to tolerate the insults?" As far as the east is from the west. How many times do we turn the other cheek? As many times as it is slapped. How long must I remain silent before my tormentors and accusers? As long as the sheep remains silent before his own slaughter.

How can we endure such persecution? How can we hold up? By loving as Christ loved. Selfless love. Not looking for reward, not looking for vindication, not looking to be proved right in the end, but being proved as one who is able to love as Christ loved, knowing that Jesus counts all who love in this way to be his friend. And Jesus will never abandon us.

How is it that this friendship is to be defined? What makes it different, and why is it not reciprocal? Look at the last verse which we read today. "No longer do I call you servants, for the servant does not know what his master is doing; but I have called you friends, for all that I have heard from my Father I have made known to you." There are those who are able to obey the commandments. They're servants. They don't know the mind of the master. They obey because they have to obey.

We find those in the Christian Church who are striving in works of righteousness, seeking to obey the letter of the law, but never understanding the relationship of love, and so they remain servants. And Jesus says, "But you will not be my servants. You are my friends."

And a friend has had an explanation revealed. Why do we obey? We cannot be saved by obedience, so why do we obey? Because it's the nature of the one indwelled by the Spirit of God. It's the nature of a Christian to obey. It's not external to us; it's internal to us. And we know that we obey because of the love relationship we have with One who has called us a friend. Why a friend? Because there is no better Friend than One who would give his own life for the sake of the one he calls his friend. That privilege belonged to Christ alone. Only Christ could give his life for those he calls his friends.

I, in claiming him to by my Friend, cannot give my life to satisfy any debt. Only he as our Friend is able to satisfy the debt. And so therefore, for his friends, those he claims as his friends, he satisfies their debt by his death on the Cross.

My grandmother who has passed into glory could only bang out one song on the piano. And I use the word *bang* quite literally. She had all the chords right, but that piano suffered mightily under the strength of that woman's arms. She only could do one song, and whenever she babysat for us, I got to hear that song. And actually it was a treat. It was a song written in 1855 by Joseph Scriven, and I'll bet you know it.

> "What a friend we have in Jesus,
> All our sins and griefs to bear!
> What a privilege to carry
> Everything to God in prayer!"

The fact that Christ has called us friend has been a treasured comfort for generations of Christians, a treasured comfort because it implies a closeness in proximity. It implies genuine concern, not as one who is elected far off in an office who will do something to benefit our lives, but One who has an intimate association and an intimate concern with the realities of my life. If I have a good friend, my good friend knows the issues of my life. That is friendship. Your spouse, who is your friend, ought to be aware of the issues of your life. That is friendship.

Perhaps it was just this sort of assurance and comfort that Karl Barth had in mind when he was asked one time, "What is the greatest thought you ever had?" Karl Barth, who is in some quarters a bit scandalous as a theologian, had some ideas that not all agreed with, but he certainly was a lover of Christ and a follower of God. And he wrote a dogmatic theology consisting of more pages than I can carry, much less ever read in my life. I have no idea how some are able to do that.

Barth could have responded in innumerable ways, but in all seriousness he said, "Jesus loves me; this I know for the Bible tells me so." So I ask you, *consider your own life. Examine your own life. Is it characterized by love? It is characterized by a love that is demonstrable? Not just an idea of love you'll get to one day. Do you actually have love in your life walk?*

Friendship

You know where you can test yourself. Not with those who are easy to love, but those whom you already know that you struggle with loving. Those whom you don't want to love, but you know they're believers, and you have to love them. You don't want to love them, but while we were yet sinners, Christ died for us.

Will we diminish his love and say the offense against us is so much greater than our offense against a holy God? Will we not love because Christ has commanded that we love? We must love or else question our own testimony because if our testimony is to be void of love, then we've lost the crown of the Christian testimony, which is to be love.

Is your life a living testimony? Do you love not with a love of the world, but with the deep, abiding love of Christ, a love that can cover a multitude of sins? Do you know this friendship of Jesus, where his love to others flows through you? Or are you still a servant, not really understanding the mind of the Lord on this, just simply seeking to obey in the ethics and the morality of the Christian religion? Without love, we remain servants. With love, he calls us his friend.

16

Realizing the Real Purpose of Our Appointment

John 15:15–17

"No longer do I call you servants, for the servant does not know what his master is doing; but I have called you friends, for all that I have heard from my Father I have made known to you. You did not choose me, but I chose you and appointed you that you should go and bear fruit and that your fruit should abide, so that whatever you ask the Father in my name, he may give it to you. These things I command you, so that you will love one another."

HERE IN JOHN 15, we find a summary of the teaching of Christ. As I was planning this study, I couldn't help but think of the success of that book by Rick Warren, *The Purpose-Driven Life*, subtitled "What on Earth Am I Here For?" And this passage in fact would answer that very question. What Warren has given in an entire book has some merit of course, but Christ has taught us here in such a smaller amount of space.

That book of Rick Warren's reveals the dilemma of the modern mind. He has touched on a nerve, hence the expanded and the continuing expanding sales of that book. I couldn't even find an accurate figure. When I did a search on the Internet, I came up with different years and different numbers as it continues to sell. It's well over 40 million.

Today, people are born. They're nurtured. They're educated. They're provided remarkable opportunities in this world. But more and more, as children become adults, they seem to have no idea why they are here at all. It seems the more opportunity there is the more lost we

Realizing the Real Purpose of Our Appointment

become. So we go through life simply doing what we have to do, never really knowing where it'll take us, never really learning the context that we are supposed to be living in, just carrying on as if we're part of a great machine called *humanity*, and never really feeling fulfilled in our lives.

In John 15, verses 15 through 17, Christ answers in two or three short passages the greatest questions of our lives lived here on this earth? In Ecclesiastes, chapter 1, we find essentially the voice of the generation we now have among us. There we find an introduction to postmodernism, a sense of directionlessness, a sense that it doesn't really matter where you go or what you do as long as you go somewhere and do something, that nothing really has connection with purpose, nothing has connection with calling. Just do a little bit over here now and do a little bit over there later. What does it matter in the big scheme of things as long as I have enjoyed the day in which I lived?

But isn't that the message of Ecclesiastes? It's ironic how Solomon himself perhaps was the first postmodern, except Solomon because of his wisdom did arrive at the right answer. But the toils he went through, the journey he went through to arrive at that answer is heartrending. "Vanity of vanities," he says. "Vanity of vanities! All is vanity. What does man gain by all the toil at which he toils under the sun? A generation goes, and a generation comes, but the earth remains forever."

Isn't that the voice of the generation in which we now live? They say, "We live, and we die. Our days are short. They're brief. Why should we labor? Why should we not have fun and excitement? They're so short. They're so brief. Life is so vain. At least I will indulge myself today and know that today I had fun." And that becomes the measure of a successful life, that we had fun today.

"The sun rises and the sun goes down, and hastens to the place where it rises." Solomon is talking about nature. Streams flow into the ocean, and the water continues to flow. But to what end and for what purpose? Just to fill the ocean? The postmodern would say, there is no glory in that. There is no wonder in that for the postmodern mind.

In Ecclesiastes chapter 2, verse 16 and 17, Solomon continues, "For of the wise as of the fool there is no enduring remembrance, seeing that in the days to come all will have been long forgotten. How the wise dies just like the fool!" Can you not hear the student in a school saying, "It doesn't matter if I study and get smart, or if I don't study and stay dumb; we're all going to die in the end"? Don't we hear the echoes of Solomon even in the days in which we live? And the result is the same in verse 17. "So I hated life, because what is done under the sun was grievous to me, for all is vanity and a striving after wind."

We live among a people who do hate life. They hate life. How do we know? Look at the exploding suicide rates that we see. Look at the people who are in counseling for depression. Look at the wandering and the wasted lives. Look at the seduction of the flesh and how people will seek pleasure through money, through flesh, through drugs, through whatever indulgence they can find to try to find something, and all of those just take more and more away from life. They don't contribute. So in the end, they are left an empty shell saying, "I hate life. I hate it. It has nothing for me. It took me nowhere, and I ended up with nothing but bad memories, a sullied conscience, and a knowing that I am not right before God." And so they hate life.

Pink Floyd sang an old song, "All in all, we're just another brick in the wall." Is that our view of ourselves, that we're just a brick in the wall? We're just another passing day and life? We reject educational establishments. We reject family. We reject the church.

And still even after all of that rejection, we have no idea why we are on earth. All we know is that we reject everything. We have no idea why we're here. We just know it's not for anything that is put before us. So we have a generation agreeing with Solomon. "Vanity of vanities! All is vanity. All is striving after the wind. There is nothing to be gained under the sun."

But Jesus Christ answers that dilemma, and he answers it in the passages we are examining in this chapter. Our Lord Jesus answers and gives to Solomon an answer. He gives to us an answer as well. Jesus has been transitioning the Disciples from aimlessness in their life to purposefulness. And I can't emphasize that enough. That almost is a sermon in itself.

He has been transitioning the Disciples in his teaching of them and in his walking with them from a people who were aimless to a people who have purpose. He has removed their desperation that is due to the end of all things because he has been telling them, "I'm leaving you." They have oriented themselves and geared themselves completely to being his Disciples. Now he is leaving. It would seem that now it is all over. So once again, they're aimless, but he is saying to these Disciples,

Realizing the Real Purpose of Our Appointment

"Your discipleship was not vanity of vanities because it continues on into eternity." He gives them an expectation of continuing with him.

If the Disciples continued ministering with Christ as disciples after the crucifixion and resurrection, then so do we in the same way. Not in an apostleship, but in discipleship, we also continue with him in the same way.

So these words and this assurance that was given to the Disciples are valid for us today if we will seize upon it. Or we can continue to labor with Solomon and vanity of vanities, knowing that we also will end up like all of those who've come before us who've chosen to live a vain life. We also will end with the same. But it does not have to be.

In verse 14, Jesus has made clear to the Disciples by calling them his friend, that because they are his friends, they have a common aim and a common outlook they share with him. He says to them, "If you do the things which I command you, you are my friend." He revealed the Father's mind to them. All the Father has told them, he has revealed to them.

Revelation and likemindedness, rather than their simple obedience, are what characterizes their friendship with him. There has been a transition from where he said, "Just do what I tell you," to where he says, "Now you share my mind. Walk with me, not behind me as if I still carry a whip to drive you along. But walk with me because now you share a mind with me."

Jesus has a right to command them. He is the Lord. He could command them to do what he says. But instead, he is calling them his friends. That doesn't diminish his power. It doesn't diminish his right. But he is seeking their transformation. He is not seeking a servant. He is seeking transformed lives, disciples who follow him and have an obedience that is desired but not forced, because obedience doesn't *make* them his friends. Obedience *characterizes* or identifies them as his friends.

Whereas a servant, just like a child, is expected to do those things they are told, the one Jesus calls a friend is a co-laborer, fully aware of the mind of Jesus, and bound by a relationship of love rather than simple, legal obligation. You could think of it as a free obedience.

But the friendship is not reciprocal. We don't say Jesus is our friend. He calls us his friend because we can't say of him that if he does what we say he is our friend. That is why he called Moses and Abraham his friends, but they never called the Lord their own friend. We are to have the mind of Christ. He is not to have our mind. We are now his bondservants, those who serve willingly, not those who are in captivity.

Their transformation from servant to friend is accomplished by his confiding in them the fundamental idea of his life. They are brought into the work of a disciple through thought and motive, through revelation and love. Jesus is essentially setting them free if they are only his servants, but binding them to him eternally if they are his friends.

This is a moment of liberation for them. They have a choice. Jesus is leaving. They can leave if they choose. They can abandon him. They can abandon the calling they have in life. They can abandon it all. They can walk away. They are no longer under obligation except in their soul and with their conscience.

Judas walked away. Judas left. Judas betrayed the Lord. Judas left to do something else. They are not under legal obligation, but they are under a moral obligation because our Lord has invested his life in them. They're free to run away and they're free to stay and travel the road Jesus has laid before them.

John Peter Lange explains, "The name of 'Friend' is placed in connection with joyfulness and death. Friendship with Christ is co-partner in his loving, in his self-sacrificing, in his dying, courage in the strength of self-sacrificing love."[1] Jesus is showing them that if they love him they will follow him unto the end.

And he said the same thing in John 13:1. "When Jesus knew that his hour had come to depart out of this world to the Father, having loved his own who were in the world, he loved them to the end." How can so great a love as Christ's be expressed? If this is the love of God poured out to us through the life of Christ, how can that actually be expressed? The greatness of his love is shown in his own impulse to love us first.

Here he is speaking of their apostleship. They were fishermen. They were tax-collectors. Only one was a doctor. None of these, none of these Disciples had anything that caused them to be a marvel to Christ, that caused the acquisition of their discipleship to be a boon to his ministry. They didn't even know that they ought to love him when he called them and when he prepared them to go and to serve.

---

1. John Peter Lange, *Commentary on the Holy Scriptures*, p. 466.

Realizing the Real Purpose of Our Appointment

But of course, man always feels the initiative is his own. We always feel that it was our choice. It was our prerogative. It was our initiative. But Jesus assures us here that that is not the case. Normally a disciple does in fact choose to be attached to a particular rabbi. It was the culture where the people of Israel would hear a man teaching, and they would associate themselves with that teaching, and they would take sometimes even the name of the teacher, and they would follow that teacher.

But we are entering into a relationship with Jesus which is by birth, or rebirth if you will. Just as a baby doesn't choose parents, so we don't choose Christ on our own initiative because we come into that relationship by birth, not by choice. He first loved us before we loved him. He chose us before we chose him.

Augustine says, "See then how he chooses not the good, but makes those whom he has chosen good."[2] This is Christ's work in us. Not only did he choose us, but also he appointed us to our work. The first work of a disciple is to be an emissary for Christ, to be one who testifies, to be one who brings the gospel to people.

The second work of a disciple is to bear fruit, and that is where we've been focusing on most of our teaching, to bear fruit. And the fruit of a disciple isn't simply a flash in the pan project. It's not something that just hits and goes. It remains. It abides. It bears fruit that lasts.

But how does it remain? How do we perform a ministry that has fruit that abides, that is, fruit that extends into eternity? Anyone can do something good for the church. We can make something happen. We can perform a ministry. We can put on a concert. We can put on a play. We can do a project. We can build something. We can teach a class or a seminar. We can cook a meal. We can provide a carpool for someone.

The only way those have eternal significance however is if they bring the gospel of Christ into contact with the soul of man. Then you've done something that does indeed have an eternal significance, a fruit that remains.

Any fruit we bear for our own glory will start to fade the moment it's created. Ecclesiastes 2:11: "Then I considered all that my hands had done and the toil I had expended in doing it, and behold, all was vanity and a striving after wind, and there was nothing to be gained under the sun."

---

2. Augustine, Nicene and Post-Nicene Fathers: First Series, Volume VII, p. 356.

The Last Sermon of Christ

One thing Solomon did that most of us avoid is he reflected on his own life. He reflected on the work he had done. He reflected on his own study. He reflected on his own contributions. He reflected on how he had spent his time and his days. And then he had the courage, perhaps the audacity, to judge them, to consider, "Are these worthy or not, and did they have any lasting influence?"

And what he determined is, "Everything I've done has just withered away. It has faded, and it has floated away, and it means nothing. It's all vanity. All of my investments of my time, all of my investments of my resources, all of my investments of everything I have done is now fading away. And all the glory that was mine, every round of applause I got after some wonderful achievement has now faded into history and is not remembered anymore."

But fruit for God's glory that increases the kingdom and builds the Church remains because the kingdom of God alone is eternal. You want fruit that remains? Then invest yourself in the progress of the kingdom.

As D. A. Carson points out, "Our purpose of election then is that the Disciples who have been so blessed with revelation and understanding should win others to the faith. That is fruit that will last."[3]

So we've discovered the purpose of life. It's all here in verse 16 of John, chapter 15. "You did not choose me, but I chose you and appointed you that you should go and bear fruit and that your fruit should abide, so that whatever you ask the Father in my name, he may give it to you."

Here is the purpose of life. How do we translate that into real life though, that we should bear fruit and that it would abide? We should bear fruit and that fruit should abide. So we have to attend to two matters in our life—are we bearing fruit, that is, the fruit of God, and does that fruit abide?

We begin with the idea of the vineyard in our teaching on the fruit. Jesus had a cumulative teaching approach to them. He taught by building one idea upon the others, like math class when I was in school. You begin with simple numbers and a number line maybe. And then perhaps you go to addition, and then subtraction, and then to multiplication, and then division, each one growing incrementally upon the other. But if you never learned addition, or if you never paid mind to multiplication, you would never be able to factor when you got to

---

3. D. A. Carson, *The Gospel According to John Eerdmans*, p. 523.

Realizing the Real Purpose of Our Appointment

Algebra because it requires those easier functions for you to be able to do the more complex functions.

So Jesus begins with an illustration of a vineyard, and he teaches them about a branch and a vine, and how the branch needs to produce fruit or else the branch will be pruned. But it's pruned so that the next year it grows even more fruit. Verse 2 speaks of fruit. The branch is to produce fruit because it's the nature of the branch to produce fruit. With the indwelling of the Spirit, our fruit will naturally be the fruit of the Spirit.

What should be the fruit of the Spirit manifested in our life? Primary, and chief among them, love. And then joy, and peace, and patience, kindness, goodness, faithfulness, gentleness, self-control. If we live by the Spirit, let us walk by the Spirit, so the Scriptures teach.

The Lord goes on to say that we are pruned so that our own fruitfulness will increase. So the second lesson is not just that the Christian should bear fruit because we are one with Christ and unified with Christ who is the vine, but as that unity is true and as we are indwelled by the Spirit, the fruits of the Spirit become manifest in our lives. But that is not static. There is an increasing of those fruits of the Spirit through all of our lives.

This removes the possibility, any possibility, of complacency as a Christian virtue, such as was found in the church of Laodicea. Feeling they had their fill of the Lord, they had become lukewarm, and the Lord spits them out of his mouth. For the church, pretty good is never fruitful enough, for the fields are white unto harvest, but the laborers are few.

In verse 8, Jesus expands his teaching to our call to be fruitful, saying that in bearing much fruit we will glorify God. Not in getting by, not in knowing that fruit exists, not in hearing sermons on fruit, or watching other people bear fruit and supporting them in their fruit bearing, either by praise or even by giving a financial gift. It's not the support of others bearing fruit, it's through our bearing fruit. Not a little fruit, but much much fruit. We will glorify God. Implied is the end verse that bearing only a little fruit does not glorify God. It is in bearing much fruit that we glorify God. There is no virtue in bearing only a little fruit.

Verse 16 demonstrates the final characteristic of fruitfulness. By possessing the fruit of the Spirit, love being cardinal among the fruits, and by living those fruits as expressions of our transformed character, we will produce fruit. How do you produce fruit? By living according to, and your character being framed by the fruits of the Spirit.

If you live out the fruits of the Spirit, you will produce fruit in your life. A transformed character will produce fruit, and that fruit will increase, and it will bring God glory, and it will bring us joy, and it will cause us to have fruit that abides, that is, lasts forever.

Forever you say? Forever? You mean that really love, joy, peace, patience, kindness, goodness, truth, faithfulness, I can live that way and have fruit that endures forever? There is only One who is eternal, and that is the triune God, Father, Son, Holy Spirit, and he dwells in the eternal city, and only his work lasts forever.

Scriptures teach the grass withers, the flowers fade, but the Word of God remains forever. "What is your life?" the Scriptures ask, "For you are a mist that appears for a little time and then vanishes." How can we have fruit that lasts forever? The work which he blesses is the work which we do in his name that flows from his Spirit, which is renewing us daily to do his will. It's no longer I who live, but Christ who lives in me. It is the Spirit of Christ working to build the kingdom which is eternal, and we are partners with him in that.

Jesus concludes by repeating again the new commandment he has given to them. Haven't we studied it enough? Haven't we emphasized love enough? Over and over throughout John, the topic of love comes up. Surely the Disciples had heard it from our own Lord's lips better and with more clarity than I can present it. We cannot leave it off. We dare not leave it off. We must not leave it off because our Lord did not leave it off.

The Scriptures teach us that God is love. Paul tells us that without love we have nothing. Jesus tells us that we must love one another, and he repeats it again and again and again to burn it into our hearts and to burn it into our minds. And even after the resurrection, he comes to Peter, and he asks him three times straight, "Do you love me? Do you love me? Do you love me?"

So we ask simply, "Well, then how do we love?" If it must be about love, how do we love? We pray for one another because we love one another. We remain faithful to one another, and we deal in good faith with one another. We support one another emotionally, spiritually, and materially whenever we have opportunity.

Realizing the Real Purpose of Our Appointment

And so now we have it. What answers the postmodern dilemma in life? The view that all life is vanity? It comes, and it goes, and we pass along. The answer is in people being transformed into Christ's likeness, manifesting the fruits of the Spirit, obeying the command of Christ, sharing the gospel, glorifying God, experiencing genuine joy in a community of love.

And so I ask, *who wouldn't want to be a part of that?* Who would rather drift along aimlessly just seeking a pleasure here or there in life? If you walk in the Spirit as living disciples in the way of the Lord, you will not labor and die in vain. Your life will bear fruit into eternity.

17

Taking Their Hate Out On You

John 15:18–25

"If the world hates you, know that it has hated me before it hated you. If you were of the world, the world would love you as its own; but because you are not of the world, but I chose you out of the world, therefore the world hates you. Remember the word that I said to you: 'A servant is not greater than his master.' If they persecuted me, they will also persecute you. If they kept my word, they will also keep yours.

But all these things they will do to you on account of my name, because they do not know him who sent me. If I had not come and spoken to them, they would not have been guilty of sin, but now they have no excuse for their sin. Whoever hates me hates my Father also. If I had not done among them the works that no one else did, they would not be guilty of sin, but now they have seen and hated both me and my Father. But the word that is written in their Law must be fulfilled: 'They hated me without a cause.'"

THERE IS A SIGNIFICANT shift in the themes on John which we've been following up to this point. This is continuing the farewell discourse which Jesus is having with his disciples. He has been offering words of comfort to them.

As he described to them his departure, he promised to them he was preparing a place for them and they would join him there. And then he followed that with teaching to the disciples about their identification and unity with him and their appointed duty to bear fruit as a ministry to the glory of God.

They've been called out of the world, he has taught them, separated in the name of Christ to do the work which is eternal in a world which is temporal. Jesus taught them that because of him they could ask for whatever they needed in pursuit of this ministry God has called them to in his name, and that he as their mediator and advocate would see that their needs were indeed met. It would be provided.

They're commanded to abide in him, to stay in him by keeping his Word in them. They would abide in him as his Word was found in them, and they were further to manifest the fruits of the Spirit, love being chief among them, listed first and expounded in so many other Scriptures. Love is the fulfillment of the law itself—the letter of the law, that is—and they were to express that in the fellowship of the saints. That would become the testimony of the Church.

Martin Luther, the great Reformer, said, "He points out to them how Christendom must live together, what its fate will be, and by what sign true believers, or Christians, are identified. Christ makes this so urgent because he foresaw how many false Christians there would be who would vaunt their faith with excellent words and strong outward show, but without a foundation.[1]"

We can see this concern of Martin Luther's worked out in the Scriptures in Acts 19:15. There is a story there which would be funny if it weren't so tragic, a story of seven priest's sons who take it upon themselves to perform an exorcism of a demon-possessed man. The evil spirit speaks to them in that passage, saying, "Jesus I know, and Paul I recognize, but who are you?"

The humor would be that at that point we're told the evil spirit which is in the man then causes the man who is possessed to fall upon the seven sons, and he gives them what we might a good whuppin'. But unfortunately, it can't be funny because of the nature of the story.

So we can conclude that where there are only words, Christ is not present. No matter how great the profession, no matter how great the liturgy, no matter how involved whatever the ministries might be, if they are only words, then though the lips may praise, the hearts of the people are far from the Lord.

We might wonder why Jesus is teaching so much and so long on a single subject, this subject of love within the Body, love for one another, love for God. It would seem that for the believer that would

---

1. Martin Luther, Luther's Works vol. 24, Concordia 1961, p. 264.

just naturally flow. And so by simply stating it or giving us the truth concerning love, that would be sufficient, but Jesus has continued to elaborate and to approach it from several different perspectives in order that his teaching on love would be clear to the disciples.

He emphasizes their unity with him and the foundation of love that that commits between them, and because of their unity with him, they also have a unity with one another. Why would he emphasize this? Why push so hard this idea of unity with him and love within the Body? Because as we are seeing in the passage above, he is now telling them the world will seek to destroy them, that they are in a hostile environment. And if the household is not strong, if it is not firm, if their inclusion in the Body is not one where there is unity in the Body with the Head, which is Christ, then the Body will be destroyed.

I imagine that as Jesus is speaking to them, there is a movement toward the Cross. At first, Jesus was simply explaining it, but then we're told they leave the upper room, and will go to the garden for prayer where Jesus will be arrested. Could it be that our Lord would even be looking down the road and in his mind's eye seeing the Cross, or at least the shadow of the Cross beginning to fall upon his own shoulders, and knowing as he is talking with the disciples that the Cross which he now is beginning to feel, the coldness of that shadow being fallen upon him, is also a cross which is meant for the disciples?

Because the world is the enemy of the Church, Jude will warn in his writing, in his Scriptures, that incorporating worldliness in the Church will bring division. Because the people of God have nothing to do with worldliness, we are called out from that. Worldly people are devoid of the Spirit because they are committed to ungodly passions. And that has no place in the Body of Christ, and there is nothing that is worldly that can knit together a Body where it is perceived that the love of Christ has failed.

The love of Christ is not received by the world because the love of Christ is the antithesis to the love which the world understands. The world loves what the Christians must recoil from, and the Christian loves what the world naturally hates.

Five times in a single verse, Jesus uses the word *kosmos*, or it's translated as *world*—five times. Five times he uses that word *world*. In doing so, he uses a literary means of teaching where he is making sure that that concept of world is not lost in the conversation.

We do the same thing in our conversations. When we want to make a point, we might say something, and then we might reiterate it. Or then we might say, "Did you actually hear what I'm saying?" And the person might repeat it, and you might realize that even in their repeating it, they haven't grasped what you're really trying to say, and you might repeat key words in your sentence to make sure they understand.

We know after the resurrection, Jesus and Peter are in conversation, and he asks him three times, "Do you love me?" to the point that Peter is almost desperate to understand what is it that the Lord is driving at because he answers easily to begin with. All Jesus does is repeat the same question, and each time it goes further and further to the soul of Peter.

Here in this sentence, Jesus is using the word *world*, and in doing so, he is making sure just what he is speaking of that the disciples must, must understand, that the world with its ambitions, the world with its goals, the world with its pleasures are all a danger to them. They had already experienced hatred against Jesus, and now they would begin to experience the hatred of the world coming first through the Jews, but then as we also learn to experience as we stand for Christ against all Christians in all places.

Jesus had to leave Judea because the Jews were planning to murder him. We find out in John, chapter 8, verse 59, that there they're trying to stone him, and they did that again in chapter 10, verse 31. Is this anything at all contemporary to us? Is there anything about the warning that is given to the disciples here that we can translate into our own experience?

I read in the news that there was a young Muslim Christian who was dating a young lady who was herself a Muslim, practicing in the religion of Islam. When her brothers discovered the fact, they came to the young man requiring that he convert and marry the young lady. He agreed to the marriage, but he would not agree to forsake the gospel in the name of Christ. So they abducted him and very cruelly tortured him over a long period of time until they left him dead.

Now we might say, "Well that is far off, and we know that they could be very cruel because of a lack of conversion because of this one who stands for Christ." Why is it that we can't post Ten Commandments in public places when our very legal system is based upon the Commandments? Why is it that we are offended if one bows their head to pray, and then if one does pray if they use the name of Christ? Because the world hates the faith which we hold.

And anytime it is symbolized in anything, anytime there is any reminder or any encouragement to those who would worship the same, it is to be squashed, and it is to be cast out. It is to be repressed. Do we not see it? Do we not understand it? Yet, the Christian Church continues to accommodate herself, as her ministers do, to the world.

And so we do restrict our expressions. We do fall back away from the front lines of the battlefield as it were in the cause of Christ. We do step back so we aren't offensive in our proclamation of the gospel. If we were to be honest, wouldn't we say that many times we don't speak about Christ, or we don't share the gospel because we know it would simply offend others. However, it is their rejection of Christ that condemns them to hell; having been offended by us is nothing compared to what they will suffer in hell.

Now that doesn't mean we need to try to purposefully be offensive, but it means that by holding off sharing the gospel of Christ, we are helping no one. The world is not our friend. We are called out of the world, not as punishment, but for our salvation.

Paul explains the separation of a Christian from the world further in Ephesians, chapter 2, 12 and 13. He says, "Remember that you were at that time separated from Christ, alienated from the commonwealth of Israel and strangers to the covenants of promise, having no hope and without God." Where? In the world. "But now in Christ Jesus you who once were far off have been brought near by the blood of Christ."

An interesting story in Scripture that illustrates this is the story of Lot and his movement to the good lands; Lot and his movement with his family towards Sodom in the plains where they were fertile and where people had begun to populate. He moves from the mountains and remote areas, separating from Abraham. He goes into the plains just outside the city. He sets up his tents.

We're not sure exactly when it happened, but eventually he finds himself inside the city, and based on the description of the house as the angels of the Lord come to bring Lot out of that city, we can say that he has moved away from tents and perhaps bought himself a town house as it were inside Sodom itself. He is well aware of the nature of the city and what goes on in the city, but he has decided that somehow, I suppose psychologically, he has been insulated from that, and that he can live a Godly life in an intolerable circumstance even though he should be separated from it.

So Lot lives in the city with his relatives. The angels come, finding him at the gate. He takes them to his own home, and they tell him of the approaching judgment of God. They tell him to warn his family to get out. Lot goes to his family members who think he is joking. They laugh at him, and they will not leave. Lot himself, the next morning we're told, was lingering. Even told by angels whom he recognized as being messengers of God, told by angels of judgment, he still lingered.

So intoxicating is the affect of the world upon people, upon Christians, that even though in our minds we are aware of the truth, you might still, because of a love of certain worldly activities and certain worldly functions and worldly vices, be searching for some way to rationalize within your own mind a way to hang on. You want to linger—linger in the lostness of what is worldly because of an appetite that has been placed within us and has been fostered and allowed to grow. We love that which is of the world even though God hates that which is of the world.

And so we return to it over and over again, somehow excusing it, or just pretending to be ashamed of ourselves in a humorous kind of way for a laugh, and professing that we're weak in the flesh and hope all understand. But there is nothing funny about that anymore than there was anything funny about the seven priest's sons who were bludgeoned by an evil spirit because they were not walking with the Lord.

James makes it clear what the nature of the world is in chapter 4, verse 4. "You adulterous people! Do you not know that friendship with the world is enmity with God? Therefore whoever wishes to be a friend of the world makes himself an enemy of God." If that wouldn't sober the mind of any Christian and inspire him to flee everything that is worldly, then there is nothing that will. To love the world is to make yourself an enemy of God.

Jesus makes it clear to the disciples that living in service to God and in unity with Christ will necessarily bring hostility from the world to Christ and to all who follow him. Seven times he uses the word *hate* or *hatred*. Just as Jesus called them to love, he now warns them of the world's hate.

Hatred of God's people isn't new. It's historical. Even the psalmist in Psalm 35:19 lamented, "Let not those wink the eye who hate me without cause." Isn't that the mystery of it all? In Christ's ministry, he healed the blind and made them to see. He made the lame to walk. He fed 5,000 when there was no food. He stilled the storms. He healed and cleansed the leper. He explained the Scriptures and without fault. There was no rebuke against his teaching which they could make stick. Everything was explained thoroughly. People marveled at his teachings. They saw his miracles. And yet they hated it. They hated it.

Though he taught clearly and plainly, though he acted in their midst with integrity and hid nothing from them, they hated him. Is there any more testimony we need than that and any more mystery in our own mind as to why—why—would the world hate those who seek to do good? Why does the world hate the true Christian Church? And it does.

Wasn't it the Church that founded most of our nation's hospitals? Wasn't it the Church that founded most of the orphanages when our nation depended on those? Wasn't it the Church that founded most of the institutions of education and higher learning which now have gone completely secular? And yet the world hates the Church and the gospel. The truth of the Scriptures has been pushed out as the very institutions she founded were taken over by the world. And the Church retreated one step after another away from that which she had begun.

The ministries which our nation and which all of civilization have enjoyed since the Church was born are the same ministries which Christ himself performed when he was walking in the streets of Jerusalem. And the Church has experienced the same hatred that Christ himself experienced.

Why? There are two reasons. First of all, because of the words of Jesus. Jesus taught in meekness. He taught in humility. His teaching was always in accordance with the Scriptures. And he was to teach men the way of salvation. Jesus taught clearly throughout his ministry, and their sin was now turned to judgment.

As he came to those who were wallowing around in their own lives, by his revealing to them clearly the will of God, their sin then translated into judgment. It may have been scandalous in the ears of the Pharisees, but it was never slanderous. He didn't slander them even when he told the truth about them.

Why did his word elicit such a strong response? Because before Jesus came, men felt comfortable with mediocrity. Men prefer mediocrity.

They're comfortable in mediocrity. You want to see when a minister begins to get pushed back from his own flock? It's when he calls them to stop living with mediocrity. When he says, "Let's deal with the fact that we are sinners, and let's commit ourselves to live unto God and to forsake sin," and then when he calls them to the mission which Christ has given them, and he calls them to study God's Word.

"Let's not study. Let's presume. Let's go with what we've already known. Let's stay with mediocrity. Let's not go out and wrangle and unsettle people with this proclamation of the gospel. They know I go to church. They'll ask me if they want to go. Let's not talk about sin so much. It's depressing. I said it once. That's sufficient. Let's not go there anymore. Let's stay with the level of mediocrity. Don't challenge me on any front whatsoever. Don't challenge me with the mortification of sin and the flesh. Don't challenge me with being on the mission for Christ. Don't challenge me to grow deep in my understanding in the study of God's Word. Leave me in my mediocrity, or else you will find me a difficult customer to deal with." Such is the way of those who are not comfortable with walking with God.

James Montgomery Boice says, "Before Christ came and spoke, men and women could get by with relative goodness. They could have a little arrogance, but not too much. They could have a little selfishness, but not too much. They could have a little meanness, a little hypocrisy, but after Jesus revealed it for what it is, sin, and people hated the exposure."[2] Isn't that what irritates the world? The exposure the gospel brings.

As the light of Christ shines upon the lives of men, they are exposed for what they are, and so they seek to either crawl back deeper into a hole, or to extinguish the light. They're not comfortable with the light of Christ.

So you find the churches getting busy with many ministries that have very little to do with the light of the gospel shining to be a transformative power in the lives of men. You find a lot of busyness. You find a lot of pleasures. You find a lot of religious traditions. You find a lot of people involved in a lot of religious action. But you don't find the light of the gospel transforming their lives.

Ask yourself and ask those whom you know, "What work is the gospel of Christ doing in your life now? Where is it in your flesh that is

---

2. James Montgomery Boice, p. 1192.

being mortified? That is, where is it that you are putting away sin and growing more in Christ likeness?" Or is it that the power of the gospel is so weak in your own life you can't define or identify where it's having its work? Is it that you can't really recall the last time you were so moved by the gospel that you experienced some significant transformation in your life?

Long-time pastor of Moody Memorial Church in Chicago, H. A. Ironside tells a story of a missionary that I think illustrates the condition of the world and the response of the world. There was a chieftess in a tribe, an African chieftess, who visited a mission station, and while she was there, she saw hanging on a tree outside of the missionary's hut or his building that he had a mirror.

It was just on the tree. She had never seen a mirror before. She walked up to the mirror, and she looked at it long. And then she went over to the missionary, and she asked him, "Who was the ugly person inside the tree?" The chieftess had war paint on, and the paint that they had applied to them was to make them look fierce, was to make them look evil in a way to strike fear and intimidation into the hearts of the enemies. And as she saw her face for the very first time, she saw what looked to her to be an evil and an ugly person.

The missionary explained to her that it was a mirror. She would not believe what she was seeing until he took it down and put it in her hands. She moved it around and could see that indeed that was a reflection of herself. After she sat with the mirror for some time, she decided she must have it. She offered to buy the mirror.

The missionary didn't actually want to sell the mirror that she was holding, and so he resisted. But it became clear that if he didn't sell it, there was going to be trouble. So he set a price, and he sold the mirror to her. She paid for the mirror, and immediately she took the mirror and she threw it to the ground. She said, "I will not have it making faces at me again."

Such is the nature of the world when it comes to the gospel. They think they want all of the hope the gospel gives them. They want to have an eternal life, but that only comes with the recognition that we are sinners and we are far from the righteousness of God, and that we receive Christ, and in receiving Christ, we are then clothed with his righteousness. But it doesn't end there.

Taking Their Hate Out On You

Though our salvation is secure in Christ, the rest of our lives are about the work of the kingdom, which involves the transformation of our entire person that we might love God more and glorify him by being involved in that work of transformation which is by the power of the Spirit.

This is precisely how people respond to the gospel. They want those promises of the future, but when they discover they have to deal with their sin, they want absolutely nothing to do with it—nothing. The words of Jesus reveal our true selves, and the world just won't tolerate it.

The second reason the world hates Jesus, he mentions, is his work. There are many who've come and gone, claiming to enter and to speak for God, or speak to God, or sometimes even to be God when they speak, but none of them have signs and miracles that validate what they claim. The words of Jesus can't be dismissed because the signs of God cause even the unlearned to know that this man is telling the truth.

That which goes along with the proclamation of the gospel which Jesus brings to them bears testimony that the words of Jesus are true because no man could do what Jesus has done. Signs such as the healing of the blind and the cleansing of the leper show our spiritual bankruptcy just as much as his words did. Perhaps beyond even the words and the signs however, the world which we live in today can see the purity and the authenticity of genuine Christian love that is found in a Christian community, and that also will invite persecution.

So much of the world's pursuits involve an inappropriate pursuit of love. We can't say that the world wants nothing of love. The world is *desperate* for love. And they see the love that is shown in the Church from one Christian to another, and they see the love of a Christian for Christ, and they can't apprehend or grasp that love for themselves.

So rather than have a diminished quality of love of their own, they seek to destroy that which they can seemingly never apprehend. When the love of Christ is seen in the lives of his people, it makes the love of the world be seen for what it is. It's filthy. It's inadequate. It's perverse. And it is dead. And so the love which is shown in the Christian Church steels away the false pretensions of love which the world tries to create.

So the world believes that by shutting out the love of Christ, they'll once again be satisfied with that love which they have learned from the world. The bottom line is found in Christ's words, "They hated me without reason." We'll never be able to make it make sense to us. No matter how horrid the cult may be, no matter how vilified a particular leader may be, those associated with the Christian Church are hated more.

No matter what abominable practices a particular religion may have, no matter how many heads our enemies may saw off with their knives, it's the Christian who is vilified as being deceptive and leading people astray. It's the Christian's sin which will be used against the Christian Church to seek to demonstrate hypocrisy and falsehood.

They hate us without reason. But we can be warned to not accommodate ourselves to those who hate Christ. We don't simply want them to love us just because we want to be loved. Our love need is fulfilled in Christ. We don't need to turn to the world. We don't have to become like Lot who took his own family from the safety and security which they enjoyed down to the plains and eventually assimilated into Sodom itself, moving from the suburbs to the city until an angel of God came to tell them to come out. And then he heard his own relatives laugh at the warning, and he himself delayed because of his own affection for the things of the world.

First John 2:15: "Do not love the world or the things in the world. If anyone loves the world, the love of the Father is not in him." We cannot love both. We cannot be both. We cannot be in and of the world and also in and of Christ.

Consider these questions. Are you living too closely to the world? Are you living at the outskirts of Sodom, or have you moved into Sodom itself? Do you sit in the gates of the city and marvel at the sin around you while at the same time being in amongst it yourself?

Is your testimony diluted because of your affection to the world? Is it hard for you to profess Christ while you at the same time are participating in loving all of the life that those who are lost enjoy? Does your love for Christ and his people contrast so strongly with the brokenness of the world that you find those who reject God also rejecting you? And do you find because of the way you live your life that those who God is calling are drawn to you because they recognize in you the voice of Christ as you proclaim the gospel?

We should live in imitation of Christ, not doing anything to earn the hatred of the world except on account of our unity and love for Christ and his love for us.

18

Part 1, Pass It On

John 15:26–27

"But when the Helper comes, whom I will send to you from the Father, the Spirit of truth, who proceeds from the Father, he will bear witness about me. And you also will bear witness, because you have been with me from the beginning."

THE CHURCH HAS SEEN a loss of authority. When the Church speaks, people do not necessarily listen. In fact, people are free in their own minds, certainly not by the counsel of God, but in their own mind, they are free to dismiss the Church, dismiss the Church's teaching, dismiss the worship of God, dismiss all things Christian. They feel that sovereign, divine authority in themselves to be the Church and to decide what is right and wrong concerning the Christian life.

The Church has lost authority not only in this century, but it has been cyclical. The Church has seen its authority wane, and then be recovered, and then wane, and be recovered again. The Church addressed this loss of authority in the 18th century with what was called the Boyle Lectures at the time.

Having lost its impact on people, the Church sought to remedy it, and the way they sought to remedy it was through apologetics, and through lectures, and through teaching to put the Scriptures before the people and say, "The Scriptures are solid. The Scriptures teach truth." Appealing through teaching to the people, the Church sought to reestablish its authority, not through fear and intimidation, but by causing people to once again look upon the Scriptures.

The Last Sermon of Christ

In the 19th century, the Church again sought to establish authority, or to reassert its authority by remodeling the Church, that is seeking to redo the Church aesthetically, and ended up with what we might call a proto-Catholic appearance. It created ornate vestments for ministers, and it recessed the pulpit into a nave in the church, and established once again the appearance of an altar, seeking to give an air of dignity to the Church, hoping that the beefed-up ministerial training would also impart confidence to the people as they came to hear the clergy in the church.

So through sight and through sound and through stringent educational requirements, the Church sought to reestablish people's confidence in what the Church is and what the Church stood for. But none of these really slowed the decline of the Church until around 1857 when there was a revival that broke out in America, a genuine spiritual revival.

Today, we see churches on quest for authority again. We see the searching for authority as even the most faithful are so quick to dismiss the church and their God. Some are using money and publicity as enticements to bring in the people. Others are focusing again on academics and lectures. And still more are looking solely to what we might call a hyper-spirituality or a romantic view of the Church either through ecstatic gifts or through concert-style musical programs. But still the Church loses ground.

Despite every attempt, and despite all strategies, the Church continues to lose ground, born out by recent statistical evidence that has been taken. Martyn Lloyd-Jones notes that Hegel's dictum about history is true. "History teaches us that history teaches us nothing."[1]

We seem determined to repeat all the same errors of our forefathers. We see those who neglected the faith to their own ruin, and seem to somehow think we are able to do the same to our own glory. We seem determined to take the same path and others who struggled.

We seem unable to appreciate the exclusive authority of the Scriptures in our lives and at the same time rely on the exclusive authority of the Holy Spirit. We seem to struggle with either Spirit or Scripture. We seem to think it either needs to be spiritual or academic. Ours is a historic error, but one that is to our own detriment.

First Peter 1:12: Things "announced to you through those who preached the good news to you by the Holy Spirit sent from heaven,

---

1. Martyn Lloyd-Jones, *Glorious Christianity*, 176.

things into which angels long to look." Things announced to you through those who preached the good news by the power of the Holy Spirit. In this verse, 1 Peter 1, we find yoked together the Scripture—the preaching, the study of Scripture is exhorted in the Scriptures themselves—and also the Holy Spirit.

Martyn Lloyd-Jones considered the authority of the Holy Spirit one of the most important areas of study concerning authority from a practical standpoint. We can talk about the authority of the Church, we can talk about the authority of Scripture, we can talk about the authority of Christ, but unless the Holy Spirit himself is authoritative, then the Scriptures will never open up to our eyes and our hearts to God.

It's practical because the authority of Christ in Scripture is simply academic unless the Spirit opens our eyes and changes our hearts—a study of the Holy Spirit, the work of the Holy Spirit. In the 17th century, Puritans divided into two camps over the action and the work of the Holy Spirit, over a disagreement concerning the authority of the Spirit and the authority of Scriptures.

There were those who said that nothing mattered except the Spirit. They became known as the Quakers. They felt there was nothing that mattered except the internal light, or the internal testimony of the Spirit. And this position resulted in a depreciated place of the Spirit in the midst of mainline Protestants as they began to react to this hyper-spirituality of the Quakers.

And so as the Quakers began to push one way with this exclusive look at the Holy Spirit with a disregard of the revealed Scripture, the response to it in the Puritan community was to devalue the work of the Spirit and to focus solely on a study of the language and the words of the Scripture.

The work of the Holy Spirit, the person of the Holy Spirit, and particularly in the passage of this chapter, led to the controversy that split the Church east and west. We might think that it's of no consequence, but imagine what the Church would be today if there wasn't the Eastern Orthodox, and then the Western Church, as it was originally in the Roman Church, and then ultimately the reform that led to multiple protestant denominations.

The *Filioque* clause, as it's called—*Filioque* is simply Latin for *the son*, or *from the son*—is about where and how the Holy Spirit is sent. In the text, it says that Christ will send the Holy Spirit, but it says that the Father sends the Holy Spirit. Christ asks, and the Father sends.

The Nicene Creed, which is in many hymnbooks—originally simply said that the Holy Spirit proceeds from the Father. The Western faction of the Church became concerned that that was depreciating the doctrine of the Trinity, and so they said, "From the Father and the Son together," because the Father and the Son are united in the Godhead.

The Eastern faction of the Church said, "No. You have to be literal from this verse." So the Western Church was taking a theological approach in saying, "All of Scripture testifies to the unity of Trinity, and we can't take one verse of Scripture and then devalue the Trinity by trying to make a formal statement that doesn't include the idea of the Trinity." But the Eastern Church was resolute and said, "The Scripture at that point does not state it the way you have. Therefore we will not include it in the creed."

The Western Church included it in the creed. The Eastern Church rejected the clause, choosing to emphasize that the Son and the Spirit both come from the Father. And so there became a question of the eternal generation of the Son and the Spirit. The clause became a major flashpoint between east and west until 867 when Constantinople declared it a heresy, and a full schism occurred after a number of attempts at reconciliation in 1054. There have been many attempts to reunite since then, but the Eastern and Western Churches remain separate to this day.

Why bring up this historical point? Well as Christians, it's important we understand our own family history and certainly division of the Church. Just as we might joke about Hatfields and McCoys, the separation of the east from the west has been a feud that has continued to this very day! And there is very little communication between the east and the west. You will not find much success of the Western Church in the east, and likewise much success of the Eastern Church in the west.

This is our history. This is who we are. This is how we came to be who we are. And it was over a controversy on the Holy Spirit—his purpose, his work, and even where the Spirit came from and how we came to receive him. The Holy Spirit is, if you will, the fulcrum of salvivic history—certainly of salvivic mission.

Chapter 15, verses 18 through 25 teach there is a hatred of the world that is turned toward Jesus, and that hatred will continue towards him through the Disciples. It's hatred of Christ that turns people on the Disciples. We might wonder why. If Jesus is going away, why would that hatred continue? Why wouldn't they simply dismiss the disciples as just one more cult they can ignore?

Acts 9 describes that hatred in detail with a familiar figure to us. "Saul, still breathing threats and murder against the disciples of the Lord." Deep was the hatred of Christ. Luther observed, "The Spirit of truth opposes lies and false arguments for the world too is full of its spirits. As the saying goes, Wherever God erects a church, the devil builds his chapel or tavern next to it. That is, wherever God's Word springs up in purity, the devil ushers in sex, factions, and many false spirits who also deck themselves in glory and in the name of Christ and his Church.

Luther observed that the enemies of the gospel are often those who appear to be members of the gospel itself, members of Christ. And yet they are the enemies of Christ.

As Jesus describes the persecution and hatred of the world against himself and the Church, he interrupts himself. As he is going on with the Disciples about how bad they can expect life to become after his ascension, he interrupts himself and connects the attitude of the world with the work of the Spirit.

Some have wondered why Jesus suddenly stops after he says, "They hated me without a cause." The next two verses talk about the wonder of the Holy Spirit, and then Jesus returns to the difficulties of walking in the way of Christ. He is connecting the attitude of the world with the work of the Spirit and the position of the apostles with their place in the Spirit and the coming of the Spirit.

For the New Testament age, the Holy Spirit is again the fulcrum of our salvation life. The Holy Spirit is described by Jesus first as a helper or a comforter. So Jesus is first striking a tone. After this phrase, "They hated me without a cause," Jesus is now taking a tone of consolation by introducing the Holy Spirit as the *Paraclete,* the One who would comfort them.

He is telling the apostles that their struggle will not be theirs alone, but that the Holy Spirit will come alongside them in their duty to him, that the Holy Spirit will not abandon them, that Christ himself will not abandon them. Calvin, a great Reformer, said, "In opposition to the wicked fury of these men, that is, the adversaries of the gospel, Christ

The Last Sermon of Christ

produces the testimony of the Spirit. And if their consciences rest on this testimony, they will never be shaken."[2]

What a promise the Lord has given. He is telling the Disciples, "You will carry the gospel forward. You will continue the ministry I have begun. And you will do so in the face of horrific persecution. But you will not falter, and you will not faint because I will give to you the Holy Spirit, and the Holy Spirit will walk with you to assure you and to strengthen you and to empower the words and work of your ministry."

Their success will not be based upon their ingenuity and strength of the flesh. It will not be based upon their ability to wax eloquently and to speak well. It will not be based upon a particular strategy for church growth or a particular plan. Instead, it will be based on the converting power of the Holy Spirit in the hearts of those who have ears to hear the Word the disciples deliver. The work of the Paraclete is to establish their confidence, to shore them up and encourage them in the face of extreme circumstances.

I think a wonderful example of this from the Scriptures comes from the book of Daniel. In chapter 3, Nebuchadnezzar had made an idol of gold and demanded that all people in all places would worship this idol of gold. The Chaldeans came to Nebuchadnezzar, and they told him there were a people, the Jews, who were not worshiping his idol exclusively as the only god.

Shadrach, Meshach, and Abednego were brought forward and were called on the carpet for their not bowing to this idol. Nebuchadnezzar is described as being "filled with fury" against them. He ordered the furnace heated seven times its usual heat. The three were bound, and still in their clothes thrown into the fire alive.

But when Nebuchadnezzar looked into the flames, he saw four men, not three, walking in the midst of the fire. And the fire had not harmed the three. They were delivered from the flames.

This is the experience of the one who would serve Christ. Do you think the world is excited to hear that there should be a conviction for the sin they love? That they should repent and turn away from the desires of the flesh? It's the desires of the flesh. It's what they want! It's what they live for. Such things are their goals and their ambitions.

Do you think the gospel is welcome to a people who find that the gospel pulls them in just the opposite direction—a direction of

---

2. Calvin, *Commentary on the Gospel According to John*, 130.

selflessness, of humility, of service, of duty? Those are the exact opposite of what we're born to. We're born to live for self, to seek pleasure and happiness, to fulfill our own desires, to go after whatever we want to go after. That is the way of the flesh. It's the way of Satan, not the way of the Lord.

Do you think the gospel which calls people to feel the guilt of that sin will be welcomed? Do you think the gospel which calls them to repent and turn away from what is most familiar to them, the work and love of the flesh, do you think that will be received well? Of course not.

So what will the world do? Will it allow you to continue to point out the hypocrisy in their sin? They'll do one of two things. They'll run away from you, or they'll seek to destroy you. Either they'll get away from you, or they will seek your silence. They'll either seek to put you out of their community if they don't want to move, or they'll seek to simply discredit you, or they'll seek to silence you through persecution, leading ultimately to death.

As John Calvin describes it, "When the world rages on all sides, our only protection is that the truth of God, sealed by the Holy Spirit on our hearts, despises and defies all that is in the world, for if it were subject to the opinions of men, our faith would be overwhelmed a hundred times in one day."[3] Just that alone is worthy of our taking a moment to ponder.

If it were left to my will without the aid of the Holy Spirit, at least a hundred times a day I'd forsake the faith. I do not have the power in my own flesh to do the things of God from my own will. And I prove it day after day.

But thank God Almighty there is the Holy Spirit, and I am called back, and I do repent, and I do return to God, and he does forgive and restore me, and I'm left with an assurance because of the Holy Spirit that though I stumble and though I fall, my God still loves me. Without the Holy Spirit, I have no such assurance at all. I have only my sin, the sin which I love, which God hates, which will not put me in good stead with the Father.

Martin Luther said, "Behold this work of the Spirit, this presence of the Spirit, leads to a confident and staunch heart that can scorn the devil with all his terror and torment, defile his might, and say, 'Sin, if you want to condemn me, you will first have to condemn Christ my

3. Ibid.

dear Savior, Priest, and Intercessor with the Father. Death, if you want to devour me, you must begin on top with Christ my Head. Devil and world, if you want to torment and frighten me, you must first pull him down from his throne.'

"In brief, I will fear nothing, for Christ is mine with his suffering, death, and life, the Holy Spirit with his comfort, and the Father himself, with all his grace. He sends the Holy Spirit to preach Christ into my heart and fill it with his consolation. So we can conclude that because the Spirit of God is with us, not only are we not overcome by the world, but we press on knowing that even the gates of hell will not prevail against the Church."[4]

What a confidence we as Christians have. What a confidence we have as we serve Christ and his Church. This Comforter whom the Lord has sent is not only our encouragement, but he is our key, our power, our only means to victory. Not only are we assured of our forgiveness of sins in Christ, but also we are assured of our eventual victory in Christ. Already the victory is sealed, but we will be raised in glory and see for ourselves that which has been promised. And what purpose does the world have of this because the world's end is to end? Nothing built in this life, no kingdom that is built, no pleasure is lasting.

Ecclesiastes is an ancient book with a modern impact. Ecclesiastes could have been published in the past few years with a title appealing to a post-modern world, and nothing in the text would need changing. Ecclesiastes deals with the loss of meaning for life. It is written for those looking for something solid, something to hang their hat on, so to speak, and after all their seeking and grasping for meaning, they find that brokenness is all this life can offer them. No matter what the promise of passing pleasures or success, every hope the world can give will at the same time crush them.

And ultimately, God willing, at the end of their life, they will learn that it is only the gospel and only Christ that can give them any happiness, joy, and hope. Tragically, they're left with the scars. Tragically, they're left with a past that brings them shame to mention it. But that becomes a testimony, a testimony of a life that was truly lost and has now been found.

The work of the Holy Spirit, which we will continue to explore at least for one more time together in this passage, is to take the Word

---

4. Martin Luther, *Luther's Works*, 292.

of God, to make it alive to the hearts that have the hand of God upon them. Not the Spirit alone, but the Spirit with the Word. Not the Word alone, but the Word with the Spirit.

And with the Word being proclaimed by the apostles, those without the Spirit are opposed and will persecute. And those with the Spirit will rejoice for the day of their salvation has arrived.

19

Part 2, Inspiration and Illumination

John 15:26–27

"But when the Helper comes, whom I will send to you from the Father, the Spirit of truth, who proceeds from the Father, he will bear witness about me. And you also will bear witness, because you have been with me from the beginning."

THIS PASSAGE CONTINUES TO unpack the remarkable teaching of Jesus as he continues his disclosure of the work of the Holy Spirit." Even with such clarity in these verses, there is still a great deal of confusion that exists in the Church of Jesus Christ about the Person, work, and our experience with the Holy Spirit.

There are those who feel that the work of the Holy Spirit is to come upon an individual from time to time, to anoint them with some special grace from time to time, that they might experience some ecstatic gift from time to time. There are those who pray that the Holy Spirit would be poured out for revival. And while the sentiment is clear, the Holy Spirit has already been poured out—it was so at Pentecost. And so are we praying that a Spirit who is far removed would be poured out again? What exactly are we praying for?

The sentiment is true enough. We do pray that God would revive his Church, and we do know that that is by the Holy Spirit. But we must be careful in our language else we train each other and the world to view the Holy Spirit as away, and we are asking him to come. The Holy Spirit is here. What we need is to be a people who are surrendered unto the work of the Holy Spirit, looking in the right place for the work of the

Holy Spirit, lest we become confused even in our own devout yet errant theology concerning this, the third Person of the Trinity.

What is the Holy Spirit is doing? We mentioned in the previous chapter that Jesus' farewell discourse is moving in close to that great high priestly prayer at chapter 17, but teaching vitally about the work and the Person of the Holy Spirit.

We mentioned in the preceding chapter that this work of the Holy Spirit in the face of persecution from the world is to come and comfort, to come and be One who abides with believers, to be a Helper to the people. The word *Paraclete*, One who comes alongside of to bring counsel and advice, and to comfort, to strengthen and give resolve. We concluded that because the Spirit of God is with us, not only are we not overcome by the world, but we press on knowing that even the gates of hell will not prevail against the Church.

In saying that, we acknowledge the gates of hell will rail against the Church, that the gates of hell will fire whatever volleys and rounds and darts and temptations it can muster against the Church. The gates of hell will also shout against the Church words of discouragement and words of temptation. Just as in the story of sailors who heard the siren song that caused them to shipwreck on the rocks of the islands, there will be those songs that are sung to the Church, seeking to draw the Church away from the true gospel of Jesus Christ.

But the Scriptures are clear that none of that will prevail. None of it will prevail because our God is greater than Assyria. Our God is greater than Babylon. Our God is greater than hell, and so none of that will prevail against Christ's Church. There is power, and there is an authority in God's Church that is only slightly understood by God's people. And not only is it slightly understood, but it is seldom relied upon by God's people.

We turn to human devices. We turn to our own wisdom. Seldom do we know how rightly to call upon God in the power and the work of the Holy Spirit, to be empowered by God through the Spirit, to use that which God has given us in the ministry and work of the Church. Perhaps that is why the ministry of the Church is so anemic at points because we are relying not upon the strong arm of the Lord, but upon our own arm and our own feet and our own voice.

The Church of Jesus Christ is a Church with a mission and an advantage. The power of God is at the Church's disposal in the Person of the Holy Spirit. Jesus describes the Holy Spirit as a Comforter and as a Spirit of truth. The weapons of Satan and the world are sin and death, temptation and despair, but he makes our resolve to crumble while God makes our hearts to be strengthened. He causes our hearts to melt, but the Spirit says, "Go on and do as you are commanded. God desires to save."

So in the face of temptation, in the face of despair, in the face of crumbling resolve, instead of adjusting ourselves to the world so we no longer feel the tension, the Spirit of Christ says, "Be strong and go as I have taught you. Go as I have commanded you, and you will not fail, and you will not falter, and you will not stumble as long as you keep your feet on the path which I have set before you."

But what are the means we actually utilize to accomplish this? We must wonder, *how? How does God do that? How am I to know that is actually what happens? Is this a promise simply for the future that we cling to now, and just that clinging is what keeps us secure? Or is there an actual working of the Holy Spirit, an activity of the Holy Spirit that causes me to realize these strengths and truths and resolves now?*

When we say the ministry of the Holy Spirit is the fulcrum of salvation history, we go further and say the Holy Spirit is life to a believer. It's the fulcrum of salvation history and is life to the one who is in Christ. We've made the Holy Spirit central and essential to Church doctrine and practice when we say that.

If we say, "You must have the Holy Spirit to be saved," then we are saying our ministry must have some concept of how that is accomplished; otherwise, when we preach the gospel, what are we expecting people to grab hold of if we lack any understanding of the Holy Spirit in our practice as a church?

The Holy Spirit's work is a preserving work as our Comforter, which we've already explored. But in addition to that, the Holy Spirit has a prophetic work and a transforming work because this is the work and the power of God. The Church has a power to carry the gospel to all nations by the witness of the Spirit through the apostles.

Most would agree with a statement that a dead church and a dead religion is one that is devoid of the presence of the Holy Spirit. None would advocate a dead church. None would advocate a dead religion, one that has simply form, but no substance, one that powerless for the edification of an individual, much like any radio program or television program would be.

One seeks to have in their church a life, not simply a representation of something else. One seeks to have a church that is infused with the life of God in the Person of the Holy Spirit, not simply a form of religion, but one that is true.

Some have proclaimed the idea in their seeking of these manifestations of authenticity, in their search for a continuing apostolic ministry, that there is still a God speaking to his people just as he spoke to the apostles. In essence, there is still direct revelation from God. But this is simply not true.

Some seek to empty their minds. Some go into dark places. Some will recite a single verse over and over to empty their minds so that God can speak to them, learning through different sorts of meditation that are more Eastern in their origination than they are scriptural. And in so doing, they hope to hear God speak in a dream, or in a vision, or to fill their mind because it is empty.

But nowhere in Scripture is there any example or command that would say, Empty your mind. "Be quiet and silent before the Lord" simply means, "Close your mouth and quit speaking from your own mind and seek out the will of the Lord." It doesn't say, "Have a mind that is empty." In fact, the warning is there are many spirits that will whisper in the ears of anyone who has a vacant space for them to fill.

There used to be in the time of the Reformers a group that was called Enthusiasts. Now we know them as Charismatics, but it was the same essential theology. They were people who were on a quest to know God by the Spirit, and they wanted to know his will, and they were seeking earnestly after that. And we have no fault against that seeking.

However, they did so in a hyper-spiritual sense. Instead of looking in the right place, they looked within themselves. And in looking within themselves, they were not hearing the Spirit of God, but they were hearing their own conscience, their own inner voice, whatever you might choose to call it. But God instructs us as to where he speaks and how he communicates to his people.

While we may suffer from a deficit of practical knowledge about the Holy Spirit, misunderstandings continue to divide the Church. And so we must find clarity on this issue of the Person of the Holy Spirit.

The Last Sermon of Christ

The question is not whether the Holy Spirit comes and works, but how he comes and works, and how he operates with his people. We wonder how he is doing that. God is not sitting idle. God is active, or else the Church wouldn't even exist today! But his people have been derelict in their duty to understand what God is doing with his people and how he is doing it.

Most agree with Romans 8:9, "Anyone who does not have the Spirit of Christ does not belong to him," but disagree on how what is dead becomes living. What are the means of the Holy Spirit's work? That is really, I think, what we're asking. If we get down to the kernel of truth, we can make statements, we can put forth propositions, and we can assert what is true about the Person of the Holy Spirit, but what we really want to know is, *What are the means God uses with the Holy Spirit to cause that which is dead to become alive?*

What are the means God uses? Is it simply something supernatural, or are there means that are employed? Does it simply happen, or does God use a device or means to accomplish his will?

We would find the answer in the great battle cry of the Reformation, *sola scriptura*. Scripture alone is the means, the written Word, not simply internal feelings or impressions or some significant experience. In John 16:13, we read that "When the Spirit of truth comes, he will guide you into all the truth."

So what does this work of the Spirit look like then? What does our verse teach us about the work of the Spirit? The first thing it teaches us is the doctrine of inspiration, and secondly, the doctrine of illumination. Look at the passage. "When the Helper comes, whom I will send to you from the Father. . . ." Here we have the sending of the Spirit. "The Spirit of truth. . . ," this now establishes the content of the Spirit's ministry.

And it "proceeds from the Father." It has a mission from God. As Christ was sent from the Father with a mission, so the Spirit is sent from the Father with a mission, and that is to "bear witness about me." The Holy Spirit is a testifier, and testifies about Christ. How does he do that? "You also will bear witness, because you have been with me from the beginning."

Is he speaking here of you and of me? We know we are to bear witness. We have the Great Commission, so no one is in anyway seeking to either water down or rebut that. But here he is speaking particularly of the apostles. Were you with Christ from the beginning? Were you there as he ministered in Judea and Jerusalem? I was not. While I'm indwelled by the Holy Spirit, and I have his Word, and I have the narrative of that, it was the apostles who were there with Christ from the beginning.

The inspiration of Scripture is the directing of the writing of the Scriptures which are the testimony concerning Christ given by the Holy Spirit through the apostles. Inspiration is the work of the Holy Spirit to use a human witness to record God's Word. Second Peter 1:21: "No prophecy was ever produced by the will of man, but men spoke from God as they were carried along by the Holy Spirit."

Now inspiration is not possession. Jesus said, "The Spirit testifies and you," that is the apostles, "will testify," because they had been with him from the beginning. What is the significance of their having been with him from the beginning? The apostles had a treasure that was unique to them, and it was not given by the Holy Spirit.

Do you know what that treasure, unique to the apostles, not given by the Holy Spirit is? A first-hand knowledge, a historic knowledge of the ministry of Jesus. Is that important? Of course it is. In Acts, chapter 1, when Judas, the one who betrayed Christ was to be replaced, the requirement was that he would be selected from one who had been with Jesus from the beginning. The requirement for the new twelfth apostle was that it he needed to be one who had firsthand knowledge of the ministry of Jesus Christ.

The Holy Spirit didn't teach the apostles history, but he revealed history's meaning to them, and gave them remembrance of all of those things which they otherwise would have forgotten. The gospels are the history of their knowledge through experience of the Lord Jesus Christ. The epistles are their explanation of what that history means.

Martyn Lloyd-Jones criticized the conflict in the minds of some people between the authority of Scripture and the authority of the Holy Spirit; such is a false and unnecessary conflict: 'The Bible suggests, therefore, that the Holy Spirit normally speaks to us through the Word. He takes his own Word, he illumines it, and takes our minds and enlightens them, and we are thus made receptive to the Word.... It is not right, therefore to speak of the Spirit or the Word, but rather of the Spirit and the Word, and especially the Spirit through the Word."[1]

---

1. Gregg Allison, *Historical Theology: An Introduction to Christian Doctrine*, p. 97.

The second work of the Holy Spirit is illumination. If anything is illuminated, that means that it has light shown upon it. It is made so that we can understand it.

If you're stumbling along in the darkness, you might take a flashlight, and in turning it on, you illumine the way before you so you won't stumble or fall. Or you might flip the light switch to illuminate the room so that you can see where the things are that you need; otherwise, you trip and you fall. You have accidents.

The same is true in the spiritual life. Without illumination, we will trip, and we will fall. We'll have accidents, and we'll stumble. We may even be in the wrong room and never even know it without illumination. What is truly sad is when those who are blind believe they see when they truly see nothing at all.

The Holy Spirit inspired the writers in the past, but he continues to bear witness today. The Spirit testifies today. The Holy Spirit is sent on mission from God to man. The work of the Holy Spirit is to bear witness concerning Christ. So his witness can be considered as that of an advocate, speaking to support the testimony of Jesus, and through his Word the apostles.

As the disciples tell the story and explain it, the Holy Spirit brings light to the truth of revelation, and that illumination takes place in the mind of the listener to understand the word. That truth then weighs on their conscience. That is the process by which we are saved.

The Spirit, working through the apostles, rendered to us an accurate account of the work and ministry and teaching of Christ. Then those same apostles, still because of the illumination of the Spirit in their own life inspiring them as it were, write in their epistles, their letters, the truths revealed concerning Christ and explain them, giving us the doctrines which we know and which we live by.

Then the individual believer, post-apostolic, takes up the Scripture or hears the gospel preached, and in hearing that gospel, the Holy Spirit illumining the mind of the listener, the believer now becomes aware of sin and the need for salvation lest he/she stands under the judgment of God.

The conscience being burdened, the individual then, with perhaps hands out and heads raised, calls out to God for mercy through Jesus Christ. But the person would not know to do that, nor would he/she have a will to do that if it were not for the transforming power of the Holy Spirit in the hearts of people.

The work of the Holy Spirit is experienced by everybody who truly believes. No one who truly has believed in Christ has been without the work of the Holy Spirit. First John 2:20: "You have been anointed by the Holy One, and you all have knowledge."

Does that mean we know everything as if we are the Internet, devoid of all of its errors of course, which would probably make it less than half its original size? No, we don't have all of that knowledge in our head. That is not what he is talking about. You have all knowledge necessary for salvation.

First Corinthians 2:12 through 13: "Now we have received not the spirit of the world, but the Spirit who is from God, that we might understand the things freely given us by God. And we impart this in words not taught by human wisdom but taught by the Spirit." Imparted with words, not informed by human wisdom, but by the Spirit.

Notice the dynamics. Words, words, words. The preaching of the gospel, the ministering of the gospel, the testimony of Christians is in words, and then those words are taken up and used by the Spirit. "Not taught by human wisdom but taught by the Spirit, interpreting spiritual truths to those who are spiritual."

That which is spoken anywhere the Scriptures are truly preached with anything other than simply headline statements, where the Scriptures are unfolded and opened before the people is not understood unless it is by the power and work of the Holy Spirit because there is no place where our humanity can empathize with the power of God. It's all so distant from us unless the Holy Spirit draws it near.

What does the Holy Spirit do in illuminating us? What is it actually going to accomplish as far as the change in our life?

First of all, *comprehension*. The truth concerning Christ is to understand and believe. Like the Roman guard who was before the Cross, we will say, "Surely this Man is the Son of God." That is not something that is learned by the flesh. It is something revealed by God. Just as when Peter said, "You are the Christ," then Jesus said, "This was revealed to you by the Father. You did not come up with that on your own." It's revealed by the power and the work of the Holy Spirit.

Our comprehension is when the Holy Spirit alone gives true understanding. In First John 2:27, John was dealing with those antichrists, people who had been in the church, and though many thought they actually were converted and they had been accepted as converts and believers, now they had gone out of it because as the gospel came in, they went out from it. They had never been true converts.

Like the seed on rocky soil that sprang up quickly, perhaps even presented a wonderful and a beautiful flower on its head, they withered just as fast. First John 2:27: "We have an anointing of the Holy Spirit that abides in us to teach us all things."

Conviction is the second accomplishment. If we truly understand who Jesus is, we will at once see ourselves in a new light. We will sing "Amazing Grace" with a sober mind, and we will identify with the word *wretch* in that song. We'll be broken like David when he said his sin was always before him.

And then third, we will believe and we will *commit*. We have several examples of belief and conversion in the Scripture. One is Nicodemus, a learned man of the Jewish religion, steeped in the Scriptures themselves. Nicodemus felt his problem was one of understanding. He thought that Jesus' teaching was simply at a more advanced stage than his own understanding.

He knew Jesus was from God because of the miracles Jesus performed, and no man could do these. He simply wanted what he needed in addition to what he already had. But Jesus tells him, "You can't get there from here. You can't simply add to what you already thought you had. You were born wrong. You started from the wrong place. You were born of flesh, and what is born of flesh is flesh. What is born of Spirit is Spirit."

When Paul went to Europe, he met with a small group of women outside the city gate of Philippi on a Sunday afternoon. Lydia, a woman who worked with purple cloth, was in that group. And in Acts 16:14, we read, "The Lord opened her heart to pay attention to what was said by Paul." She was the first European convert to Christianity, but she wasn't saved by Paul, but by the power of the Holy Spirit working through the Word.

That is supported in 1 Corinthians 12:3. "Therefore I want you to understand that no one speaking in the Spirit of God ever says 'Jesus is accursed!' and no one can say 'Jesus is Lord' except in the Holy Spirit." Without the Holy Spirit, there is no work in a person's heart. The heart lies dead.

We will believe in the atoning and saving work of Jesus when the gospel has its work by the power of the Holy Spirit. We'll believe in God's grace being extended to us, and we'll commit ourselves to the Lord. This is the Word that is nearest in our mouth and in our heart. This is what we preach—the truth of God recorded by the apostles. This is the wonderful truth we bear witness to today.

This is your testimony. This is my testimony. But what makes this even more powerful is that this is the Spirit of God's testimony. As Isaiah said in 59:21, "'This is my covenant with them,' says the LORD: 'My Spirit that is upon you, and my words that I have put in your mouth, shall not depart out of your mouth, or out of the mouth of your offspring, or out of the mouth of your children's offspring,' says the LORD, 'from this time forth and forevermore.'"

The Word that the Lord has put in our mouth is there by the power of the Holy Spirit. When the Word of God goes out, it doesn't return void because of the power of the Holy Spirit and the ministry of the Holy Spirit. The Word of God was given to us by inspired writers who had been with Jesus in the beginning, thus nullifying any claim for continued apostolic ministry.

We are disciples, not apostles. We haven't been with Jesus to understand in history with our own eyes his walking among the Jews, and heard with our own ears his teaching, which then the Holy Spirit working uniquely would cause us to remember and to reflect upon and to record accurately. That belonged to the apostles.

What we do have are the Scriptures. We have that story. We have the Christ who is real and living, and we have him through the power of the Holy Spirit with us this very day. "Wherever two or more are gathered," Jesus says, "I am with you there." And we know that the Holy Spirit works to take the hearts of unbelievers and illumine the Scriptures to them to bring them life.

So what is our imperative? Our imperative is to take this Word of God and keep it open before the world that any whom the Holy Spirit is working with will come to know Christ through the agency of the Scriptures, through the agency of preaching and teaching, through the agency of witnessing and testimony, and then conversion comes by the Holy Spirit.

Some have sought God somewhere besides his Word. Some have heard the voice of a spirit, but not the Holy Spirit. Some listen to God

The Last Sermon of Christ

in his Word. Some preach God from his Word. Some believe God as he has revealed himself in his Word, and those come to know the truth of God.

So sound again, we say, the battle cry of the Reformation, for this is the only tool, this is the only device, this is the only work of the Church—preach the Word of God that men may be saved.

20

Perseverance: Running on Fumes

John 16:1–4

"I have said all these things to you to keep you from falling away. They will put you out of the synagogues. Indeed, the hour is coming when whoever kills you will think he is offering service to God. And they will do these things because they have not known the Father, or me. But I have said these things to you, that when their hour comes you may remember that I told them to you."

THESE VERSES ON PERSECUTION are nested in Jesus' teaching on the Holy Spirit. The Holy Spirit will be empowering the ministry of the apostles, and Jesus has been giving them in chapter 14 words of comfort. In chapter 15, he gave them words of admonishment, and in 16 now, he is giving them some predictions.

The work of the Spirit takes place through Christ's church today, and the church ministers while living even as an alien in this world. The apostles are going to have to come to realize that they, in their becoming persons saved through Jesus Christ and being a citizen in the kingdom of heaven, will now be aliens in the world, and that the world in which they have dwelled, the world of Judaism, the world of Israel, will no longer be their safe abode, but because of the gospel, they will now become enemies even of that place which gave birth to Christ. From where that ministry came, it will now turn upon them. The Spirit hasn't come and isn't called a Comforter because our journey is easy, and neither was theirs.

The Last Sermon of Christ

It's not a journey that will take place over wide-open plains and unobstructed, straight paths. Our ministry, as the apostles' ministry, takes place in what we might rightly call the "fog of war," a fog of resistance, a fog of temptation, a fog of oppression, a fog of persecution, and all of these are greater than our own strength. It is only by the power and the ministry of the Holy Spirit that we will not only persevere, but also be successful and victorious in the cause of Christ. We will persevere.

I remember driving as a young man. My father had an old GMC Suburban, and the gas gauge in that truck didn't work, and neither did my billfold when it came to buying gas. So I would take this big Suburban, which probably got three miles to the gallon, and I would try to do the math computations (math, not my greatest skill), and I would drive downtown.

On my way home, thankfully this particular GMC—I love good American ingenuity—would give you a warning that it was going to run out of gas. It would cut off once about two miles before you were completely out of gas. You could re-crank the engine, and you knew you only had a very short time to find some gas. It would never fail that I would be able to coast into a gas station. I would just run on fumes until I coasted into a station to be filled back up.

How much that has instructed me on the Christian life. Seldom do I feel that my tank is full and I can take on the world and travel the distance because I topped it off at the last stop. I always feel spiritually I'm running on fumes, and I know I would be left stranded except by the power and the work of the Holy Spirit that causes me to persevere.

With all that Jesus had promised the apostles, (he had given them these words of comfort) the apostles may have easily believed their work was going to be easy, or at least well-received. Think for just a moment about what they're hearing. Jesus begins after the Lord's Supper, and then they journeyed into Jerusalem, and there were throngs waiting for him as they laid down palm branches, and they sang, "Hallelujah." They were on an emotional high with great anticipation.

Then we have the celebration of Passover, which is a positive celebration of God's redemptive work among the people, but it was there at the supper that things began to become strange for them as Jesus put a towel around his waist to teach them servanthood. Then Jesus predicted that he would be betrayed, not only by Judas, but that all of them would flee when his name was called against them.

Perseverance: Running on Fumes

Judas leaves mysteriously, and they're confused. Then Jesus announces the time has arrived, that he is going to be leaving them. Despair has begun to set in, but he says, "Don't despair because I'm going to prepare a place for you, and that place will be greater than the first." So now they're excited again, and Jesus says to them, "And after I leave, I will send you a Holy Spirit, my Spirit. I will dwell with you, and you will accomplish great and wonderful things for the Lord in my name as long as the Word abides in you, and you obey my commands."

So as they are set for this, and they're beginning to think they're going to take this great Word in the power of Christ to the nation of Israel and to the people of Jerusalem, they must anticipate there will be a great reception, just as they saw on the day of the triumphal entry. There is an anticipation of success, and so Jesus has to correct them and say, "There is something about this ministry that you need to know. You won't be received well. In fact, they're going to throw you out of the synagogues, and then failing to silence you, they'll even plot your murder. You will be so irritating to them that they will have to put you away from them, and then they will not be satisfied with that, but want to crush you as well."

Jesus doesn't want them to be shattered by a false optimism, so he begins to warn them. Unfortunately, the church has not embraced this truth as something to be taught today, and so we are probably guilty of some false advertising when it comes to our message.

I'm intrigued by the drug commercials I see on television because they try to convince us that if we take this whether we need it or not, life is going to be good. Then we hear this voice in the background, almost unintelligible, speaking in a monotone. For us, it might say something like this: "Serving Christ may result in conflict, job loss, division in families, relocation, or loss of friends. In some Christian service, commitment also results in sleeplessness, personal sacrifice, and in rare occasions, imprisonment, torture, execution, and death. As with all life commitments, read the Scriptures before making a commitment."

Unfortunately, we don't actually advertise that way. We may say it subtlety as we've read the message today, but we don't really make that kind of an application, do we? Jesus has already spoken of persecution however in a broader sense in chapter 15, and all Scriptures agree. In several places, we read about it.

The Last Sermon of Christ

Matthew 5, in the Beatitudes, verses 10 through 11: "Blessed are those who are persecuted for righteousness' sake, for theirs is the kingdom of heaven. Blessed are you when others revile you and persecute you and utter all kinds of evil against you falsely on my account."

In 1 Peter 3:14 and 4:14: "But even if you should suffer for righteousness' sake, you will be blessed. . . ." "If you are insulted for the name of Christ, you are blessed, because the Spirit of glory and of God rests upon you." Even in Philippians 1:29, the book of joy, the book of optimism: "For it has been granted to you that for the sake of Christ you should not only believe in him but also suffer for his sake." It's been granted to you, not only that you would believe, but also that you would suffer for his sake.

In chapter 15, Jesus had promised them the hatred of the world, and that hatred would come from the world's hatred of him. The world hates the followers of Christ because they hate Christ. Because of Christ's command to them that they must obey his commands, they refuse. They would like to have a Christ that would save them without the necessity of transformation, without the necessity of obedience to him, without recognizing his lordship over their lives. They'll take a Christ who is a soft sell, but not one who causes them to have to live according to his design.

He told them they couldn't expect to be treated any better from the world than he himself was being treated, and he was on his way to the crucifixion, and that the harder they tried to make the case for truth, make the case for light, make the case for peace, the greater the persecution would become as a reaction to the stinging of their being convicted of their sin.

You want to make some people angry? Talk to them about their sin. You want to cause people to rail accusations against you? You want to cause people to want to shut down your ministry? Start talking about their sin and the necessity of them dealing with their sin, and you will then find out where people in their relationship with the Lord.

In this, the apostles join a good company of prophets, like Jeremiah who came to God's people, just as evangelists, pastors, and missionaries come to Christ's church today. Jeremiah called for the people to repent and to serve God. For his troubles, they threw him into a well. They burned his book, and they threw into prison.

Martin Luther paraphrases Jeremiah's response, saying: "'Why should I continue to preach in vain?' Jeremiah would say. 'What reward do I have except to be constantly mocked and reviled and plagued? What devil can endure such groundless hatred, contempt, and torment from the world? But when such thoughts entered my mind and such malice almost induced me to be offended and stop, then I felt as if there were a burning fire in my heart and in my bones, that as I became so terrified and so sick at heart that I felt as though I were lying in a red-hot stove, and I thought I would surely die if I kept silence.'"[1]

So we're all tried by the devil. We're all tried by the world, even as both are found to exist in the visible church today, for wherever lust and strife and malice and deceit and threats and cursing and division are found, we can say these things come not from God, but from the spirit of the world which is brought into the household of faith.

In verse 4 of our passage today, he says, "I have said these things to you." Jesus here almost sounds sorry that he has to tell them of the horror and the darkness that lies ahead of them, but he wants them to know here at the last what it is they're about to face in the most immediate sense. While Jesus was with them, the apostles had hardly been noticed. All of the attention had been given to Jesus. He had provided for them cover and protection. Just by virtue of his teaching and his miracles, all eyes were upon Jesus, and the apostles were just part of the background, but now he tells them they will be exposed, and they will be targeted by those who are enemies of the gospel. They'll be excommunicated, and they'll be murdered.

We know from the book of Revelation, in chapter 12, that this is true, and it provides there in figurative language that the dragon would seek to devour the child, then next the woman who gave birth, and then her seed. In Acts, the prophecy of chapters 15:18 through 16:4 is fulfilled in every detail.

The threat against them was first excommunication. They would be thrown out of the Temple. Being put out of the synagogue meant more than what we feel when a member is dropped from the rolls of the church. It means the same, but we don't feel the same about it because we can simply go find somewhere else to go. We don't deal with the issue that caused us to be dropped. We just go somewhere else where we

---

1. Martin Luther, p. 301.

might be accepted. So the impact of being cast out of the household of faith is not felt in the excommunications of today.

It means for them, for the apostles, separation from the spiritual life of Israel. There are no other places to go. There simply will be no worship of God, not collectively. There'll be no sacrifices that are offered, no priestly duties for them. There won't even be a reading of the Scriptures as there were no private citizens who owned copies of the Scrolls. There were no more opportunities for them to exercise their faith as they had always known it. Their social life would be devastated, their economic potential ended, and they would even be denied a proper burial.

All this suffering was to come from the religious community. Not from those outside of the community, not from Babylon or Assyria, not from any of those traditional and ancient enemies of the people, but from the religious community itself. The place they had called home now would turn upon them.

For most of us, the inverse is true however. While yes, there are some within religious communities who will oppose the true work of Christ, our real fear of excommunication is not from the church, but from the world. We are so afraid of being cast out of the world that we will sacrifice our work in the church to stay in the world. A commitment to Christ will cut us off from the world's music, and its drinking, and its carousing, and its gambling, and its fleshly indulgence, and we may certainly suffer social and economic isolation as a result of our commitment to Christ.

What do we do? What is our remedy? We compromise and secularize the expressions of our faith. We avoid persecution from the world by accommodation, and so we seek to maintain some sort of a dual membership with Christ's church and the world. Can we manage some kind of a dual membership, however? James 3:10: "From the same mouth come blessing and cursing. My brothers, these things ought not to be so." This is double mindedness. We cannot maintain this sort of a dual membership with two entities which are at odds with one another.

There is an ancient Middle Eastern tale of two enemies, a scorpion and a fox. A great river was cutting through in a rainy season a part of the desert, separating the animals on one side of that river from the food which was on the other.

Perseverance: Running on Fumes

A fox came up to the river, and he was seeking a way across the river. As he stood there considering his place, his life-long enemy, a scorpion, also came up to the river. Standing there with the fox and looking across, he said to the fox, "I have been up and down the riverbank, and I have seen a place where it is shallow, and the waters are calm, and it's easy to cross. I'll show you where that is if you will help me to get across. If you'll put me on your back, and you'll take me across, I'll show you the place."

The fox looked at him, and he said, "Do you count me a fool? If I were to put you on my back, surely you would sting me, and I would drown." The scorpion said, "If I were to sting you and you were to drown, then we would both drown because I cannot swim across the river alone." The fox thought for a moment. The scorpion's words were logical, so he went to the place under the scorpion's instruction. He lowered himself down. The scorpion got on his back, and they began across the river.

Halfway across the river, the fox felt a sharp sting between his shoulder blades. Shocked that he had been stung by the scorpion, he turned and he said, "What have you done? Now we both will drown." The scorpion, with a quiet voice, said, "I couldn't help it. It's simply my nature."

What is the nature of the world which has always been in opposition to Christ? The threat to Christian fidelity has been persecution, prejudice, physical danger, and some day it may be those things again. We may face the sword for our commitment to Christ, but the contemporary danger to Western Christians is not yet one of being murdered, but infidelity to Christian comes in our accommodation to the world, our love of the world.

Jesus warned the apostles so they wouldn't go astray. Like a mouse that sees nothing but a feast on a mousetrap until the trap is sprung, Jesus didn't want his children taken by surprise when the world showed them its hatred of God.

In Mark 8:34 to 36, Jesus said, "If anyone would come after me, let him deny himself and take up his cross and follow me. For whoever would save his life will lose it, but whoever loses his life for my sake and the gospel's will save it. For what does it profit a man to gain the whole world and forfeit his soul?"

The Last Sermon of Christ

You want to see where the battle is fought? Look at the lives particularly of our young people. Watch it on the news. Look at the programs. Talk to some of them. Teach a class. There you will see where the battle is being fought. Just as our young people are on the cusp of adulthood, they are caught between the faith they've been taught and lived under their parents and the new faith they've seen in the world.

In seeking some peaceful resolution to these two conflicting philosophies of life, too many will accommodate the world, believing they have both, but it's just simply not possible. What part does death have to do with life, or light with darkness, or heaven with hell? Absolutely none, but under such tremendous pressure from the world and the soft sell of Christianity they have learned through their youth, the incentive to avoid the mental and social affliction given to them by the world is simply too great.

Jeremiah Burroughs, in his book *The Evil of Evils*, wrote, "It is a very evil choice for any soul under heaven to choose the least sin rather than the greatest affliction. Any affliction is better than to be under the guilt of the slightest sin."[2]

Burroughs continues in the next chapter, "Servants of God who have been guided by the wisdom of God to make their choice, but have rather chosen the sorest and most dreadful afflictions in this world rather than willingly commit the least sin. For example, if you would turn your thoughts to what you have read or heard of the martyrs, what hideous and grievous torments they suffered, the boiling of their bodies in lead, laying their naked backs on gridirons, rending and tearing their members in pieces with horses, pulling the flesh off with pinchers, and others by red-hot burning tongs, enduring their flesh to be scorched by being broiled first on one side and then the next. Yes, even the weakest of women have endured this, to have their flesh harrowed with stones and sharp irons, to have their bodies slain and thrown into rivers of cold ice, and a thousand more things. Whatever hell and wicked men could devise, they were content to endure all of this and more rather than to act against their consciences and commit the least sin; they embraced the tortures rather than embrace the sin."[3]

So Burroughs surmises at the end. "Many of you," he says, "when it comes to it will be more loath to lose a coin than commit a sin, more

---

2. Jeremiah Burroughs, *The Evil of Evils*, p. 2.
3. Ibid, p. 5

loath to endure the least shame or a nickname than to commit a sin. Are there not many who would tell a lie rather than suffer a little shame even in your own family?"[4]

So should we protest and run when afflictions come? Paul says he was whipped. He was put into stocks. They kept him even without clothes in public humiliation. He went without food. In 2 Corinthians 4:17, he calls this suffering "light momentary affliction is preparing for us an eternal weight of glory beyond all comparison," but when it comes to sin, he doesn't call that a light momentary affliction. When it comes to his sin, he says, "O wretched man that I am!"

Rather than being an offense to God, what affliction on earth would there be that we would forfeit the honor of God for our own personal comfort? In John 16:4, again Jesus says, "When their hour comes." The prophetic Word from Christ places all affliction under the sovereign hand of God. He is here making a prophecy. He is not saying, "If"; he is saying "When," and *when* in all of history belongs in the hand of a sovereign God. Knowing God is sovereign thus means that all of the affliction we are to endure is a part of God's sovereign plan.

Then we cry out. We say, "Doesn't the Lord love us? Why would the Lord cause us to suffer, his own people?" Isn't that the same cry echoed by the people of Israel all through the pages of the Old Testament? "Where is our God? Why do the unjust seem to thrive while those who are called God's people seem to suffer?"

The evil present in the world ought not surprise us. Has the world ever been a friend to Christ or to his people? Evil parses out the wheat from the tares, God's own from the lost. Satan's attack, which is meant to destroy the church, actually in God's sovereign hand purifies and strengthens the church.

The worst Satan can do to us is leave us to ourselves. Perhaps that is what David meant in Psalm 119:71. "It is good for me that I was afflicted, that I might learn your statutes." Failing an assault on our bodies, we can expect an assault on our conscience. It was the first subtle attack in the Garden, making a fruit that is forbidden appear to be so essential to the good life that it can't be turned down. The result of falling in love with the forbidden fruit was that all the good fruit God had supplied seemed to be bitter in comparison.

---

4. Ibid, p. 6.

The Last Sermon of Christ

This persecution in the form of temptation results in sin. Jesus was a Man of Sorrows, beaten, shamed, and killed, but would have rather let the world perish than to sin against God. He would endure even the shame of the cross as an act of obedience to the Lord, but he would not have committed the first sin against a holy God.

Persecution even in the form of moral temptation is a refining fire in which God is purifying his people, the church. There is a beautiful illustration told by Billy Graham, and later quoted by James Montgomery Boice. A man who was overwhelmed in the time of the economic depression had lost his job, he had lost his wife, he had lost his personal fortune and his home, but he had a strong faith even in such dire circumstances.

One day as he was wandering the streets, he passed a construction site where a large church was being put together, and he watched as a man was working with stone, as he was chipping away. It was a triangular piece of stone, and he walked up and he asked the man what he was doing. The man pointed up to a high spire on the church, and he said, "You see that hole up there at the very top? I'm fitting this stone for it." As the man walked away, he realized that even in these difficult circumstances, God was perfecting him for heaven through earthly tribulation.

Today we see nations that once embraced Christianity turning away. Some have adopted persecutions against Christians like that of the Imperial or Papal Rome. We might be discouraged when we can't display the Ten Commandments or we can no longer pray in Jesus' name. Jesus promised us it would happen. Why would we act surprised?

The question is not whether persecution will come or whether temptations will assail us or whether evil exists. The Lord has promised us all of these, and history has proved him right. The question is: *What will we do in the face of all of these things?*

Paul and Silas sang in prison when all others in the prison were in despair. When God released them, the jailor who had been watching them fell at their feet and said, "Sirs, what must I do to be saved?" May the testimony of our fidelity to Christ cause others to see Jesus in us as well.

21

The Spirit and the World

John 16:5–11

"But now I am going to him who sent me, and none of you asks me, 'Where are you going?' But because I have said these things to you, sorrow has filled your heart. Nevertheless, I tell you the truth: it is to your advantage that I go away, for if I do not go away, the Helper will not come to you. But if I go, I will send him to you. And when he comes, he will convict the world concerning sin and righteousness and judgment: concerning sin, because they do not believe in me; concerning righteousness, because I go to the Father, and you will see me no longer; concerning judgment, because the ruler of this world is judged."

WHAT SHOULD BE THE focus of a church ministry? What should we be doing as first priorities as a church? We know the short answer to that, and our first priority, is the activity of worship. We do also know there is the activity of discipling and discipleship of families and of one another in our different places of life, different stations of life, and we do that through various means. We also know there is the activity of outreach and evangelism that we are called to be doing. We also confess we are a little reticent oftentimes to do that, but nevertheless, we acknowledge that worship and discipleship and evangelism are the activities of the church, the manifestations of the church's calling with the Great Commission.

Well what is our philosophy behind all of that? Where is the theology behind all of that? Would we have to do lengthy studies on each one simply to arrive at the answer that the church should be about worship, discipleship, and evangelism?

I think it would be much easier for us if we began to think, as the church is the Body and Christ is the Head, that that which concerns the Head concerns the Body. Now we might live a bit of a schizophrenic life where our head tells us to do things with our body which are inherently unhealthy. Hence, many of us will have medical conditions, or many of us will have weights that aren't exactly where the doctor says they should be, and on and on, or injury because oftentimes our head takes our body in the wrong direction, but not so with Christ.

Christ, who is our Head, has a perfect sense of mission and direction for his church, which is his Body. How would we then organize around that as a philosophy? What sort of direction does that give us? Christ, in his ascended position at the right hand of God, serves as Prophet, Priest, and King. Here we find the focal point of the church's expression in the world.

The church gives expression to the work in ministry of Christ as *Prophet* through the proclamation of the gospel, through the warning of the judgment which is to come. The church gives expression to Christ's function as *Priest* by praying for all men in all places and by interceding for them and by administering to them Word and sacrament as the means of grace. The church also provides expression to Christ's role, his office of *King* because in declaring the law of God that all men are subject to, we are declaring his divine rule.

Now what does that have to do with the passage considered in this chapter? Jesus is laying a template for the disciples, and you'll notice he says he is leaving and sending his own Spirit, the Holy Spirit, which will convict, or convince, men of sin, of righteousness, and of judgment. This is what we preach. This is the message of the church. As we give expression to Christ's person as the Prophet, the Priest, and the King, the message we take is that the Spirit would be convincing men of sin, of righteousness, and of judgment.

Now we may feel we have much else to say, but here Christ is saying that the Spirit will be about this business. The Spirit will be working in men's hearts and in their minds to convict them of sin, to teach them of righteousness since Christ has ascended to the Father, and to warn them of the impending judgment because the ruler of this world has been defeated. That is what the Spirit is doing, and he has called the

The Spirit and the World

church to be the agency through which that occurs. So while we may be busy about other things, this is what Christ has considered his business and his message.

As we look at our passage however, we find the apostles were more confused about this than today's Christians might be. When Jesus begins his discourse here in verse 5, he starts by saying simply, "But now I am going to him who sent me." "But now" are words of change. He had been with them, but now he is going away. "I had been there," and he has been telling them in the passage we considered in the previous chapter that the attention for persecution was not on them because it was upon him, but now he is leaving, and they can expect that persecution to now be directed towards them rather than towards him.

What has been their response to his leaving? They're filled with grief. They're looking down in their shoes, so to speak. Why are they filled with grief? After all, he has told them, and he has promised that the Spirit will come and that he is going to prepare a place for them, to build many mansions for them, there should be a great expectation, but they are not filled with expectation. They are filled with grief.

"Because I have said these things," Jesus says to them. "Because I have said these things, you are filled with grief." He has described his separation from them, and he has described the persecution in the conflict which is to come, and because of these two facts, these apostles are filled with grief. As the disciples' minds and hearts become completely overwhelmed with their despair, they begin to sink into that despair. They begin to sink into a depression. They begin to lose their way in darkness as one who is in the water begins to sink, and looking up, watches the light fade as the depths begin to swallow him. The disciples are beginning to sink into that darkness of despair.

They weren't looking any further into the future than their own immediate peril, their own immediate loss with Christ. Sorrow is filling their hearts. Now the Lord is upbraiding them for their distractions and for their despair.

We wonder, *Why even mention the hard times? Just let them come. Why tell them about all of these difficult times ahead? Why cause them to be in despair and so distracted that they're not able to pay attention to what he is saying? Why tell them this and cause them to be so disconcerted at a time when he has so much to say?*

The Last Sermon of Christ

Perhaps you've read John Bunyan's classic allegory of the Christian life, *The Pilgrim's Progress*. There in the story, it tells of our main character (we could call him our hero), Christian, who has left the City of Destruction to travel to the Celestial City. Along the way, he and his companions slip into a very miry sludge, a swamp if you will, more likely a bog. It was a place called Despond.

They wallowed around a while, and Christian, because of the burden which he carried on his back (we know that was his sin), began to sink into that Slough of Despond. His partner who was with him however, was able to struggle to the side and was able to pull himself out, and he began to run back along the path of life, reversing his course, to return home to the City of Destruction without helping Christian out.

Christian is left there alone, struggling and sinking deeper and deeper into despondency when a man arrives called Help. We recognize in this allegory that Help is the Holy Spirit. Help pulls him free and sets him on firm ground. Christian asks why the bog hasn't been filled. Why is it still there? Why isn't it repaired so that travelers who are coming along won't fall in? Help responds that it cannot be filled, and it cannot be repaired. As long as there are people who will travel from the City of Destruction to the Celestial City, they will have to negotiate this Slough of Despond.

William Tyndale was a man martyred so that we can have a copy of the Bible. The Scriptures which you appreciate and which you study and which we explore together are possible for us because of men like William Tyndale. He was asked about persecution. He was asked why in the world he would tolerate such persecution, and he responded with this simple phrase, "I never expected anything else."

When it comes to the things of God, and when it comes to the transformation of the soul of a person and their character and their mind, do we not expect there will be inner turmoil and external persecution? As we begin to separate ourselves from the things which were of this world, would we not expect there are parts of this world which we grew to love that we will despair in losing? Will we not also expect that the relations we had in this world, perhaps even the vocation we had in this world, as we begin to withdraw in order that we might be holy unto God, that we would not experience persecution and charges of judgmentalism because we have judged a particular activity or life or vocation or friend to be evil and not of God? Do we expect anything

The Spirit and the World

other than persecution, and will we too sink into despair? Will we too sink into worry?

The question is not whether a Christian is going to encounter difficult times, but rather when, and more importantly, what will be our response? Jesus had begun his farewell discourse reminding the apostles to trust in him, but their thoughts were on nothing but themselves. They were absorbed in their own grief, their own sorrow, the things they would encounter, the circumstances of their life.

We can see this in our own lives whenever we have attended a funeral of someone when we are there with their family. We will intuitively walk up to them and say without any coaching, without a great deal of spiritual depth and understanding, "He or she is in a better place." We understand intuitively that at the moment of greatest despair, there is a need to lift up our heads and to look beyond the despair to the hope which lies ahead. Not that we are saying the person didn't really die, you don't really feel grief, or your heart is not really broken. We would be appalled if we heard anybody say anything like that, but we are always comforted when we are reminded there is a hope beyond the grief.

Don't dwell in the grief. Don't sink into despair, but look beyond that to something that is beyond which is true. Jesus is seeking now to lift their eyes again towards himself by this simple question, *"None of you asks where I am going?"*

Now we might protest as would the apostles. Peter, in chapter 13:36 did ask. He asked, "Where are you going, Lord, because I want to go there?" Thomas, in 14:5, also said, "Show us the way. Tell us how we can go." But these questions were mere expressions of their own grief and actually were more of a protest than any real inquiry.

How can we understand that sense of the language? As a child, you might have planned on going with your father on a trip, perhaps a fishing trip or perhaps you were simply going for a walk, and your dad was called away to work. The child might observe as the father has said, "I'm going to have to leave. I'm not going to be able to go with you on this trip."

The child might say, "Ah, Dad, where are you going?" Is the child really asking, "Tell me the details of your trip"? It's a form of protest. "Dad, where are you going? Why are you leaving? Where are you headed? What's up?" It's more of a protest of "I'm so disappointed because I

The Last Sermon of Christ

was so looking forward to our journey together, our trip together, our activity together. Where are you going?"

Jesus has heard the disciples' questions in the same way. "Lord, where are you going? Where are you leaving?" They haven't really received an understanding of the place which Jesus is going. These questions, expressions of grief, and protest came before Jesus described his going to the Father. They came before he described his sending them the Holy Spirit, his own Spirit, and now actually at this moment would be the appropriate time for their question because now the question is informed with some facts and truth, but the apostles have now forgotten to ask, and all they can look at is the ground as they sink into despair.

If they had turned from their own sense of loss and followed carefully the words of Jesus and asked perhaps for an even greater revelation, they would have forgotten their own personal despair and begun to consider his glory which was to come. So here is the lesson we learn from this first of passage we've explored. We learn that perseverance in hard times and what we can call spiritual resiliency among Christians comes not from looking inward for strength. It comes not from clearing our mind and meditating. It comes from focusing all of our attention on Christ. That is where we receive our spiritual resiliency and our strength to persevere in difficult times.

Jesus continues teaching them. He tells them that it's better if he goes. It's better for them if he leaves. They should lose the form of a servant as the Word made flesh and learn to love him as glorified rather than carnally in flesh. They should come to associate and relate to him spiritually as he ascends to the Father and is seated at the right hand in that role of Prophet and Priest and King. They should learn to form their love around Jesus as he will be in a glorified state rather than simply as flesh.

We see this again after the resurrection when Mary comes, and we know she grabs his feet, and Jesus says, "Don't cling to me. I will not be carnal for you any longer. I will not be of flesh for you any longer. You must relate to me in a resurrected state. You cannot hold me to the earth."

He will be returning to the divine state which was his before the incarnation. He'll be at God's right hand as our Advocate, serving as mediator between God and man. He says, "You'll see me no more in the state of humiliation, never again earthly, but only glorified."

The Spirit and the World

His exaltation is explained to us in many passages of Scripture, but it's certainly worth considering two. Philippians, chapter 2, verses 9 through 11: "Therefore God has highly exalted him and bestowed on him the name that is above every name, so that at the name of Jesus every knee should bow, in heaven and on earth and under the earth, and every tongue confess that Jesus Christ is Lord, to the glory of God the Father."

Consider for just a moment these apostles are most intimately acquainted with Christ. Christ is soon to be resurrected, sitting at the right hand of God after the ascension to rule over all the earth, and that ultimately on that last Day of Judgment which is to come, every knee will bow and confess, "Jesus is Lord." The apostles, who are closest to Christ in his earthly ministry, are despondent and in despair.

Brothers and sisters, if the apostles so close to Christ can so easily fall into despondency and despair, we also should be carefully on our guard lest even though we have this revelation before us, we too fall into despondency and despair in the world in which we live because we take our eyes off of the glorified Christ. In taking our eyes off of the glorified Christ, we are left as one sinking in the water, losing the twilight from the surface above, being enveloped in the darkness descending deep below.

One other verse on the exalted Christ will help us to have an appreciation and an excitement about the place of Christ: Hebrews 1, verse 3: "He is the radiance of the glory of God and the exact imprint of his nature, and he upholds the universe by the word of his power. After making purification for sins, he sat down at the right hand of the Majesty on high."

This is what Christ is seeing as he talks to the disciples. This is where Christ is headed as he talks to the disciples, and as he looks out to them, he says, "Have you no concern over where I'm going, over what lies ahead for us? Is all you can see my prediction to you that I'm leaving and that you will encounter persecution? You'll see me no more, never again in a state of humiliation, but only in glorification."

The second thing he tells them is that he'll send the Holy Spirit to them. We already know he has told them he is not going to leave them alone, but he is going to send the Holy Spirit as a Comforter to them. Already, he has introduced that Spirit as Comforter which will bring to their mind remembrance and understanding, but the Spirit will also have a ministry to the world. He will show the world the truth concerning sin, righteousness, and judgment. This is the mission of the Comforter: to convict, or convince if you will, the world of sin, righteousness, and judgment.

H. A. Ironside says, "The Spirit comes to convince the mind, to exercise the conscience, and to cause the will to act in accordance with the desires of our blessed Lord. The Holy Ghost has come to give such power to the Word that men will believe it and act upon it."[1] We can say right now that without the Spirit, men cannot understand the truth about sin, righteousness, and judgment. Their eyes will have as it were scales over them, and they will be blind to what the nature of sin is, and to the nature of righteousness versus their own self-righteousness. They will also be blind to the nature of judgment, to the fact that the prince of this world which the world still follows and obeys has been vanquished and defeated, that those who follow this worldly prince follow one who is dying and whose day of termination is set.

First, there'll be conviction of sin because men do not believe in and receive Christ. If this sin remains, that is, unbelief in Christ, then all other sins remain. We might say, "But there are so many others. We have those listed in the commandments. We have all of those sins of spiritual evils and woes and vices that are listed in the Bible. Do those not count?" Yes, of course they do, but if the sin of unbelief remains, they remain, but if that sin is remitted and we believe on Christ, then all others are also forgiven as well.

The sin of unbelief is the sin that is not able to be pardoned. The blasphemy of the Holy Spirit is a blasphemy against the Spirit of Christ whose work is to change the hearts of men. It is saying, "Be gone! I will not listen. I will not obey." It is rejecting the words of Christ; it is condemning the work of the Spirit of Christ whose function is to teach us the truth concerning sin, and Christ, and his righteousness, and judgment.

We see this work in Acts, chapter 2, on the day of Pentecost, this work of the Spirit. The disciples go down into the streets of Jerusalem, and they begin to preach Christ. Peter explained how Joel's prophecy concerning the coming of the Holy Spirit has been fulfilled, and that men and women would call on Christ, and that they would live. Remember, just shortly before in this very city on these very streets, our

---

1. H.A. Ironside, p. 691.

The Spirit and the World

Lord dragged a cross to Golgotha, and here in these streets of Jerusalem, the Spirit makes them understand.

Acts 2:36 and 37: "'Therefore let all Israel be assured of this: God has made this Jesus, whom you crucified, both Lord and Christ.' When the people heard this, they were cut to the heart and said to Peter and the other apostles, 'Brothers, what shall we do?'"

When Jesus came, he gave sin a newly refined focal point, and that is disbelief in him. Sin is rebellion against the government of God. It is sedition. Jesus lived in perfect conformity to the rule of God. He was purity among the impure. He was truth among liars, and he took the sin of the world to Calvary to restore righteousness. To refuse God's work in Christ to restore righteousness, to refuse Christ who is God incarnate is the greatest sin.

The world looks on unbelief as intellectual sophistication, however. They prefer someone who is not decided about Christ, but who remains open minded. The world values an open mind rather than one who is resolved in their commitment to follow Christ. The world can't understand the sin of disbelief without the convicting work of the Holy Spirit. How upside down a world we live in when disbelief would actually be considered a virtue, a sign of great intellectual prowess, instead of living in darkness and uninformed in the ways of God.

Secondly, the Holy Spirit convicts men concerning righteousness. I'm reminded of a story I once heard of a man on an airplane who was trying to share the gospel with one next to him. He took out a napkin, and as they were talking, it was clear that the one who was riding with him in the seat to his right was not really buying this whole idea of sin and his need of forgiveness. He considered himself a moral and ethical man. By world's standards actually, he was a good man, and he had a fine reputation.

The evangelist, taking that napkin, wrote on one corner, the upper corner, "God," then he drew a diagonal line from one corner to the other, and he asked the man to imagine the worst sinner he has ever thought of in his life, one he is sure just would never be found in heaven. We confess, of course, only God knows. We cannot condemn men here, knowing their true spiritual condition, but as we imagine history and as we imagine men like Stalin and Pol Pot and Hitler, we can imagine that somehow out of all of these, there will be those who will not be found in heaven.

The Last Sermon of Christ

The man was encouraged to think of one of these and to write his name in that bottom corner, showing on that scale God is the greatest good and the worst is the most evil of men that has ever existed. The man in the airplane decided to write Hitler in the corner, and then he was encouraged to think of these names, Billy Graham and Mother Teresa, and to take these great saints who've worked for the kingdom, and to put them somewhere on that scale of righteousness where he thought they might be in the view of God as far as righteousness goes.

The man placed both of them not all the way at the top, but in the top third. He put them on the scale being certainly far away from Hitler. Then he was asked to place himself on that scale. Recognizing the challenge from modesty here, he couldn't put himself above Billy Graham and Mother Teresa, so he moved down to around the fifty percent mark and decided he didn't even really want to appear to be so immodest as to put himself at fifty-one, so he went more forty-nine or forty-eight percent, showing he still had a little ways to go. He was not quite there yet.

The evangelist took the napkin, and he said, "You have it all wrong concerning the righteousness that you judge Graham and Mother Teresa. They actually are much closer, in fact, indistinguishable in their place at the bottom end of the scale as they would be judged according to their own righteousness."

There is no way to move up the scale at all in our own righteousness. It is only the righteousness of Christ that takes us on the scale, and then it takes us all the way into heaven. There is no place to put someone based on his or her righteousness in being acceptable to God. Matthew 5:20: "For I tell you that unless your righteousness surpasses that of the Pharisees and the teachers of the law, you will certainly not enter the kingdom of heaven." In Matthew 5:48, "Be perfect, therefore, as your heavenly Father is perfect."

There is only one degree of righteousness accepted by God in heaven, and that is perfect righteousness. The resurrection and the ascension show us there is one whom God calls righteous, and when the Spirit reveals that to us, we pray with Paul these words, "That we may 'be found in him, not having a righteousness of my own that comes from the law, but that which is through faith in Christ—the righteousness that comes from God and is by faith'" (Philippians 3:9).

Number three, the judgment. In a progression from seeing ourselves as dead in sin and in need of a righteousness that is alien to us, but that belongs to Christ and is imputed to us by the power and the work of the Spirit, it follows that there'll be some day of reckoning, some accounting for this, a judgment of righteousness.

No one naturally looks forward to judgment. One of the worst characteristics or characterizations you can give to someone is to call them judgmental. Sometimes the apparent delay in the Day of Judgment however can make it seem as if it is more imagined than it is real.

Scriptures show us God's judgment in the Garden, in the days of Noah, at Sodom and Gomorrah, and at the cross. The poet William Wordsworth Longfellow translated a poem by German poet, Friedrich von Logau,

> "Though the mills of God grind slowly,
> Yet they grind exceeding small;
> Though with patience he stands waiting,
> With exactness grinds he all."[2]

Second Peter 2:9: "The Lord. . .hold the unrighteous for the day of judgment, while continuing their punishment." For new creatures in Christ, Scripture declares we've been judged already. That is the relief of the Christian, isn't it? We who are in Christ have been judged already, but there remains yet a Day of Judgment, and why is that Day of Judgment sealed and sure? Because any protection the unrighteous may believe they have under the protective covering of the prince of this world will not hold because the prince of this world was defeated already at Calvary. He no longer is able to exercise any protection over them.

The natural mind again would not be convinced that there is to be a day of accountability, and so people around us in this world are content to eat, drink, and be merry, but a Christian is shown the truth by the Holy Spirit. So what does all this mean for us? First of all, the church should take seriously the work of Christ in the Holy Spirit, and rather than seeking to simply be creative and imaginative and flashy, should seek to join him there in the work the Spirit is doing, proclaiming the lostness and sin of rebellious man, the want of righteousness except as it is found in Christ, and his return in judgment, and his victory over the prince of this world.

---

2. from *Bartlett's Familiar Quotations*, p. 247.

The Last Sermon of Christ

Knowing that being judged righteous in Christ requires a conviction and repentance of sin, and knowing that the natural mind can't grasp these truths, we ought to pray that we ourselves would be convicted of our sin and made righteous in Christ, and we ought also to pray that the Holy Spirit will convict the world concerning sin, concerning righteousness, and concerning judgment. This is the ministry of Christ as he has explained it to the apostles, and so it is the ministry of the church.

22

The Unity of the Trinity in Revelation

John 16:12–15

"I still have many things to say to you, but you cannot bear them now. When the Spirit of truth comes, he will guide you into all the truth, for he will not speak on his own authority, but whatever he hears he will speak, and he will declare to you the things that are to come. He will glorify me, for he will take what is mine and declare it to you. All that the Father has is mine; therefore, I said that he will take what is mine and declare it to you. A little while, and you will see me no longer; and again a little while, and you will see me."

WE'VE MADE SO MUCH of trying to understand the disposition and the situation of the apostles, their place and their lack of understanding, their bewilderment and their panic, really, as Jesus is seeking to comfort and to teach them that I'm beginning to empathize with them as their conversation with Jesus winds down. It will be their last conversation with Jesus as chapter 17 becomes his prayer to the Father.

This is the Word of God for the people of God. This is the fifth and final passage where Jesus is teaching on the coming of the Spirit. It's the fifth and final passage of the coming of Spirit delivered by Jesus in this final discourse, and this teaching focuses on the completion of the revelation of Jesus. He is telling them, "I still have many things to tell you. You're not fit right now, literally, to take what I need to tell you, but you will still receive what I need to tell you because the Holy Spirit will give it to you."

We're going to seek in this chapter to work through this final teaching. Jesus wants to prepare the disciples. He wants to strengthen and forewarn the disciples against that trouble that will come to them by the adversaries of the gospel, and he has sought to explain what the Holy Spirit will accomplish with them and through them, but the disciples will not fully grasp his words until the Spirit applies them to their heart. They hear, and the words are there, but they can't apprehend those words completely without the Holy Spirit really making their hearts able to receive, making their minds able to comprehend what Jesus has taught them.

Some have confused the concept of inspiration and illumination, which we've covered at some length already, with continuing revelation. When we read that verse, "I still have many things to say to you, but you cannot bear them now," some have taken that to mean that there will be a continuing, new revelation outside of the Scripture.

Martin Luther chronicles the misuse of this passage to justify the claims of the Roman church prior to the Reformation in some detail. The Roman church prior to the Reformation took this verse especially early to say that there were continuing edicts and laws that were being delivered through the church that were binding just as Scripture, tradition which holds even to today. The Roman church says that Scripture *and* tradition are both authoritative, but tradition oftentimes has teaching that is found nowhere in the Scripture, thus their willingness to accept extra-biblical revelation. That is not anything they would be shy about. They would affirm, "Yes, there is a delivering through the pope, a word from God that may be new to the ears of his people."

Teachings on Purgatory, for example, and penance all come from an interpretation that suggests the Holy Spirit continues to reveal new doctrine. In those days, the pope added commandments to the teaching of Christ himself. "They have demanded that everything they said be regarded as articles of faith necessary for salvation, although, in fact, these statements are not at all related to the kingdom of Christ and the Holy Spirit has nothing to do with them."[1] In this whole body of teaching, we need to observe that Jesus has not given one new law. He has defined the law in love and the whole concept of love (love for one another and love for God), but he has not given to them an eleventh or twelfth or thirteenth commandment. He has spoken to them words of comfort, words of promise, and words of hope.

---

1. Martin Luther, p. 353.

The Unity of the Trinity in Revelation

Men have sought salvation in a knowledge of God without God or his revelation since the beginning of time, but the distortions didn't end with the Reformation. Extra-biblical requirements have been added to the gospel in every age, from snake handling to Pentecostalism and the issues of what happens with the Holy Spirit and at what point you can actually say you are saved. These distortions continue.

We read about them in Acts 15 where circumcision was required before you could actually say you were saved in Christ. Whether it's a legal requirement or whether it's some experiential requirement, whether it's some public action or private devotion, men have consistently claimed that the teaching of Jesus is not enough, not enough for salvation, but Scripture is clear that we know nothing except by the revelation of God in Christ. There is nothing we can add that comes from God. All that is necessary for salvation is delivered to us by God in Christ and delivered in the Scripture which we understand by the Holy Spirit.

With Jesus' second teaching on the ministry of the Holy Spirit, back in chapter 14, he ends all such speculation on extra-biblical revelation. John 14:26 reads, "But the Helper, the Holy Spirit, whom the Father will send in my name, he will teach you all things and bring to your remembrance all that I have said to you." We discussed at length that it was the disciples' remembering the teaching and actions of Jesus that formed the foundation of their exposition of the doctrines related to those things Jesus had taught and done.

The epistles explain the history which is recorded in the gospels. Written long after Jesus had left them, these epistles are the remembrance—inspiration, if you will—revealed to them by the Spirit of Christ. Our understanding of it is illumination. The Spirit is occupied with bringing Jesus' teaching to the remembrance of the apostles and instructing them as to the fullness of its meaning.

For whatever reason, men have sought to know God without the revelation of God in Scripture. There almost seems to be a deliberate seeking of God outside the Bible. Folks want to find God outside the Bible. For whatever reason, there is this desire to prove that you can find God in numerous other places than the Bible, even if God himself has said it shall not be.

While I cannot locate the exact quote, it is said that in the third century, Tertullian responded to the heretic Marcion saying something like, if you suggest God can be known through human surmises . . . or human thinking, . . . I answer that a God cannot be known except by his showing. Otherwise, the man might appear greater than God, for he would be dragging God out into the public by human power. Human insignificance has found it easier to invent gods than to attend upon the true God.

Here, I believe Tertullian is simply saying that if man declares God will be known by some way other than what God has said, then man is declaring himself superior and dragging God out to show him forth in a way that God has not designed as if God belonged to man much like a pet or some other object a man might pull out to impress his friends. Karl Barth, more contemporary to us, said, "God is known through God and God alone. God speaks to man in his Word, and thereby he gives himself to be known."[2]

How then is God to be known? Jesus is the Word of God made flesh. He is the apex or the climax of God's revelation to man. All revelation before and since Jesus walked among men has pointed to him. Hebrews 1:1 to 2 would teach us as much. "Long ago," it reads, "at many times and in many ways, God spoke to our fathers by the prophets, but in these last days. . ." which we now are in, ". . . he has spoken to us by his Son, whom he appointed the heir of all things."

Note again verses 13 and 14. "When the Spirit of truth comes, he will guide you into all the truth, for he will not speak on his own authority, but whatever he hears he will speak, and he will declare to you the things that are to come. He will glorify me, for he will take what is mine and declare it to you."

Jesus calls the Holy Spirit the Spirit of truth over against a spirit of lies and deception. Isn't that the implied contrast? The Spirit of truth is truth which stands against lies and deception. The Spirit will show them more about Christ which can do nothing but glorify his name. Each revelation of the Spirit concerning Christ glorifies Christ. A test of true teaching may very well begin with the question of where is the glory set in the teaching. Is it Christ who is glorified, or is it man?

Much of preaching today is therapeutic, by implication signaling that it is man and his psychological health that is at the center of God's will rather than the glory of Christ. It is a great temptation to turn the scriptures on their head and speak to the carnal needs of man rather than to seek the truth of the matter in spiritual terms and submit to the teaching of the Holy Spirit. That learning that is required of one

2. Karl Barth,

who will preach the gospel isn't such that a man can determine in a day that he will preach the deep things of God. No, a man must take time to know the Scriptures in order that the Holy Spirit will illumine his mind to understand them and then, after understanding will come the teaching. And even in this, Christ assures us that the message brought forward by the work of the Spirit will never be without the validation of the Scriptures. Verse 13 assures us that the Spirit of Christ will carry the message of Christ which is to illumine the teaching of Christ that is found in the Scriptures. There is no new revelation, only illumination and understanding of the teaching of Christ. And that is only with total dependence on the Holy Spirit. The Spirit confirms to the heart the truth of Christ's teaching.

Martin Luther paraphrases Jesus in these passages, "Even though you've already heard much about this, you will never understand or believe by your own strength that it will and must be as I have told you and that what is to be proclaimed about me through you is true and right, and you would never have the courage to begin such preaching and to persist in it if the Holy Spirit himself did not come to preserve and guide you in this truth."[3]

Jesus is outlining the Christian's dependence on him for testimony and teaching. We have no testimony and no teaching outside of the revelation of God in Christ delivered in the Scripture, and without the work of the Holy Spirit to show us the teaching of Christ and bring it to our understanding, our testimony and teaching fall far short of the glory of Christ.

> "All things have been handed over to me by my Father, and no one knows the Son except the Father, and no one knows the Father except the Son and anyone to whom the Son chooses to reveal him" (Matthew 11:27).

So where else will we go to learn of God?

This takes me back to 1988. At that time, I was a great Armenian. A good Calvinist would not have even had lunch with me. I was struggling to learn. I wanted to know, and I was opening the Scriptures for two years, seeking to answer a question. I was going to be a schoolteacher. Seminary was far from my mind. I was still in my undergraduate days, and I was seeking to understand the sovereignty of God. I was

---

3. Luther, p. 366.

seeking to understand predestination, and I was opposed to it. I didn't know much about it except that I didn't like, and I was "agin it" as they say back home.

For two years, I was against it. Even though evidence continued to pile up, and I could really find only single strands of misapplied Scriptures to make my case, I had in a notebook, which I still have, page after page after page of evidences from the Scriptures which I was seeking to disprove. That is why I was recording them. I wanted to find some answer to these Scriptures.

Finally, late in the night one evening in 1988 while living in Irmo, South Carolina, I was reading through Romans chapter 9, and I came to verses 20 and 21. "But who are you, O man, to answer back to God? Will the molded clay say to its molder, 'Why have you made me like this?' Has the potter no right over the clay, to make out of the same lump one vessel for honorable use and another for dishonorable use?"

I had read those verses before, but it wasn't until that moment that the veil was lifted, that light burst into my mind, and a wave of relief and cognitive rest came over me because now the revelation of God that had been laid out before me in the pages of my own notebook and in the pages of my own Bible came together, and all the months of study came together into one coherent truth, and it was all to the glory of God.

There was nothing that came to me at that moment that I had not read or heard or been told before. I had sat in sermons and listened to it before, but like the disciples in the time of Christ, each teaching was laid in front of me, but I could not bring them together. Like a 5,000-piece puzzle, I couldn't find the edges, and I couldn't find the outline, and I couldn't distinguish between the colors. It was all there, but I couldn't put it together until that moment. Why that verse, why that moment, I can't explain. All I can say is that the Lord God revealed to me the truth concerning this matter which changed the entire course of my life, bringing me to where I am today.

I would venture to say that while God could have used anything else, it was at that moment that the course that brought me here was set. Had that moment come earlier when I did not have exposure to all of those Scriptures, I can't say that I would or would not have come to the same understanding. I can't know that, but what I can know is that all I had written and all that I had read and had not understood, the

The Unity of the Trinity in Revelation

volumes of pages suddenly all made sense, and it all came together in a wonderful way.

Just as Jesus never spoke or acted on his own initiative, so the Spirit only speaks what he hears. God pulled together by the power of the Spirit not something new for me, but the teaching of my Lord Jesus Christ in a way that I could understand. But not every spirit has God's glory as the goal. Just as there is a Spirit of truth, there is also a spirit of lies.

First John 4:1: "Beloved, do not believe every spirit, but test the spirits to see whether they are from God. . .By this you know the Spirit of God: every spirit that confesses that Jesus Christ has come in the flesh is from God, and every spirit that does not confess Jesus is not from God. This is the spirit of the antichrist. . . ." Who is this deceiver? Revelation 12:9 says, "Satan, the deceiver of the whole world." What are his tools? What are his devices? Colossians 2:8: "See to it that no one takes you captive by philosophy and empty deceit, according to human tradition, according to the elemental spirits of the world, and not according to Christ."

The spirit of antichrist says, "Look around at the glory of man. Look around at the world he has created. Look and enjoy all the benefits of modernity. See his cities. See his technology. Indulge in his entertainments and every material and fleshly indulgence you can reach and take for yourself," just as in the garden when Satan said, "Take and eat. Surely you shall not die." Modern man without the Spirit of Christ is still hearing the echo of those first words of temptation to man, "Take and eat. Surely you shall not die."

The Spirit of God says, "Take your eyes off the glory of man. Take your eyes off seeking your satisfaction in the things of this world, and look up and behold the beauty of the Savior." The disciples learned, as the martyrs and the faithful have borne testimony since, that the world has no tolerance for truth. Thus, Jesus told the disciples that in that moment with their hearts breaking over the loss of their Teacher and Friend that they couldn't bear all the Spirit would reveal later.

This brings us now to ask what the Spirit will teach. We say the Spirit is going to teach us; well, what does the Spirit teach? Let's summarize it in three categories—history, doctrine, and the things to come.

History: The Spirit guided the apostles in all truth, giving them remembrance and understanding of Jesus and his life and teaching. We have that recorded for us in Matthew and in Mark and in John as he guided the apostles into understanding the life of Jesus, of recounting and recording the life and the teaching of Jesus in a historical sense. This was the experience of the disciples traveling home on the road to Emmaus. Discouraged they encountered a travel companion who opened up the meaning of the Scriptures to them beginning in the Old Testament and leading them straight through to Christ. "The whole Old Testament finds its focus in Jesus Christ, His death, and His resurrection. The Apostle Paul says the same thing in different words: 'For no matter how many promises God has made, they are "Yes" in Christ. And so through him the "Amen" is spoken by us to the glory of God (2 Corinthians 1:20)."[4]

Here is a distinctive mark of Christianity—that it is set in history. It isn't conceived in mythology. It isn't simply the thoughts of philosophy or speculation or intuition. It is not simply a pattern of ideas developed systematically into a religion. It is a theology, and it is set in the days of men when Christ was incarnate as a man. It's a story of redemption that puts a real man on a real cross on a real hill in a nation called Israel.

The Bible begins with God's speaking reality into existence, and the New Testament is God's last word spoken in the presence of his Son, by whom he made all the worlds and who is the radiance of his being.

The second of our categories is that of doctrine. He gives us history. He tells us the story of Jesus and the story of Israel, the redemptive history of man, but then he tells us what it means. The Spirit takes what belongs to Jesus and makes it known to us. Beginning with the book of Romans, the Spirit unfolds the true knowledge of God. Having shown what God has done, he shows us what it means. We say Jesus lived, but then we say, "What does that mean?" We say Jesus died on a cross, but then we ask, "Why, and how will we relate to that as a fact?"

The epistles tell us about the atonement. They tell us about the resurrection, they tell us about the kingdom that is to come, and they tell us not only that it is a fact, but also what it means. They define for us the righteousness of Christ in the atonement applied to men because he is the second Adam. They teach us it was for sin that Jesus died and from sin that he saved us, that it was vicarious, substitutionary, atoning, and redemptive. The Spirit tells us what the history of redemption means.

Thirdly, there is a prophetic work of the Spirit. Jesus told them that the Spirit would teach them about things to come. So we read in

---

4. Vern S. Poythress, *The Shadow of Christ in the Law of Moses*, p. 5.

The Unity of the Trinity in Revelation

1 Thessalonians 4:16, "For the Lord himself will descend from heaven with a cry of command, with the voice of an archangel, and with the sound of the trumpet of God. And the dead in Christ will rise first." Was this new revelation? Of course it was not. You have in Daniel the prophecy of the Son of Man descending on clouds. You have Jesus' own words when he said, "Tear the Temple down. I'll rebuild it in three days. My kingdom is not of this world," and then his promise to return. Now the apostles, by the power of the working and the illuminating effect of the Holy Spirit, are able to tell us of things to come, such as in Revelation 21, that there will be a new heaven and a new earth, and every tear will be wiped away. Sin will be no more. In revealing the things to come, the Spirit is continuing to glorify Jesus.

So only one last question remains for us. Why, if there is one God and if there is one Lord and there is one Spirit, and if there is one truth, why don't all who are in Christ apprehend that same truth together and remain in agreement? Why is there discord among people who hold to this same central doctrine of the inspiration of the Scriptures and the work of the Spirit in illuminating our understanding?

The Lord promised the apostles a knowledge, an understanding, which they could not yet bear. He said, "I have so much more to tell you, but you can't bear it right now." In other words, there wasn't found in them a fitness to be able to receive the truth which was yet to come.

The great Augustine points out that at that time the apostles were not even fit to die for Christ. Later, in the history of the church, there will come a day when lesser men than the apostles, when women and children, will sing praise to God even as the flames are licking their bodies. The apostles themselves would one day stand firm for Christ, but not one living soul on earth was found fit for the Lord on the day of his arrest. Not one was fit to receive all that God had to tell them.

Perhaps this solves a mystery for us as to how a person can hear the gospel for years, or even a lifetime, but in the end still be unable to possess any sound doctrine. They may become acquainted with the religious history of Christianity, but in the end, as with the 5,000-piece puzzle before me, they still cannot apprehend a sound doctrine. It still makes no sense to them. They still can't put it together.

What makes them fit is the coming of the Holy Spirit, not their intellectual prowess, not their years of exposure to the story of redemption, but the Holy Spirit. It is the carnal mind that puzzles at the truth

The Last Sermon of Christ

of God. To the worldly wise, Jesus is an inspiring figure, a great Man, and a moral teacher, a model of love, but all the Spirit had to reveal still remains beyond their reach.

Again, Augustine helps here. "Some things there are indeed in the holy Scriptures which unbelieving men both have no understanding of when they read or hear them and cannot bear when they are read or heard; as the pagans, that the world was made by him, and yet he was crucified; as the Jews, that he could be the Son of God; as the Sabellians, that the Father and the Son and the Holy Spirit are a Trinity; as the Arians, that the Son is equal to the Father and the Holy Spirit to the Father and the Son; as the Phoenicians, that Christ is not only a man like ourselves, but God also, equal to God the Father."[5]

If the disciples could not bear to know and the world doesn't have the capacity to know, then what hope is there for you and for me? If the apostles who had been with Jesus could not be found fit to receive the truth, and the world does not have the capacity to contain this knowledge of God, then what are we to do? Seek first the kingdom of God, seek to grow in love, a love that is deposited by the Holy Spirit, and learn to apply yourselves to the study of Scripture, prayerfully asking that God would show you his truth and reveal himself to you. It is in them that God speaks and it is from them that understanding comes.

Do you want to understand yourself or the world? Do you want to understand the people around you, your children, or your parents? Then turn to the Creator of both and not to man. What can man tell you about man when man is yet puzzling over himself? Turn to the Creator and ask of the Creator. Learn to love spiritual rather than carnal pleasures. Take your delight in the Word of God rather than in the vocations and preoccupations of man so that you may see with and not through the eyes by a spiritual light to discern that Word which carnal man cannot bear to hear.

If you so commit yourself and apply your energy to seek out the Lord through the Spirit of Christ, he will teach you all things, and you'll be able to bear it. As the Scriptures of Ephesians and Romans teach, be renewed in the spirit of your minds so that you may discern what is the will of God, what is good and acceptable and perfect.

---

5. St. Augustine, p. 372.

23

In a Little While

John 16:16–21

"A little while, and you will see me no longer; and again a little while, and you will see me." So some of his disciples said to one another, "What is this that he says to us, 'A little while, and you will not see me, and again a little while, and you will see me'; and, 'because I am going to the Father'?" So they were saying, "What does he mean by 'a little while'? We do not know what he is talking about." Jesus knew that they wanted to ask him, so he said to them, "Is this what you are asking yourselves, what I meant by saying, 'A little while and you will not see me, and again a little while and you will see me'? Truly, truly, I say to you, you will weep and lament, but the world will rejoice. You will be sorrowful, but your sorrow will turn into joy. When a woman is giving birth, she has sorrow because her hour has come, but when she has delivered the baby, she no longer remembers the anguish, for joy that a human being has been born into the world. So also you have sorrow now, but I will see you again, and your hearts will rejoice, and no one will take your joy from you."

HAVE YOU EVER WONDERED whether you might have been able to figure Jesus out just a little bit quicker than the Disciples? Have you ever thought that perhaps they just weren't on the ball or maybe they were a little distracted? How many times has Jesus explained his mission and his purpose to them? Time and time again, he seems to have laid it out plainly, laid it out sometimes explicitly, even used figures and stories to help teach them and to show them what he is there to communicate and the gospel itself. There is enough in several single explanations already given for us to explain far more than the disciples understand just hours before the end of Jesus' incarnational ministry on earth. Yet the disciples are puzzled over the words "a little while." Seven times Jesus tells them, "a little while." The words seem so simple to be so difficult to understand.

Henri Bergson, a professor at the College of France, published a small essay back in 1903 titled *Revue de Métaphysique et de Morale*. It's simply referred to later as *An Introduction to Metaphysics*. Now that is a long and a complicated title as is often the case when a college professor is writing to define something very simple: *How do we know what we know?*

In the first pages of this essay, he defines two ways of knowing. He says this, "The first implies that we move around an object, and the second that we enter into it. The first depends on the point of view at which we are placed and on the symbols by which we express ourselves. The second neither depends on a point of view nor relies on any symbol."[1] So the first he calls *relative knowledge*, and the second he calls *absolute*. We sometimes use the word *intuitive* to say it's how we come to know.

So the first is a way of knowing through observation, through relation of one object to another. You might meet someone, and you might say, "I have this fellow sized up. I know what he is all about," because you know someone else whom you think is a lot like that person. You can't really know the inner workings of the individual. You can't really know how their mind is operating, but you're taking some guesses based on deductions. You have a relative knowledge of that individual.

You can walk around the individual, that is, you can observe their life, you can listen to their words, you can learn their history, you can observe from a distance, and draw some conclusions. We call that *stereotyping* sometimes. We can call that being *prejudiced* at times. Sometimes, we draw conclusions based on very little information, based on color or race or based on ethnicity. We may look at people and decide we know all about what motivates them based purely upon appearance or dress, and yet we really don't. We really don't know what makes that person who they are. That would require us almost to enter into the personhood of that individual. To really know what is coming out of someone, we would almost need to be that person.

1. Henry Bergson, *An Introduction to Metaphysics*. Knickerbocker Press, NY, 1912, p. 1.

Relative knowledge is gained by observation and deduction while absolute knowledge, what we also would call *intuitive* knowledge, is acquired by entering into a relationship with that object by identifying with it, by seeing from that object's perspective.

How many of us thought our parents were harsh or antiquated or narrow-minded loons? We were shocked they could be so far up the evolutionary chain when we come from their genes. We thought at best they were boring, but more likely, they were intentional killjoys. Then we became parents, and we wished we knew half of what our parents did when we thought they were out of their minds.

The disciples are having trouble relating to the words of Jesus. They're having trouble understanding what to us seems to be so clear. Jesus is telling them, "I'm going to the Father." That seems clear enough to us, and it actually is a language they can understand, a Man saying he is going to his Father.

We understand going to the Father in a way that is unique to Christianity, a unique religious phrase, but unique to Christianity. So when we speak in terms of going to the Father outside of our Christian environment, how will other religions or secular people hear it? How will a member of the Muslim religion hear us when we say we're going to the Father? Or how will someone who is Jehovah's Witness, or someone who is non-Christian even in the carrying of the Scriptures hear us say we are going to the Father?

It's a term that is unique in its application to Christianity, so while we may say a phrase is easy to understand, we may find a number of different perspectives and definitions when that phrase is actually used. I would contend that much of our lack of results in evangelism comes from our using an institutional language we understand because we're on the inside and that simply has no point of reference for people who are outside the church.

The disciples can't understand it, and they admit they don't know what he means. When Jesus says, "In a little while," it's a simple phrase, "A little while." It seems to have reference to time, but they confess to one another, "What does he mean a little while?" This is Christ's expression, and all who belong to him sense what he means.

Luther, the great Reformer, explains, "Christ's going or being sent from the Father means nothing else than that he, the true Son of God from eternity, became a true man and revealed himself on earth in

The Last Sermon of Christ

human nature, essence, and form, that he let himself be seen, heard, and touched, that he ate, drank, slept, worked, suffered, and died like any other human being. On the other hand, his going to the Father means that through his resurrection from the dead, it is declared that he sits at the right hand of God and reigns with him forever as eternal and omnipotent God."[2] This is what that phrase means.

"I am going to the Father," means that our Lord Jesus Christ was resurrected from the dead, glorified, ascended to the Father, and sits at the right hand of God the Father Almighty in glory to return to judge the living and the dead. All of that is contained in the phrase, "Jesus is going to the Father."

This, the disciples will come to know as the Spirit of God, gives them understanding, but in the hours before the arrest of Jesus, it was too much for them to comprehend. It was too much, as Jesus says, for them to bear. "A little while," is a phrase that puzzles them.

John's repetition of the term emphasizes it as central to the teaching of this passage, so we must turn our attention to the meaning of "a little while." The disciples have heard Jesus is soon to leave. That is comprehensible, but he said he would die, so how will they see him again in a little while? Do you see how Jesus' phrase, "In a little while I am leaving," can be understood, but then he turns right around and says, "In a little while you will see me again"? That is breaking down barriers of their understanding of reality.

They understand a Man is going to die. How were they to understand, having never seen, never experienced, and never imagined that they would, even conceptually, perceive a Man rise from the dead and then have a relationship with him again? This is beyond the disciples' ability to comprehend. They have no mental framework for this teaching. Doesn't that bring some compassion to us then as we read these disciples? We don't think of them as dunderheads anymore because it just didn't come to them as easily as it does to us.

"In a little while," Jesus says, "I'm leaving." Yes, they know. He has been comforting them over and over again to try to help them understand that his leaving would not be the end, that he is going to prepare a place for them. He is stretching their eyes heavenward and causing them to look into the afterlife, and they are beginning to understand

---

2. Martin Luther, p. 375.

In a Little While

there is a sense of eternity in Jesus' words, but now he injects into the equation, "But in a little while you're going to see me again."

So they're going back and forth. Jesus is with them, and he is the Messiah, and he is establishing the kingdom. "Oh, Jesus now is going to die very soon, and he is going to be leaving us, but Jesus is telling us there is a place we're going to go where he is building a home for us, and we will be there in eternity with him, but now he is telling us that in fact we are going to see him very shortly. What does all of this mean?" How can they fit this on a linear time line? "He is with us. He is leaving us. He is going way out here, and yet he will be with us again."

Frederic Godet captures the disciples' puzzle. It's not one of belief; it's one of understanding. He says, "Where for us all is clear, for them all was mysteries. If Jesus wishes to found the messianic kingdom, why go away? If he doesn't wish to found it, then why return?"[3] You see the logical breakdown they're having. There seems to be an illogical sequence of events. Could one of the roadblocks in our Christian testimony be that we presume too much of a logical flow for those who have no concept of a Messiah, of a kingdom, of death and the propitiation of sin, and the necessity of a resurrection, and the historical fact of a resurrection and what it all means, and then pointing on towards Pentecost, the coming of Christ in Spirit, and eternity resting forever in God's grace?

So the disciples are perplexed, and we might add, again, but none will ask Jesus a question. You notice that this time around? No one brings it up to Jesus. Who can blame them? In John 13, verses 37 and 38, and in 14:5 through 10, and again in 22 and 23, Peter, Thomas, Philip, and Judas, not Iscariot, had each asked a question in turn of Jesus, and they were told the reason they didn't understand was because of sinful ignorance and carnal mindedness, that that is the root of their misunderstanding and their questions. So instead of setting themselves up again, they just whisper to one another, but Jesus knows they need this answer. They need to know what this means because even if they don't understand on this night, they need to hear his words to reflect on them later.

So what is Jesus telling them? "A little while, and you will see me again"? First, Jesus is speaking of his arrest and his crucifixion. "A little while, and you will see me no more." This is the eve of his arrest. We are at the threshold of his arrest. He has spoken of it before. John 13,

---

3. Frederic Godet, Commentary on the Gospel of John, p. 315.

The Last Sermon of Christ

verse 33: "'Little children, yet a little while I am with you. You will seek me, and just as I said to the Jews, so now I also say to you, "Where I am going you cannot come."'" They've already been prepared that Jesus is about to leave.

John 12:32 and 33: "'And I, when I am lifted up from the earth, will draw all people to myself.' He said this to show by what kind of death he was going to die." So he has been leading them into an understanding of and acceptance of his quick departure, his imminent departure by way of crucifixion. This brought the Disciples their sorrow. Death and separation were entirely in their mental framework. They could understand that, and so their sorrow was deep, and it was real. That they grasped. "The One whom we love, the One whom we have followed is soon to be unjustly persecuted and crucified." It was from their despair over this that Jesus is now seeking to rescue them.

They sorrowed because of personal loss. Jesus was their Teacher and their Friend. With him they had seen and accomplished things that they would never have believed possible before. They believed in him, and they believe in him now, but have no idea what they will do when he is gone.

Secondly, they sorrowed because they sensed the end of the messianic journey. They had come to Jerusalem, there had been the triumphal entry, the messianic expectation reached its apex, its crest, its climax, and the Jews who opposed Jesus were going to win, and Christ would die. They who persecuted Christ and their disciples would rejoice while the disciples would be left to mourn.

We can see a profound example of that in Luke 24. After the crucifixion, the disciples were leaving Jerusalem. They were all going back to their ordinary lives, traveling on the road to Emmaus. Jesus appeared to them, but they did not recognize him. However, they engaged him in conversation, and what were they talking about? They were talking about Jesus, and they said this, "We had hoped he was the One who was going to redeem Israel." You get a sense of the loss, you get a sense of the sadness, a sense of the despair on that road to Emmaus.

Jesus is telling the disciples that all of that sorrow is going to turn to joy when he returns. He compares it to childbirth, by giving them a parable, saying that in those moments of a woman entering into the pangs of childbirth, when the contractions begin, when everything is beginning to move into place, when the bones are being adjusted

In a Little While

because a woman is going to give birth, those incredible and massive changes in a woman's body bring grief and pain, and yet when the child emerges, and life begins, and there is the sound of the cry, all is forgotten, and there is joy, and the baby is held, and sorrow and grief and trial give way to joy and happiness and hope.

After the resurrection, you'll notice in your Scriptures, there is no reference to the crucifixion in the New Testament that is punctuated with sorrow. Before the resurrection, the disciples couldn't grasp the idea of atonement or propitiation of sin and the spiritual nature of the kingdom, but as the Spirit led them to put quill to parchment, the joy of salvation poured from them. The joy of the crucifixion poured from them.

In Galatians 6:14, Paul even refers to the cross as his glory, but the glory isn't established at Calvary, but at the empty tomb. The resurrection is what turns tragedy to triumph and sorrow to joy. The great preacher, Donald Grey Barnhouse, notes, "It's unfortunate that we approach the cross of Jesus Christ as though it were the climax of his life instead of a great episode that lead to the much greater event of the resurrection and all that followed it."[4]

When we approach the cross, are we in mourning and full of sorrow, or do we see the cross now through the lens of the resurrection? So even the cross is a time of great joy and great celebration. Not the celebration of a Man suffering, but the celebration of the forgiveness of sin.

But this is not all Jesus meant. Jesus promises he is coming to them, and we wonder, Is he speaking of the time after the resurrection when he appears to them again, or is he talking about Pentecost when the Spirit of Christ descends in the Holy Spirit upon the church and the church age is begun, or is he here talking about the second coming when he will return in judgment to establish the new heavens and the new earth?

C. K. Barrett sees deliberate ambiguity here, connecting death and resurrection eschatologically. That means, connecting them with an end-times' view. He sees the death and resurrection not being viewed simply as two events in history, but being delivered in the context of the end times, the last days and prefiguring the final events of the last day. All are connected—.the crucifixion, the resurrection, Pentecost, and the Parousia, or the second coming of Christ. Each one would be

---

4. Donald Grey Barnhouse, *The Cross Through the Open Tomb*, p. 13.

diminished without the other. Each one has meaning as it is connected one to the other.

While we study and we analyze each concept by itself, Jesus speaks of them intuitively, to go back to the language we discovered at the beginning, as if they are all one event, as if they were all happening simultaneously. He sees one reality, one kingdom, and we see all the parts. It's similar to being hooked up to a machine that counts out heartbeats. The doctor measures each beat, and we hear each beat one by one, but the heart itself simply knows to beat. It's not counting and analyzing. The heart simply knows to beat.

So when we study Scriptures, often we analyze and we count and we break it into its parts, but the Scripture simply tells us the mind of God. Some will protest we can't see him now; however, Jesus said he would come, so although we can't see him, we reply in the Christian church, "Yes, we do."

The Spirit of Christ has come to the church, and the spiritual is as real as the physical, and every truth that is revealed in Scripture is evidenced in life. For when we are blessed in the Spirit of Christ, we see Christ face to face in the Scriptures. Word and Spirit operate together and in connection to our resurrected Lord. This is why the answer to one who feels estranged from Jesus is not to seek him in any way other than the pages of Scripture, affirmed in Hebrews 12:1 and 2. ". . . Run with endurance the race that is set before us, looking to Jesus, the founder, and perfecter of our faith. . . ."

If Jesus cannot be found or seen, why do we have instructions to look to Jesus? Where can we do that except in the pages of Scripture? So if we were to take the letters of a name, say *J* and *O* and *E*, individually they are simply letters in an alphabet, three of 26, not special, not distinct, but taken together without separation, read together in sequence, they form a word, a proper noun. Not simply isolated letters, now they have reference to a living being who has personality, who has personhood, who has purpose in life. We can know something about Joe if we know anything about people at all.

This takes us to where we began with the difference between relative and absolute knowledge, or intuitive knowledge. We can only know Christ relatively, that is, as a figure in history, without the illuminating work of the Holy Spirit, but if the Spirit of Christ is within us, if the Spirit of Christ is within our heart and he has made us alive in Christ, then we can know Christ absolutely because it is Christ who dwells within us. It is Christ himself who reveals himself to us as he truly is. We can know the mind of Christ, not just simply observe the effects because it is Christ himself who has entered into us. In 1 Corinthians 3:16, "God's Spirit dwells within you." In Galatians 2:20, it is "Christ who lives in me." We don't become Christ, but he dwells in unity with us. Just as we cannot know Joe absolutely unless we are Joe, so we are able to know Christ because he dwells within us.

Ephesians 3:14 through 19 explains our intuitive knowledge.

> "For this reason I bow my knees before the Father, from whom every family in heaven and on earth is named, that according to the riches of his glory he may grant you to be strengthened with power through his Spirit in your inner being, so that Christ may dwell in your hearts through faith—that you, being rooted and grounded in love, may have strength to comprehend with all the saints what is the breadth and length and height and depth, and to know the love of Christ that surpasses knowledge, that you may be filled with all the fullness of God."

How do we know intuitively? Because we are indwelled by Christ. Temples of the Holy Spirit, indwelled by the Holy Spirit, we are able to know not based upon our own knowledge, but based upon revelation of Christ in himself.

There is one final dimension to Christ's teaching here though. Beyond the resurrection, beyond the church age, is the second coming. In this age, there is still sorrow, and there is still suffering, and it seems that there are wars without end. Sickness, death, abuse, immorality, they all run rampant. We sometimes wonder whether we're right about all of this. Jesus said, "A little while." Seven times John stresses "a little while" to us. For adults, the time between birthdays is only a little while, but for a child, it's an eternity. Time spent on a playground is just a little while; time spent in the classroom is an eternity.

The apostle Peter remembered what he felt like that day, and he tells us in 2 Peter 3:4. "They will say, 'Where is the promise of his coming? For ever since the fathers fell asleep, all things are continuing as they were from the beginning of creation.' For they deliberately overlook this fact, that the heavens existed long ago, and the earth was formed out of water and through water by the word of God, and that by means of these the world that then existed was deluged with water and perished.

But by the same word, the heavens and earth that now exist are stored up for fire, being kept until the Day of Judgment and destruction of the ungodly. But do not overlook this one fact, beloved, that with the Lord one day is as a thousand years, and a thousand years as one day."

Jesus was revealed to them as the Word of God in his incarnation. He was revealed to them as Christ glorified at the resurrection. He is revealed as the Spirit of God since Pentecost. He will be revealed as the King of kings at his return. We go through the travails of life now as a woman who is giving birth, but in that day, there will be no more sorrows, no more tears, no more death.

What is our hope? That in a little while our Lord will come again. Do you in fact know Jesus? Has your sorrow turned to joy because of the reality of seeing Jesus face to face by the power and the virtues of the Holy Spirit as he reveals himself to you in the pages of Scripture? Do you know this Jesus, or like the letters in the word *Joe,* do the pages of Scripture seem disconnected and discordant, and to get around this, do you avoid the essentials that God has delivered to us, making an excuse that perhaps they're not important because they seem so incomprehensible? Yet would God deliver anything unimportant to his people concerning himself?

When you look at the Scriptures, do they come together as letters that form a language and then have reference to reality, or do they remain simply that, letters standing individually with some merit and some teaching, and yet never really coming together in your own mind and in your own heart? Do you never get a sense that you know intuitively this One called Jesus Christ? Do you know Jesus? Do you know the joy of the cross? Do you know him relatively, or do you know him absolutely? Are you puzzling like the disciples, or are you rejoicing as the children of God?

24

A Loving Father Wants You To Ask

John 16:23–27

"In that day you will ask nothing of me. Truly, truly, I say to you, whatever you ask of the Father in my name, he will give it to you. Until now, you have asked nothing in my name. Ask, and you will receive, that your joy may be full. I have said these things to you in figures of speech. The hour is coming when I will no longer speak to you in figures of speech but will tell you plainly about the Father. In that day you will ask in my name, and I do not say to you that I will ask the Father on your behalf; for the Father himself loves you, because you have loved me and have believed that I came from God."

SOME YEARS AGO, I was leading a study called *Experiencing God*, by Henry Blackaby. I find it to be a very interesting study, not complete, not perfect in all ways, but certainly a study that has proved itself worthy of undertaking. In part of that study on one particular evening, there was a discussion of spiritual gifts. As we were discussing spiritual gifts around a table that one night, someone mentioned because it was brought out in the study itself that perhaps prayer is a spiritual gift, that there are certain people who are particularly gifted with prayer.

Now there was a couple who protested that prayer is not listed as a spiritual gift in the Scripture and that all Christians are called to prayer. Those who believed that prayer is a gift had in mind one particular elderly lady; she had years of walking with the Lord, and they said that this woman was able to spend literally hours on her knees in prayer and had done so for years; that her life was a life of prayer, and that not only was her life a life of prayer, but she could point, if others did not do it for her, to many, many answers to prayer; that her prayers didn't seem to hit the ceiling and go no further; that her prayers seemed in some unique way to ascend to the very ear of God in a way most of us are not able to do.

Do you ever wonder about your prayers? Do you ever wonder if your prayers make it to God's ears or if they're just utterances to try to assure yourself there is a God and perhaps he will hear and perhaps things will work out for you after all? Do you ever wonder if you pray right, or if there is a right way to pray? Is there a formula we are to follow? Is there some particular way of praying that makes a prayer work and then all other prayers fail? Are all prayers even by unbelievers heard by God? We turn to people and say they should pray, and we know they aren't believers. Are those prayers effectual when they are carried before the throne of grace?

In this passage we're reading today, Jesus is revealing even our prayer life is going to be changed in that age which is to come, that age which now the apostles were on the threshold of. Many have the idea that prayer is our striving to convince God to do something he otherwise would be unwilling to do. That is the way we pray. We may not think of it that way, but that is the way we pray. We come to the Lord to ask him to do something we desperately desire or we feel we desperately need, and our disposition is that otherwise God would not be doing it; that he is going to do us a favor or make an exception, or he is going to somehow change a little bit of history in somebody's life that otherwise he wouldn't intend to do, but because of the prayer perhaps he will do something he naturally had not planned to do.

In speaking of prayer here, Jesus is actually returning to a theme he has already taught concerning prayer. Both the repetition of his teaching on prayer and the appearance here at the close of his ministry of his teaching on prayer are emphasizing the importance of prayer. So we ask, does prayer first, come to the ear of God, and secondly, is it effectual?

Let's confess at the outset prayer (*real* prayer, *genuine* prayer, the prayer which we discover in Scripture whether you're reading in the Psalms or in the life of Christ, or whether you're reading simply descriptions of the different aspects of prayer as people delivered it) is probably the second most neglected practice in the Christian life. What would be the first? The study of the Scriptures because we often

A Loving Father Wants You To Ask

find ourselves praying without thinking about it, but rarely do we find ourselves studying the Scriptures when we're not thinking about it. So Scriptures would rank as the first neglected duty of the Christian life. Secondly would be prayer.

R. A. Torrey, who wrote a great book on prayer, lists eleven reasons for prayer.

1. There is a devil and because prayer is God's appointed means of resisting him.
2. Prayer is God's way for us to obtain what we need from him.
3. The apostles, whom God set forth to be a pattern for us, considered prayer to be the most important business of their lives.
4. Prayer occupied a prominent place and played a very important part in the earthly life of our Lord.
5. Prayer is the most important part of the present ministry of our Lord, since he is now interceding for us. (That particular point will play heavy in this chapter. Our Lord is presently in prayer himself for us.)
6. Prayer is the means God has appointed for our receiving mercy from him and of obtaining grace to help in time of need.
7. Prayer is the means of obtaining the fullness of God's joy.
8. 8. Prayer with thanksgiving is the means of obtaining freedom from anxiety and, in anxiety's place, the peace that surpasses understanding.
9. Prayer is the method appointed for our obtaining the fullness of God's Holy Spirit.
10. Prayer is the means by which we are to keep watchful and be alert at Christ's return.
11. Prayer is used by God to promote our spiritual growth, bring power into our work, lead others to faith in Christ, and bring all other blessings to Christ's church.

When we pray are we changing God's mind and God's direction? I would submit that prayer is not to change God; prayer changes the one who offers prayer. Prayer changes us.

Understanding Jesus' teaching on prayer will convince us that prayer is less a Christian obligation than it is a Christian privilege. We often think of prayer in terms of "we ought" instead of "we want." We think in terms of guilt. "You know, I really should pray more. I really ought to be praying more than I do." What a privilege we are skipping, what an opportunity we are missing when we approach it as some legal obligation instead of a door that has been opened wide by the Lord Jesus Christ. Prayer is the action that proves all of the other blessings the Lord has been speaking of.

Jesus has been telling them about joy. He has been telling them how they might receive joy, and he said, "Your joy is dependent upon your obedience. Your joy is dependent upon my love to you. Your joy is dependent upon my Word abiding in you." All of these are knit together by prayer. Prayer becomes the path the Christian travels to discover the fruits and the promises of Christ in life.

Jesus gives us a reference to time in this passage. Did you notice the words, "In that day"? That *day* is a reference to the day of his resurrection, the day that they will see him again. "In that day" is language used in Scripture to refer to the last day, the Day of Judgment, the day of the end of history. Jesus is marking here the end of history, that is, the end of redemptive history, the inauguration of the new and the final testament. The new covenant is being inaugurated. The time of his resurrection marks that day.

In Hebrews 1:1 and 2 bears repeating. "Long ago, at many times and in many ways, God spoke to our fathers by the prophets, but in these last days he has spoken to us by his Son." Jesus says, "In that day—in that day when we see him again." The day of resurrection marked the restoration of spiritual hope. In the resurrected Christ, man is reconciled to God by faith. He is our Advocate, and he is our Mediator.

Jesus now sets before us the reality and the proximity of that reconciliation in relationship with God the Father. Remember as we proceed, man has been alienated and separated from the Father in the garden. Christ has come to mediate that relationship, to make atonement for sin, and to restore man's relationship with the Father. Jesus, in this teaching now, is setting before us not only the reality of that restored relationship that we will once again be able to speak in prayer to the Father, but also the proximity, meaning the time is now. "In that day," he said. In that day. The waiting time has now passed, the Messiah has come, the day has arrived, man will once again speak to the Father, and the Father will once again speak to man through the mediation of Jesus Christ.

Jesus teaches that prayer is based on two realities. One, that he is the Mediator between God and man, and two, that our opportunity for prayer is found in our union with him. Not in ourselves as individuals, but in our unity with Christ.

Jesus goes on to say, "In that day, you will no longer ask me anything." Until sunset on this last day that Jesus was with them, Jesus had been walking with them. They had had direct and immediate access to him. They had appealed to him directly for understanding, for teaching, for answers, for the needs of life, and Jesus supplied their needs. He taught them the Scriptures. He stilled the storms that threatened their lives. He fed thousands. He healed the sick and the lame. He even healed Peter's mother-in-law, a miracle Peter actually did not even request. Now Jesus explains that God who is the Father by virtue of their adoption in Christ will supply as they have learned through Jesus.

Calvin compares the Disciples to children learning the alphabet, pausing on each word. Each new word makes them hesitate, but soon the Holy Spirit would show them the wisdom of God.

You may remember a prayer you recited as children when you went to bed at night. "Now I lay me down to sleep. I pray thee, Lord, my soul to keep. If I should die before I wake, I pray thee, Lord, my soul to take. If I should live another day, I pray thee, Lord, to guide my way." Then we would say, "God bless," and you'd start to list all the people who were important to you. It's a children's prayer, a prayer that does more to teach about praying than it does actually to teach heartfelt prayer.

Or perhaps when you sat down at the table, you said a prayer like, "God is great. God is good. Let us thank him for our food." Or perhaps you've heard a little more of a crass approach to prayer. "Pass the bread and pass the meat. Hurry, Lord, and let us eat." I don't recommend that one be taught to the children.

The point is there is a language of children, and the Scripture says, "When I was a child, I used to think as a child. When I was a child, I behaved as a child. But now that I am a man, I no longer think as a child does." We might ask ourselves: *Well, was it wrong that children express themselves that way? Were they wrong in doing that?*

The Last Sermon of Christ

I hear that same question often when we discuss aspects of worship or aspects of ministry. If we have learned to use a different expression, was the earlier one incorrect? And the answer is: *Do we grow? Do we learn?* Is it wrong when we were children and we behaved and acted as children do?

When it comes to our prayer life, have we matured in our expression? When it comes to our worship, have we matured in our expression, or are we safer with childish expressions? Do we feel more comfortable with those childish expressions that lack maturity, that lack growth? It's not a judgment against our children to say their prayers are simple. For like the children who were just learning the alphabet, the apostles can't read a whole sentence clearly and fluidly and eloquently. They stumble over each word, trying phonetically to work out the details of spiritual life, but by virtue of the working of the Holy Spirit, gradually there is a maturing of expression and growth, and in that, then there is a beauty of eloquence and expression that is made.

Reflect on your own prayer life as I would reflect on mine. Does our present practice of prayer reflect more the thinking of a child or the deep theological understanding of a mature Christian adult who knows God, who knows what the term *unity in Christ* means? So much of our Christian expression is built on that truth, and if we miss that truth, how much of our practice is off the mark? When we say God is sovereign and we say God is providential, do we truly understand what that means? If not, then much of our practice is off the mark. Much of our practice is uninformed and childlike.

Now does that mean that even as an adult, childlike expressions are wrong? Not if that is where they've begun. If you're teaching reading to adults who've never learned how to read, it is not wrong that they stumble over words in the beginning, but it's another issue if they are happy to stumble over words for the rest of their lives.

The same can be said for our prayer life. A lack of desire to grow in Christ and to understand the role of Christ and to approach God as God requires, that is the only wrong answer. The place we begin is not the wrong answer. The lack of willingness to grow as God calls us to is what is wrong.

Jesus is setting their future conversation with God on par with their present conversation with Jesus. In Jeremiah, chapter 31, verse 34: "And no longer shall each one teach his neighbor and each his brother,

A Loving Father Wants You To Ask

saying, 'Know the LORD,' for they shall all know me, from the least of them to the greatest, declares the LORD. For I will forgive their iniquity, and I will remember their sin no more."

Jesus is telling them, "You've spoken to me as a man. You've approached me as a man. You've let your concerns be known to me, and I have taught, and I have worked, and I have provided for you as a man. Now you will go directly to the Father, and I will make that available to you. It has not been available before, but it is available now."

It's not as if the Jews didn't know what prayer was. They understood prayer in its most high and exalted state, for a high priest would intercede for them. He would make atonement for sin at the altar, and go into the Tabernacle, and go into the holy of holies, and there intercede on behalf of the people. Prayer was a privilege that only a few truly offered to the Father. They understood that.

Do you understand what is meant when we say, *priesthood of believers?* That opportunity has been given to all God's people by virtue of the indwelling of the Holy Spirit. Here the Lord is saying, "No longer will you come to me, but your conversation with God will be much like your conversation with me in my incarnated state." Just as they approached Jesus, we approach God the Father.

The lesson here is that prayer is an approach to the Father based on our adoption as sons and permitted because of the mediation of Christ who has brought peace between God and man. So the beauty of a prayerful expression is in its authenticity—not its form, not its Shakespearean English, but in its authenticity, a genuine concern.

When the disciples approached Jesus, do you think they made sure they used the most eloquent speech? Or did they simply pour their hearts out before him? Was that pouring out of their hearts uninformed, or as they had learned Jesus did they approach him as he had been revealed? Certainly as they learned him, they approached him as he had been revealed. When he showed himself, they were awestruck, and you remember in the passages we've just recently studied, they even came to a point where they were afraid to approach and ask him anymore, and the Lord, knowing their heart answered the questions they didn't ask.

Twice in verse 23 we read that word *ask*. Two different words are used in the original autograph, in the original language, which is curious. The first word means if you translate it very literally, *a familiar entreaty*. That is, asking a friend. It's like asking a friend to do something for you. The second one, however, when we making a request of the Father, that word translated literally is *a petition*, a begging for help in time of need. Not a familiar entreaty, but a petition.

Rather than listening to the human voice of Christ, the disciples and all of us to this day are taught by the Spirit who illuminates the Scriptures. Thus, we learn the Word of God and appropriate the mind of Christ as our own; we petition the Father for the issues of our life. Here is where we begin to introduce in our own thinking about prayer this idea of unity.

See, in our unity with Christ, we are being transformed. We are appropriating the mind of Christ to ourselves. In so doing, our prayers will also reflect that unity with Christ. No longer will it be the man of flesh who is coming in prayer before God, but it will be one who has the very Spirit of Christ and whose flesh has been mortified through sanctification, for whom prayer plays a part as one of the means of grace. The Lord himself said, "I have not come to accomplish my own will, but the will of the Father." We too will be able to say as we mature, "We pray not for our own will, but for the will of the Father."

Jesus is impressing upon them again that prayer is to be offered in his name. He knows they haven't prayed that way yet, and the reason is clear. They don't pray in his name as they are still with him. They speak to Jesus directly, but not to the Father by his mediation. They did not yet know the full import of that name, but it will soon be revealed by the Spirit.

"In his name" is not a magical formula or a spiritual incantation. It's not something where even if an unbeliever simply prays, "In Jesus' name," amazing things will happen. Uttering Jesus' name is an appeal to the Father based on a confession of the righteousness of Christ and not our own. It's also declaring we are praying in harmony with his will. When we say, "In Jesus' name," we are saying, "I cannot come in my own righteousness, and my prayer request is in accordance with the will of the Lord Jesus Christ."

Too often, people in prayer are guilty of using Jesus' name as some sort of a magical formula. They say it at the end as some sort of sealing act bringing their time of prayer to a close. Even if someone uses Jesus' name, if the prayer is not in accordance with the will of God, then he may as well have not even used it at all for it does nothing. Yelling the name of Jesus at supposed demonic appearances is akin to holding up the cross in front of vampires. His name is employed by virtue of his role as mediator, not in some sort of Greek idea of a demigod.

In Hebrews, chapter 7, verses 24 and 25, we find that the Lord Jesus Christ as our High Priest is making prayer. "He holds his priesthood permanently, because he continues forever. Consequently, he is able to save to the uttermost those who draw near to God through him, since he always lives to make intercession for them." The resurrection and glorification of Jesus sets him as our Mediator, sets him as our High Priest. Prayer is our privilege, and that is gained not on my merit, not because I deserve it, not in my name, and not in no name at all, which is so frequently the practice in prayer, but in Jesus' name.

God is not manipulated by prayer, but chooses to give in prayer. We know our Lord stands as our Advocate because Stephen, in Acts 7 as he was being martyred, as he gave testimony to the council of the religious leaders who had continually martyred those whom God had sent throughout the years, there they rose up against him, gnashing their teeth, so frustrated and angry at him. They picked up stones to stone him, and Stephen looked into the sky, and he said, "The clouds have opened up, and I see the Lord Jesus standing at the right hand of God."

He desires prayer to be that living dynamic of believers' correspondence with the Father. We come before the Father in Jesus' name, and God doesn't deny Jesus anything, and he does answer prayer. Dr. Robert McQuilkin, who was president of Columbia Bible College many years ago, testified that they had committed to buy a large building, spending about $10,000 which in those days was a good bit of money. The staff and the trustees had committed the matter to the Lord in prayer throughout the entire process to include the finances and the fundraising.

The required money had been coming in, but on the last day of September with the note due on October 1st, they found themselves $2,121.21 short. So they went to their knees in prayer in humble submission to God that his will would be done, that their need would be met, and that God would receive the glory. They rose and went to check the donation box outside, wondering if perhaps God had answered the prayer. Inside they did find money, $21.21, which left $2,100 outstanding.

Throughout the day, money arrived. At one point, the largest gift to come in was $100 until late in the day when $500 arrived. By evening,

The Last Sermon of Christ

they had $2,121.22, one cent more than they needed. The testimony was clear that the living God had heard and supplied their need. God used people, people who didn't even know there was such a great need, people who did not know there were men and women on their knees in prayer, people who were praying. He gave joy to those people. Matthew 7:7, "Ask, and it will be given to you; seek, and you will find; knock, and it will be opened...."

The second and the final aspect is one I've mentioned already, and that is our union with him. The clearest picture of our union with Christ is his earlier reference to the vine and the branches in John 15. Our spiritual life doesn't originate in ourselves, but it flows from him to us by the converting and life-giving power of the Holy Spirit.

That relationship of a vine to branch produces fruit as evidence of the indwelling and authentic engrafting of the Holy Spirit. Love, joy, peace, patience, kindness, goodness, faith, meekness, and temperance show the inner transformation that takes place for those who are new creations in Christ. When we come before the Lord, the privilege has been purchased by Christ, and the character required for an audience with God is Christ's own character. Only our union with him gives us words for prayer. Our prayers ought to be the natural expression of a converted heart, appropriating the mind of Christ and being renewed in his image.

I love the story told by H. A. Ironside at Moody Memorial Chapel in Chicago. He talks about a battle in the War between the States. There on the battlefield lay a wounded young man. As he lay there dying, another crawled to him and tried to offer him comfort. He provided whatever aid he could, but there was nothing he could do to save the soldier's life, and so he did what he could just be keeping his company.

As they lay there together, the one who was dying was so grateful for the comfort, he told the soldier who remained with him that his father was quite wealthy and that after the war, if he was ever in need, if he would take this note, which the dying man provided, that he assured his father would provide as far as he was able for his need.

After the war, some time passed, and in fact the young man did find himself in need, and so he thought to avail himself of that opportunity. He went to the father, and sent word to him that he was a friend of his son's in the war. He was rebuffed, and there was no audience with the father. Before he left, he decided to use the note itself instead of just sending it by word. So he asked one of the servants if they would take the note to the man.

No sooner had the note been delivered than the man came out with his arms outstretched. He embraced the young man, and he said, "Why didn't you tell me that my son wrote out a note to you?" The note simply said, "Father, if you can ever do anything for my friend who helped me when I was dying, please do so." It was signed, "Charlie." The man came running out, embraced him, and did anything for Charlie's sake. God will do anything his Son desires for our sake.

What is the result of this? The attainment of joy, a joy because of this new relation to the Father as evidenced in prayer. I suppose one joy comes in answered prayer (we can't deny that), but the focus of joy here is on a spiritual joy, not carnal joy. It's not that we get the results so much as we get the audience, the conversation, the relation with the Father. In prayer, we encounter God not through a high priest or prayers that are offered to this saint or the other, but on the most personal and intimate level.

In our habits of prayer, we grow more familiar with our Father and know we are familiar to him. We're reminded of his love as he pours out spiritual blessings upon us. Our hope for eternity is renewed as we utter prayers to the eternal God who has given us life, and we are relieved to know our Father is always with us, always caring, always listening, always blessing.

So let me ask you, what is your habit of prayer? As you reflect upon your understanding of Christ, in his role as Mediator, as you reflect upon his telling of the vine and the branches in our union with him, do we approach the Father based upon these truths that we have a unity with Christ? Do we express the will of God just as Christ expressed the same will? Is it a will that is substantiated by a reflection on the Scriptures? Do we approach God knowing it is through the mediation of Christ and by virtue of his atonement we're able to make our appeal to the Father? Do you pray in the name of Jesus based on his merit, based on our union with him? Are you confident that the Lord hears your prayers? Do you have joy because of your walk in the Lord and by availing yourself of this means of grace?

Consider your prayer life. You alone are able to make proper assessment. You alone know the validity of your prayer life before the Father. You one alone know if you truly have communion with the Father in Jesus Christ. You alone know that this relational component of our spiritual life which bears evidence in prayer is not hypothetical, is not imaginary, is not a what if. Either we have this or we do not have this to the satisfaction of our own soul. Jesus has commanded that we pray by virtue of his name and in his name to the Father, this living dynamic of faith that bears testimony to the authenticity of our relationship with Christ.

25

Understand and Embrace the Incarnation

John 16:28–30

"'For the Father himself loves you, because you have loved me and have believed that I came from God. I came from the Father and have come into the world, and now I am leaving the world and going to the Father.' His disciples said, 'Ah, now you are speaking plainly and not using figurative speech! Now we know that you know all things and do not need anyone to question you; this is why we believe that you came from God.'"

IF WE WERE TO turn to a single passage and say, "Who is this Jesus and what did he do?" these verses in John 16:28–30 would be a place we could turn, and we would find summarized in four succinct points exactly who this person Jesus Christ is and what he came to accomplish.

To understand Jesus' mission, we must understand his divinity. Without an understanding of his divinity, there is not much about Jesus that will make sense. We see this in a number of different faith groups. We of course would expect those that do not hold to any theistic belief at all, those who do not think there is a personal God, would be unable to see Jesus as anything more than a figure in history the likes of a Confucius. But for those who are theistic, we sometimes stand amazed that they're able to hold to a transcendent, personal God, but have no Mediator between themselves and God. They would seek to approach him based upon their own merit, and so what would they put in place of Christ except another God? There must be One who is deity who can usher us into the presence of the eternal Father.

The Last Sermon of Christ

Now if we're going to understand Jesus' mission, we must understand his divinity, and if we're going to understand his divinity, we must wrestle and come to terms with such theological concepts as the Trinity. Isn't the Trinity the Achilles' heel when it comes to apologetics for the Christian faith? Isn't the Trinity where those who would seek to accuse us require of us an explanation before we can proceed any further with the presentation of the gospel?

It may seem they're trivializing or they know where it is we would struggle the most to explain, but I would submit to you that if we don't understand the divinity of Christ, how can we explain the gospel? If we don't understand this incarnate Son of God who is eternally existent and a member of the Godhead, how can we tell them that this is the same God who became flesh and dwelled among us to save us of our sins? We must know Christ. That is really what is at stake here. Knowing Christ. Not knowing about Christ, but knowing Christ.

Our Westminster Confession of Faith, a summary of scriptural teaching, in the second chapter begins this way: "In the unity of the Godhead there be three persons, of one substance, power, and eternity; God the Father, God the Son, and God the Holy Ghost." That simple statement of biblical doctrine of the Trinity is either not understood or rejected by most of mankind. Most of mankind throughout history has not accepted this simple statement concerning the Trinity.

Atheists, agnostics, non-theistic cults have no category for any type of personal God whatsoever. It simply is not part of their way of thinking that there is a personal God, and so there is no place for a Trinity. There is no place for Christ who is God. So we certainly would expect their rejection. Why is a concept of Jesus, the eternally existing Son of God who is of one substance with the Father, so repugnant to unbelievers? It's not just that they reject it; they are offended by the fact that we would call Christ one with the Father.

But it's not only in our own time. Wasn't the charge against Christ himself for the crucifixion that he claimed to be God? He would dare to call himself the Son of God, making himself equal with God in power and in glory. That single aspect of Christ is the stumbling block for all, for the cross means nothing without deity. The cross is injustice without deity. The cross is ineffectual without deity.

Because no religion that teaches that Christ is God can at the same time teach that man may one day be God or do anything to save himself, we find that most reject the concept that Christ is God. If Christ is God, where does that leave man? If Christ will be elevated to God, then where is man to go? All other religions have man moving upward. Perhaps some are not so bold as to say they believe he will someday become a God, but then what is the destination of man?

In the Buddhist faith, man simply becomes part of an eternal cosmic energy. Perhaps in Hindu or others there is a reincarnation aspect, but even in reincarnation there is the hope of some progress. The reincarnation/recycling process ultimately results in an ultimate but vague destiny. Christianity, on the other hand, places man in an understandable position, not desirable for the unbeliever, but understandable. We are a people, a race, who have fallen. We are outside of any hope because the kingdom of God's gates have been closed to us except as we enter with Christ who himself is King in that kingdom.

None of the errors in thinking are presented in the Bible. The confusion concerning Trinity is something of man's own creation. We can't turn to the Scripture and say, "You see, the Scriptures are all befuddled when it comes to the Trinity. The Scriptures are all confused when it comes to the Trinity." It may be true there is not a chapter in the Bible we can turn to that reads like a systematic theology to teach us about the Trinity, but the Scriptures boldly proclaim that the triune nature of God is in fact true. The Bible assumes its truth even if it doesn't go into minutiae of detail to explain it. It proclaims it, and so we turn there, and we find support and understanding, but it's not in isolation because if we don't grasp the deity of Christ as a member of the Trinity, then none of the rest of the gospel will fall into place. It all falls out of place. Men deny the divinity of Christ, but Scripture is clear. Jesus is like us and completely different from us.

Donald Grey Barnhouse, the great preacher from Tenth Presbyterian many years back, described how he was instructing some French children, and they were learning John 3:16. They were learning it in French, and the translation of John 3:16 out of the French back into English reads this way: "God so loved the world that he gave his unique Son." His unique Son, the unique Christ.

There is a uniqueness to Christ that is lost on those who will not ascribe to him deity. In Hebrews 1:3, we read, "He is the radiance of the glory of God and the exact imprint of his nature." Second Clement, in the oldest sermon we have recovered outside of the New Testament

The Last Sermon of Christ

letters themselves says, "Brethren, we ought so to think of Jesus Christ as of God."

What importance does that suggest to us? It means that this doctrine of the Trinity wasn't developed and conjured up in history; it was the assumption from the beginning. The very beginning of the Christian church was based upon the divinity of Christ. There was never a time that the Christian church did not hold to the divinity of Christ.

So the first step in understanding Jesus for us is that we would grasp his deity, grasp his person as belonging into the Trinity. Second Corinthians 8:9: ". . . though he was rich, yet for your sake he became poor, so that you by his poverty might become rich." This unique Christ, then, we can say is without equal. He is unique in that he is eternal. Before his birth in Bethlehem, Jesus existed with God. Before the manger, he revealed himself to men as the angel of the Lord in the Scriptures of the Old Testament. When he was born, Abraham rejoiced, and Jesus said, "Before Abraham was, I am."

In Isaiah 6, the seraphim call out that the whole earth is full of his glory, and in John 12:41, we're told that Isaiah was saying these things because he saw the glory of Jesus. In Daniel 3, there three Hebrews were thrown into a furnace, and King Nebuchadnezzar looked in, and instead of three, he saw four men, and he said the fourth was like a son of God.

A familiar Scripture summarizes for us very succinctly, how the preincarnate Christ became man. It is called the "kenosis" passage and is found in Philippians, chapter 2, verses 5 through 8.

> Have this mind among yourselves, which is yours in Christ Jesus, who, though he was in the form of God, did not count equality with God a thing to be grasped, but made himself nothing, taking the form of a servant, being born in the likeness of men. And being found in human form, he humbled himself by becoming obedient to the point of death.

This Christ who already existed took the form of man, took humanity into himself, clothed himself with flesh, discarded his rights as God, and humbled himself to become a servant. As Hebrews says, this One whom now God has highly exalted "became for a little while lower than the angels."

The emphasis is on the fact that Jesus took the work as our Redeemer willingly and freely. The Father didn't compel him. Satan

Understand and Embrace the Incarnation

couldn't prevent him. The first step then for us to understand Christ is again to grasp the eternal nature of his person, that he is deity. He is God.

The second step if we're to understand Christ is to consider the incarnation. Again, let me return to our Confession because it's so clear concerning the person of Christ. In chapter eight: "The Son of God, the second person in the Trinity, being very and eternal God, of one substance and equal with the Father, did, when the fullness of time was come, take upon Him man's nature." Can we not hear the teaching of Scripture reflected in this passage?

Jesus first says, "I came from the Father." *I came* is in the tense we call the aorist tense, and that means it happened once in the past. It happened at a point in time. It happened on a particular day that he was born and laid in a manger. "I came."

What is the big deal about it's being a one point in time? Jesus is not continuously being incarnated. He came one day in the flesh. He came at a point of history in flesh. He took upon himself humanity on a particular day at a particular time in a particular place. "I came from the Father." He was before, but on that day, he came in flesh. It happened once in the past.

Then he says, "I . . . come into the world." Now here is a different tense. Here is where it is good for those who paid attention in their high school English because you can keep up with the flow, and so much of interpretation depends upon understanding the emphasis and the content aside from the alignment of certain letters into words. It's the perfect tense. That means it happened in the past, but it has abiding results or it's presently occurring.

So what Jesus is saying to the disciples is simply, "I came from the Father at a time appointed by God, and I have come to you, I've come into the world," meaning from that point he was in the world, in flesh, and at the time he is speaking to them, he remained with them. Now you might wonder, why should we be concerned with these semantics of language? If it was not so, or if these tenses were actually different, then it might be said that Jesus was a phantom. He was a mirage, or Jesus was simply an apparition of God, but not really flesh.

Jesus is saying very specifically, "I came." Not, "I misted through," or, "I floated into reality," or "I appeared to you as a vision." He is saying, "I came, and it was on a day I came, and I am remaining with you now.

The Last Sermon of Christ

I came from the Father where I existed before, and I am remaining with you now." He is making a clear statement regarding his incarnation and his flesh. He was a man, and he dwelt among them in history, and yet he is God.

Jesus, who is God, willingly took on the flesh of the creation. Here is the mystery to an unbelieving ear. They might accept that we've put our faith in a man because many of them do the same. Many of them put their faith in a particular man to be an advocate in the afterlife, but the fact that the Man is also the one true God who then went to the cross and gave his life puzzles them.

The Christian Church has consistently affirmed that Christ took on the flesh of man but remained God without confusion between the two. He was fully Man and fully God but neither a God-man nor a Man-god. There was no compromise in either his humanity or his divinity. While this has been the confession of the church since the very beginning and while this is the testimony of the Scriptures before the New Testament was written, we also find in our day that still people hear this as if for the very first time, and it still eludes them as to how this can be. How can it be that this Man took on flesh and remained God?

He did so to be our Savior. Hebrews 10:4: "For it is impossible for the blood of bulls and goats to take away sins." We have been sanctified through the offering of the body of Jesus Christ once and for all. Once again, I find an illustration by Donald Grey Barnhouse to be helpful. He gives an illustration of a judge who was sitting on a bench when one day he looked up from his papers and saw standing before his bench his very own son who was arrested for reckless driving.

The judge, as he looked as his son, knew he had to continue to do his duty, and when the evidence was brought forward, it was clear, unambiguously that his son was guilty. So he weighed against his son the heaviest and the fullest of fines and punishments, and after he had rendered judgment against his own son, he then adjourned the court and he stood and he walked around and he paid the fine.

A little girl who was there listening to the illustration, being very sensitive and having a good bit of discernment herself said, "Ah, but Dr. Barnhouse, God can't get off of his bench. He cannot leave heaven."[1] So Barnhouse responded that this little girl had given him the best

---

1. James Montgomery Boice, p. 1236.

Understand and Embrace the Incarnation

illustration of the incarnation of Jesus who while being fully God has come to pay the fine that God the Father has imposed.

So in the first place, he has come to make atonement for sin. That is the purpose of the incarnation. In the second place, he has come to reveal God. John 1:14: "And the Word became flesh and dwelt among us, and we have seen his glory, glory as of the only Son from the Father." Jesus came teaching people of the Father and of the Father's will. In John 7:16: "My teaching is not my own," says Jesus. "It comes from him who sent me." Again Jesus says in John 12:49, "For I have not spoken on my own authority, but the Father who sent me has himself given me a commandment—what to say and what to speak."

Not only did he teach them about God, but also he showed them God in his person and in his life. Scripture today teaches us that no man can see God and live, so we ask, how did Jesus show them God? How can we see God and live? Did Jesus show them God? Could they see God in Christ?

In Job, chapter 42, Job is protesting because of all that has happened to him, that he is a righteous and holy man, but he was reaching a point of estrangement from God. The strain of his life and the strain of all that had come down upon him was beginning to cause him to be estranged from God. In chapter 32, verse 2, Elihu was burning with anger against Job because Job was justifying himself rather than God.

So beginning in chapter 38, God takes Job on a whirlwind tour of all of creation. Beginning with the foundations of the earth, the seas, the creatures of the deep, the land and the sky, he shows him his providence in upholding all things, even in the battles that are fought and the violence that exists. So in Job 42, verse 5, we read these words, "I had heard of you by the hearing of the ear, but now my eye sees you."

Did Job see God as a Spirit who appeared before him? Had he put Job in the cleft of the rock to observe as God came by? Did he reveal himself to Job in that way? No. He revealed himself to Job by opening Job's mind to understand the person of God and the work of God. Job had heard, but he had not seen. Was creation hidden to him? Was all of the data obscured to him? No. It was all there in front of him, just as the Scriptures are open before us now and available to any who would desire to read or to look, to see, and yet many will say from this day forward, "I had heard of this One called Christ, but now I see him. I once was blind, but now I see."

The Last Sermon of Christ

Job had seen creation, but not in the context of the person of God. The Tabernacle of the Jews could have simply been ceremony to those who could not see God in the Tabernacle. If they could not see the plight of man and the mercy of God, even the mercy seat of God, then the Tabernacle was nothing but a very particularly arranged and perhaps peculiar structure, but for those who were blessed by God with sight, they had heard of the Tabernacle, but now they could see God.

The same is true of the church. As we worship together, there are those who may feel that this is a very particular way to worship God, but for those who see, they see God. Do we see God in the print that is in the bulletin? No, but we see God because just as we walked through a Tabernacle experience where man is lost, atoned for, and then in fellowship with the Father through Jesus Christ, so the same happens in Christian worship today. So the church carries on and shows God. We do not paint God on the ceilings or on the walls, but the ear has heard, and now the eye can see God because we're placing the gospel in the context of God rather than in the context of the world.

In Mark 15, the centurion saw death in the context of God when he said, "This Man in the way he breathed his last, truly this Man was the Son of God." Jesus showed us perfect obedience, love, law, grace, justice, truth. Jesus shows us the character and the person of God.

Growing up, I was always fascinated with welding goggles. We had a family friend who was a welder, and every time we visited, I would pick up the face shield, or his goggles, and I would put them on. I thought it was amazing how he could work in these because I couldn't see anything at all. They're almost black. But without those goggles, if you weld, the bright light of the welding torch will burn and blind your eyes. With those goggles, you're able to see.

Without Christ, any vision of God that is real will only come on judgment day, and it will be like a welder's torch to those who have not known God before that day; however, for those who have Christ, it's like the welder's goggles. They are now able to look and see, in the context of the work which God is doing, the light of Christ and the love of God.

Jesus tells us in the passage that he also is returning to the Father. By the Spirit, he continues his prophetic work with us today. He has assumed official rule over the kingdom in his ascension to the Father sitting in glory. Matthew 26:64: Jesus told the high priest there that he would sit at the right hand of power himself. In Acts 7, Stephen, just before he is stoned, looks up. He sees the heavens open up and the Son of Man standing at God's right hand. His ascension to God's right hand is a public coronation that he is King. It's proof that the work of redemption is now complete. It's finished, and he has now taken his place to rule over his people.

By his rule over his people, Jesus proves that life after the resurrection is life that is not dull. It is life that is full of activity purpose. He rules. He protects the church by his Spirit, and he governs through his appointed officers. Not only is he King, but he is our High Priest. In Zechariah 6:13, "It is he who shall build the temple of the LORD and shall bear royal honor, and shall sit and rule on his throne. And there shall be a priest on his throne."

Hebrews 5:1 describes a priest's work. "For every high priest chosen from among men is appointed to act on behalf of men in relation to God, to offer gifts and sacrifices for sins." A priest mediates between God and man. Our Larger Catechism, which we use primarily in the instruction of children answers the question of Christ's priesthood like this: "Christ executeth the office of a priest, in his once offering himself a sacrifice without spot to God, to be reconciliation for the sins of his people; and in making continual intercession for them."

Hebrews 4:14 supports that saying, "Since then we have a great high priest who has passed through the heavens, Jesus, the Son of God, let us hold fast our confession." There is One who has made peace for us with God. Because Jesus makes continual intercession, we are able to hold fast by faith to our confession.

So how do we take this and package it in some way other than simply to be in awe because of who Christ is? How do we apply it so that we may worship Christ for who he is, realigning ourselves in our lives so that when we enter into worship we do so with clarity of mind, knowing for what singular purpose we have gathered? In Christ, you have the transcendent God, taking flesh to himself to dwell with men that men could know him. So we ask: *Do we know him? Have we seen God? Do we know Christ?* He came to reveal God to men, to mediate between God and man. Do we know God through Christ? It was an act of love done willingly on our behalf and to God's glory.

His return to the Father means redemption is accomplished. How do we behave in the fact of redemption accomplished? Do we still strive as if it is our own works that are earning merit with God, or do we live as if redemption has been accomplished? Do we live as if we have a Redeemer who is interceding for us every day? Do we have that confidence that there is One who daily makes intercession for his people? Do we live with an understanding that Christ is King and sits at the right hand of God, ruling with authority his people, and in so doing, do we then turn to the Word and order our lives according to the rule of our King?

Robert McCheyne said, "If I could hear Christ praying for me in the next room, I would not fear a million enemies, yet distance makes no difference. He is praying for me."[2] So we hold fast in faith to our confession, knowing that Christianity has no peer. Christ has no rival. We have heard of God with the ear, but in Christ, through the Word in the Spirit, the means of grace, we have beheld him with the eye of understanding.

Like the disciples, we don't profess to know all things, and neither did they. They said that they know that Christ knows all things. We don't profess to know all things, but we do know, as they did, with confidence that in Christ, who does know all things, we are secure. For God so loved the world that he gave his unique Son. Hold fast to Christ. Know Christ. Follow, obey Christ, for in him we live and move and have our being.

---

2. Robert McCheyne, *The works of Rev. Robert Murray McCheyne*, p. 138.

26

Peace in Despair

John 16:31–33

"Jesus answered them, 'Do you now believe? Behold, the hour is coming, indeed it has come, when you will be scattered, each to his own home, and will leave me alone. Yet I am not alone, for the Father is with me. I have said these things to you, that in me you may have peace. In the world you will have tribulation. But take heart; I have overcome the world.'"

WITH THE WORDS OF John 16, verses 31 to 33, Jesus concludes his incarnate teaching ministry to the disciples. It seems difficult to put enough emphasis on this. The Lord is concluding his teaching ministry in his incarnate state, that is, in the flesh, to his disciples. This is it. This is the last instruction they will receive before he is crucified. After all of the years he has walked with them and all of the years they have walked with him, now it comes to this. This is where the Lord is summing up. This last chapter of John is where the Lord is telling them and reminding them of those aspects of his teaching that are essential to their spiritual health and ministry.

What they have learned and what they believe now becomes crystallized in their minds. They profess they believe all Jesus has taught them. Completing this section of John, we actually have to realize that this teaching stretches all the way back to chapter 13, where Jesus began to teach the disciples those specific truths that would equip and steady them in the days and in the ministry after he had departed from them.

In the first instance in chapter 13, he taught them of love. Jesus demonstrated the humble character of love by wrapping a towel around his waist and by washing their feet, and he commanded them that they should do likewise. He taught them about heaven in chapter 14. He promised to return and take them with himself to the place which he was preparing for them. He spoke at length about the Comforter, that is, the coming of the Holy Spirit in chapters 15 and 16. He spoke about the identity, the arrival, and the role of the Holy Spirit; to convict the world, to equip the saints, to inspire the apostles, and to teach them the meaning of the Scriptures.

He spoke to them about their mission again in 15 and 16. He explained that his followers would do the same work he had been doing by proclaiming the kingdom of God. He described it in terms of fruit which they would produce. They will produce fruit because of their spiritual union with him, using the metaphor of a vine and branches. He taught them about prayer in chapter 14 and in chapter 16, Jesus explained that they would pray in his name. They would pray based upon his mediation, based upon his intercession in heaven, that he would be their Advocate with the Father, and that nothing which was necessary for their continued work in ministry would be withheld, and he gave them the conditions for answered prayer.

Concluding then his incarnate ministry to the disciples, he hears a sweet sound from their lips; those words that indicate the good fruit being produced in their hearts and in the minds of the disciples. They have said in verses 29 and 30, "Ah, now you are speaking plainly and not using figurative speech! Now we know that you know all things and do not need anyone to question you; this is why we believe that you came from God." We believe you came from God.

But as sweet as sound as that is to him, Jesus knows the Holy Spirit will complete that work. They have no more questions of Jesus it seems. They ask no further questions. In chapter 17, verse 8, Jesus affirms that what the disciples are saying is true. There he says, "They... have come to know in truth that I came from you; and they have believed that you sent me." So Jesus is not contradicting, and what follows is that the disciples do actually believe, but Jesus also knows that while their doubts are scattered now as they are firm in their belief, they themselves will be scattered later as doubts creep up again.

Here is a plain example, very practical example of what Hebrews teaches; a comparison between the life and belief of an immature believer to that of a mature believer. In Hebrews 5:11, "About this we have much to say, and it is hard to explain, since you have become dull of hearing. For though by this time you ought to be teachers, you need someone to teach you again the basic principles of the oracles of God. You need milk, not solid food. . . ."

Saint Augustine of Hippo explains it well. "They are still so far from understanding that they do not even understand that they do not understand. They were babes and as yet had no spiritual discernment of what they had heard regarding things that had to do not with the body but with the Spirit."[1] Jesus has heard his disciples. He has heard their confession of faith by their testimony that they believe, and he believes and he knows that it is genuine. Jesus acknowledges that it is genuine.

In the English Standard Version, it's translated here as a question. "Do you now believe?" But the literal sense is that it's more of a statement or a rhetorical question, if you will. He's not questioning whether they believe. In fact, part of their testimony is that they're saying, "We know you know all things." So there's not a question in Jesus' mind about whether or not they believe. The question is stated in such a way that it's a statement of their belief. "Do you now believe?" Here at this point, he's almost saying to them, "Is it that you're saying, 'Now, at this time, at this moment, you believe'?" It's sweet to his ears, and yet there's a statement here of incompleteness.

Knowing their hearts, Jesus knows the immaturity of their belief. He knows the limits of their belief. A belief stated is not a belief that is comprehensive and complete. To say you believe is to say you are beginning your journey of faith. It is not to say you have completed your journey of faith. Those limits are apparent in the scattering of the disciples, the disappointments of his followers on the road to Emmaus, and in the comments of Thomas that he wouldn't believe unless he saw with his own eyes and put his finger in the wounds of Jesus' hands. That is the belief we're talking about. Yes, they believe that they believe, but their belief is still racked with doubt because when the pressures and the challenges of persecution and tribulation come in upon them, their belief is inadequate to the testing without the indwelling of the Holy Spirit.

No, Jesus doesn't call into question the authenticity of their belief, but the depth, the strength, and the adequacy. To agree with Augustine,

---

1. Phillip Schaff, ed., *A Select Library of the Nicene and Post-Nicene Fathers of the Christian Church*, p. 392.

we would simply say they don't know the belief that is required in the spiritual battles that are ahead. So Jesus tells them what is ahead. "You believe, but you will flee, and you will scatter." This is just like the prophecy of Zechariah 13 says when it foretold, "Strike the shepherd, and the sheep will be scattered. . . ."

Jesus tells them, "You believe, but you. . .will leave me alone." When Jesus says, "You. . . . will leave me alone," he also says, "Yet I am not alone, for the Father is with me." This is somewhat in answer to the disciples words, "We know you came from the Father," but it could be implied in later teaching (if Jesus does not provide the clarification which he does) that Jesus somehow had left the Father and was out of the presence of the Father. Jesus is here saying, "Yes, I came from the Father, but the Father remains with me. I am not alone." Yet the disciples will leave him, and they will leave him without their presence or without friend on this earth. Jesus is at the center of their belief, the center of gravity of their lives, and yet they will abandon him out of fear.

The entire account is a sobering wake-up call for us in the Christian church. While the disciples had not yet received the Holy Spirit, we do have the Spirit, and we do have the Scriptures, yet how satisfied are we that our profession is the extent of our journey? How often do we find someone who is content that they said at some point they believe? We don't doubt the authenticity of that statement, but the contentedness to remain in such a state of spiritual immaturity is worthy of question. Why is it that someone would be so willing to be the victim of the pressures of this world that would cause them to flee from Christ as the disciples themselves did?

How often do we like the disciples flee to our own places and away from Christ? Where is it we go to find our comfort? Where is it we go to find our substance? Where is it we go to find our safety? Is it on bended knee to Christ, or is it to someone else? Is it to someplace else? Is it to something else? Most of the disciples fled to Bethany. Peter went into Jerusalem following Christ but keeping his distance from Christ. You and I flee too. We often lack the spiritual tenacity. When the going gets tough, we don't seek the Lord. We either attack one another to get rid of the pressure, or we flee to some other place. We run away. When the honor of God or of Christ is besmirched, we drift back away from him like Peter did, and we fool ourselves into believing that what actually is our own cowardice and our lack of spiritual fortitude is an issue of poor timing or of social grace, but the effect is the same. We leave him.

Jesus had taken the disciples as we might take a newborn. He had nurtured them on truth, on himself as the Bread of Life and the living water. The disciples were at the threshold of spiritual adulthood, but they had not yet crossed over. On this day, they were still adolescent. Between childhood and adulthood is this awkward, cumbersome age we know as adolescence. Not children, and yet not adult; confident, and yet still in ignorance. Like any adolescent, they had a great confidence in themselves. They didn't have any more questions. So indicative of an adolescent, isn't it? They knew it all, and they were incapable of helping themselves, unaware it was the hand of Christ that was holding them together.

If we compare it to our own lives, can we not see in our infancy and in our childhood, we were content to be dependent upon our parents? We followed them. They taught us. They showed us the way. They held us up, and we knew that. But as we begin to strive for independence going into our own adolescence, we fail to recognize we are only able to stretch our legs and begin to act as adult because our parents are still there upholding and keeping and securing us, and if that were removed, we would fall away completely into desperation until that day when we finally do reach adulthood and we are able to stand our own feet.

Our spiritual journey is the same way. Our profession of belief places us as a newborn in Christ. The church grows through those adolescent years believing she is doing ministry on her own strength, that she is doing things for God, that she is behaving in a way that brings God honor and glory based upon her own wisdom, her own tenacity, and yet we find that if the hand of God is removed the church crumbles and fails in an instant.

Whether it's the number of denominations that exist or the relationships in any single church, we can testify we are scattered, we are confused, and too often isolated from Christ. We're bewildered by what we don't know, but we fail to realize we don't know it. We simply go through life questioning and not understanding why God allows various things to happen to believers or in the church. We're bewildered by it not because it is not attainable or understandable, but because we remain ignorant of our own ignorance. Like the disciples, believing we know it all and have no more questions, we then set out and we judge

The Last Sermon of Christ

things based upon our knowledge, no longer asking that Christ would teach. Any lonely person in any Christian congregation can relate and know exactly what is about to happen to the disciples, for they will be as alone as they leave Christ.

Jesus presents in this passage three interesting contrasts in the verses. He says on the one hand, ". . . in me you may have peace." Three aspects: the "in me," and the second one, "you may have," and then the third one being "peace." Then in contrast to that, "In the world," and then the second, "you will have," and thirdly, "tribulation."

"In me," that is, in Jesus, versus "In the world," which will be the source of strife, the source of their pressure. "You may have," that is, if you follow Christ you may attain to it, that is, "peace," versus "You will have . . . in the world" strife and enmity and difficulty. Then the potential of peace versus what they already have which is "tribulation."

In 14:27, Jesus had already spoken of peace. He said, "Peace I leave with you; my peace I give to you." He is the fulfillment of the prophecy of Isaiah 9:6; ". . . his name shall be called

Wonderful Counselor, Mighty God, Everlasting Father, Prince of Peace."

Martin Luther imagines this is the way Jesus spoke to them. "This is his last farewell. He would clasp the disciples' hands as he bids them a good night. He concludes his sermon impressively with the thought toward which his whole sermon had been directed. He wants to say, 'This is the sum and substance of everything I have said. It's the one object to give you peace and consolation in me when strife and anxiety must be your lot in the world.'"[2]

Once again we find the contrast of life in the world and life in Christ. Johann Peter Lange points out, "As a man, Christ was keenly alive to the law of sympathy, and their temporary desertion in the hour of need when a friend proves to be a friend indeed, must have wounded him to the quick."[3] Yet man's history with God has always been one of man going his own way, doing what is right in his own eyes. Going one's own way and leaving Christ alone are synonymous phrases.

If this has been the point to which Jesus has brought us, then why do Christians so often when faced with anxiety and adversity flee not

---

2. Martin Luther, p. 414.
3. Johann Peter Lange, p. 501.

Peace in Despair

to Christ who gives us peace but back into the world where the anxiety and the strife have originated?

A young lady who has a poor view of herself and poor self-esteem will in remedy often give herself freely to others to defile her, trying to feel accepted, only to be rewarded with an even lower view of herself. Men and women with difficult jobs don't find their peace in a quiet home or in prayer to the Father, but in a glass of wine in the evening to settle them down which has no power to give any lasting peace and no power to solve their problems for the day.

The poor will take their change and they'll gamble it away on chance. The lonely will sit down at a computer and remain alone. In ourselves, we are weak, and the economy, our health, our work, and the world all loom large before us. So why do we flee to the world when we have been told and are hearing again today that it is to Christ alone that we must flee? Why go back to the place that has struck us and wounded us for peace? Why turn to the very source of our problem for peace? We may have peace if we return to Christ.

That word translated as "tribulation," has a primary meaning of *pressure*. The world tries to crowd out through pressure all true belief. The disciples and we can expect our expressions and habits of faith to be crowded out of our life by the world. The world will replace testimony and acts of faith.

It's apparent as we have battles over where the Ten Commandments are posted or where we can pray. The world continues to press faith out, and yet we flee to the world because the world gives us a check, because the world gives us a trophy. Are we so easily bought? Are we so easily purchased to believe that that is our reward and that is our peace? Are we so easily pressured into leaving Christ?

We are a people who need peace, and there's no better example of a Christian finding peace than the story told by Horatio Spafford. In 1874, a French ship was returning from America when it collided with another vessel.

On board was his wife, Mrs. Horatio Spafford and their four children. The ship was terrible damaged and sunk quickly. As the ship went down, she gathered her children around her, and they prayed. They prayed for survival and safety, and they also prayed that if the Lord would take their lives they would be made ready to accept it. The children were lost. Mrs. Spafford who was floating in the ocean was pulled out of the water by a sailor who was rowing in a boat trying to pick up survivors and saw her floating on the surface. Ten days later, she arrived in Europe. She sent her husband a message by telegram that said simply, "Saved alone."

Horatio Spafford's sadness was profound. His grief was deep, but although his loss was great, his peace was in Christ. Such is the way of the spiritually mature. He penned his soul's song in time of tragedy that we might also know the words of one who loves Christ in time of tragedy.

> "When peace, like a river, attendeth my way,
> When sorrows like sea billows roll;
> Whatever my lot, Thou has taught me to say,
> It is well, it is well, with my soul."

The Christian will look to the words of Christ for peace in the heart. The Christian will come to know the song of peace just as Spafford knew the song of peace. For those in Christ there is an inner peace, an inner quiet to the soul. Not the distress, not the turmoil, not the constant anxiety, not the soap-opera-like life that comes from those who are grabbing and grappling and searching for peace in this world with downcast face. Those who are stressed, those who are worried have not fled to Christ. They have fled to the very source of their anxiety, the devices of the world which always promise that tomorrow will be the fix, will be the repair, will be the peace. But that never comes, and yet we remain fleeing to the world with a new promise with each new day.

That inner peace secured by Christ came when he overcame the world. Notice when he says, *"I"* and when he says, *"you."* Jesus is the victor. We will have tribulation, but we are to run to him and join and be united with him in his victory. There's no victory in our work. There's victory in Christ's work, and we are to be in union with Christ so that we may also enjoy that victory.

Jesus overcame the world to save the world from what had overcome the world before, and he defeated Satan, death, and sin. Here at the end he can look back and he can say that he has conquered it. First Corinthians 15:57: "But thanks be to God, who gives us the victory through our Lord Jesus Christ." By his death, our sin was atoned for because we died with him. By his resurrection, he became the Mediator for his people and the first fruits of the kingdom. We are raised with him.

How confident are you in the victory of Christ? How mature is your belief? Where or to whom do you flee when times are hard, when tribulation and pressure come in? The disciples' belief would eventually lead them to the peace they were seeking, and that would take the character of assurance which then became courage. Does your belief lead to a peace that produces assurance and courage? Have you overcome the world, or is the world your refuge while it is simultaneously your prison?

Let me conclude with these summary words by Albert Barnes. "The world is a vanquished enemy. Satan is a humbled foe, and all that believers have to do is put their trust in the Captain of their salvation, putting on the whole armor of God, assured that the victory is theirs and that the church shall yet shine forth as the moon, clear as the sun, and terrible as an army with a banner."[4]

---

4. Albert Barnes, *Notes, Explanatory and Practical on the Gospels,* p. 364.

Bibliography

Allison, Gregg. *Historical Theology: An Introduction to Christian Doctrine* Grand Rapids: Zondervan, 2011.
Barnes, Albert Barnes. *Notes, Explanatory and Practical on the Gospels*, Vol. 2. New York: Harper, 1847.
Barnhouse, Donald. *The Cross Through the Open Tomb*. Grand Rapids: Eerdmans, 1961.
Bartlett's Familiar Quotations. Boston: Little Brown and Company, 1982.
Boice, James M. *Commentary on The Gospel of John*, Vol. 4. Grand Rapids: Baker Books, 1999.
Bergson, Henry. *An Introduction to Metaphysics*. New York: Knickerbocker, 1912.
Burroughs, Jeremiah. *The Evil of Evils*. Grand Rapids: Soli Deo Gloria, 2008.
Calvin, John. *Commentary on the Gospel According to John*, Vol. 2. Grand Rapids: Baker Book House, 1993.
Carson, D.A. *The Gospel According to John* Grand Rapids: Eerdmans, 1991.
Ferguson, Sinclair B. *The Holy Spirit*. Downers Grove: IVP, 1996.
Godet, Frederic. *Commentary on the Gospel of John*,Vol 2. New York: Funk & Wagnalls, 1886.
Ironside,H. A. *Addresses on the Gospel of John*. New York: Loizeaux Brothers, 1942
Lange, John Peter. *Commentary on the Holy Scriptures*. Grand Rapids: Zondervan, 1966.
Lloyd-Jones, Martin. *Authority*. Carlisle: The Banner of Truth Trust, 1985.
———. *Glorious Christianity*. Wheaten: Crossway, 2004.
Luther, Martin. *Luther's Works*, Vol. 4. St. Louis: Concordia Pub. House, 1955.
MacArthur, John. *Charismatic Chaos*. Grand Rapids: Zondervan, 1993.
McCheyne, Robert. *The Works of Rev. Robert Murray McCheyne*. New York: Robert Carter & Brothers, 1874.
Owen, John. "Communion with God." *The Works of John Owen*. Vol. 2. Carlisle: The Banner of Truth Trust, 1965
Poythress, Vern S. *The Shadow of Christ in the Law of Moses*. Phillipsburg: P & R Publishing, 1991.
Rogers, Henry & Sereno Edwards Dwigh, eds. *The Words of Jonathan Edwards*. London: William Ball, 1839.
Schaff, Philip, ed. *A Select Library of the Nicene and Post-Nicene Fathers of the Christian Church*. Vol. 7. New York: The Christian Literature Company, 1888.
Waters, Mark, ed. *Encyclopedia of Christian Quotations*. Grand Rapids: Baker Books, 2000.
Wimber, John and Kevin Springer. *Power Healing*. New York: Harper Collins, 1991.

www.ingramcontent.com/pod-product-compliance
Lightning Source LLC
Chambersburg PA
CBHW050844230426
43667CB00012B/2135